I0759544

Performing Transgression

Harvard East Asian Monograph Series 482

Performing Transgression

Crowds and Bodies in Heian Japan

Ashton Lazarus

Published by the Harvard University Asia Center
Distributed by Harvard University Press
Cambridge (Massachusetts) and London 2026

Published by the Harvard University Asia Center, Cambridge, MA 02138

The Harvard University Asia Center publishes a monograph series and, in coordination with the Fairbank Center for Chinese Studies, the Korea Institute, the Reischauer Institute of Japanese Studies, and other facilities and institutes, administers research projects designed to further scholarly understanding of China, Japan, Korea, Vietnam, and other Asian countries. The Center also sponsors projects addressing multidisciplinary, transnational, and regional issues in Asia.

The Harvard University Asia Center gratefully acknowledges the generous support of the Reischauer Institute of Japanese Studies at Harvard University, whose funding contributed to the publication of this book.

Parts of the introduction and chapter 3 appear in a previously published journal article: "Folk Performance as Transgression: The Great Dengaku of 1096," *Journal of Japanese Studies* 44, no. 1 (2018): 1–23.

Library of Congress Cataloging-in-Publication Data

Names: Lazarus, Ashton, 1983- author
Title: Performing transgression : crowds and bodies in Heian Japan / Ashton Lazarus.
Other titles: Harvard East Asian monographs 482.
Description: Cambridge, Massachusetts : Harvard University Asia Center, 2026. | Series: Harvard East Asian monograph series ; 482 | Includes bibliographical references and index.
Identifiers: LCCN 2025028188 (print) | LCCN 2025028189 (ebook) | ISBN 9780674303430 hardcover | ISBN 9780674304284 epub
Subjects: LCSH: Dengaku—Japan—History | Crowds—Political aspects—Japan—History | Human body—Social aspects—Japan—History | Sarugaku—Japan—History | Dance—Social aspects—Japan—History | Music—Social aspects—Japan—History | Rites and ceremonies—Japan—History | Japan—Social life and customs—794-1185
Classification: LCC PN2924.5.D45 L39 2026 (print) | LCC PN2924.5.D45 (ebook)
LC record available at https://lccn.loc.gov/2025028188
LC ebook record available at https://lccn.loc.gov/2025028189

Index by Anne Holmes and Rob Rudnick

Printed by Books International, 22883 Quicksilver Drive, Dulles, VA 20166, USA (www.booksintl.com). The manufacturer's authorized representative in the EU for product safety is LOGOS EUROPE, 9 rue Nicolas Poussin, 17000, La Rochelle, France (e-mail: Contact@logoseurope.eu).

For my mother,
Paula Anne Foster,
who would have enjoyed
flipping through these pages,
cup of tea in hand

Contents

Figures and Tables

Figures

Tables

Acknowledgments

This book grew out of a dissertation completed in the Department of East Asian Languages and Literatures at Yale University, where I learned from stellar teachers and peers. Edward Kamens was an eminently supportive and responsive advisor, and a scrupulous reader of countless dissertation drafts. Christopher Hill, William Fleming, John Treat, and Mimi Yiengpruksawan inspired me with their scholarship and teaching. Robert Goree and Brian Steininger were generous *senpai* whose work I continue to admire. Michael Chan and Joshua Frydman have been nothing short of tremendous friends throughout the years. Thank you to the many colleagues I got to know during my time as a graduate student and beyond, including Cheow Thia Chan, C. Ann Claus, Erik Cronqvist, Nina Farizova, Lucas Klein, Andrew Leong, Sam Malissa, Haruko Nakamura, Abbey Newman, Jeffrey Niedermaier, Stephen Poland, James Scanlon-Canegata, Casey Schoenberger, Patrick Schwemmer, Riley Soles, Ellen Tilton-Cantrell, Takuya Tsunoda, Rosa Vieira de Almeida, Justine Wiesinger, Naoki Yamamoto, and Yan Yang. Reginald Jackson, who opened my eyes and ears to theater, theory, and so much else, has been a source of mentorship and support over the years and from one location to the next; I cannot thank him enough for his generosity.

I spent the 2011–2012 academic year at the University of Tokyo studying and researching under the guidance of Matsuoka Shinpei, whose scholarship on performance continues to inspire. I'd like to thank him and his remarkable graduate students, including Hara Rurihiko, Hannah S. McGaughey, Inoue Megumi, Kuramochi Nagako, Naitō Hisayoshi, and Uzawa Mizuki.

I was lucky to spend my first three years after graduate school in the Society of Fellows in the Liberal Arts at the University of Chicago. Thank you to the many brilliant colleagues I met there, including Michael Bourdaghs, Susan Burns, Chelsea Foxwell, Satoru Hashimoto, Andrew Junker, Deborah Neibel, Simon Taylor, Nobuko Toyosawa, Judith T. Zeitlin, and the members of the Kuzushiji Reading Group. I would also like to thank my fellow instructors in the Reading Cultures sequence and the many sharp and creative students I had the privilege of teaching in my humanities courses.

My three years at Kyushu University shaped this book in numerous ways, not least of which was through the proximity of festivals and performances. But I am most thankful for the wonderful people I met there, including Edward Boyle, Caleb Carter, Andrew Hall, Ide Seinosuke, Inoue Narahiko, Kawahira Toshifumi, Kubo Tomoyuki, Saeki Kōji, Anton Schweizer, Shimizu Kazuhiro, Ueyama Ayumi, Ellen Van Goethem, and Gloria Yu Yang. A special thanks and enduring fondness goes to Caleb, Ellen, and Anton for their camaraderie. I am lucky to have been involved in helping to build the truly exceptional international master's and doctoral programs (IMAP/IDOC).

The University of Utah has provided me with generous opportunities and remarkable colleagues. Thank you to Vanessa Brutsche, Alexis Christensen, Nathan P. Devir, Bryce Garner, Tanya Flores, Blake Gutt, Gretchen Jude, Sae Kawase, M. A. Mujeeb Khan, Christopher T. Lewis, Joseph Metz, Ryan Moran, David Roh, Jacqueline Sheean, Cindi Textor, Deberniere Torrey, Margaret Toscano, Margaret Wan, Fusheng Wu, and John Wynne for their support. I would also like to thank the students who have taken my Theater and Performance in Japan courses; their feedback on my work, and on performance in general, has taught me so much.

This book has benefitted greatly from the willing eyes of colleagues near and far. In July 2022, I conducted a two-day book workshop with support from the Japan Foundation. The careful attention and thoughtful comments from Elizabeth Oyler, Haruko Wakabayashi, and Takeshi Watanabe was transformative. I am also grateful for Michael Chan, Takeshi Watanabe, and the members of the Junior Faculty Writing Group in the Department of World Languages and Cultures (WLC) for the patchwork of regular check-ins that have kept me (more or less) on task. Conversations with Heather Blair, Charlotte Eubanks, Michael Dylan Foster, Gustav Heldt, Charles Inouye, Terry Kawashima, Kristopher W. Kersey, Christina Laffin, Lori Meeks, Naitō Mariko, Vyjayanthi Ratnam Selinger, Satoko Shimazaki, and Ariel Stilerman have helped me strengthen many aspects of the book.

Thank you to the organizations that funded the research and writing of this book. My dissertation research was supported by a Japanese Studies Doctoral Fellowship from the Japan Foundation and a Prize Fellowship in East Asian Studies from the Council on East Asian Studies at Yale. In later stages of the project, I received support from the Japanese Society for the Promotion of Science, the Japan Foundation, and, at the University of Utah, from the Asia Center, WLC, and the College of Humanities.

At the Harvard University Asia Center, Bob Graham and Kristen Wanner made the submission and review process straightforward and painless, Daniel Lee coordinated the production with aplomb, and Adriana Cloud provided essential copyedits. I would like to express my sincere gratitude to the two anonymous peer reviewers for their helpful feedback and insights about the manuscript. And thank you to Anne Holmes and Rob Rudnick for their diligent work on the index.

Parts of the introduction and chapter 3 are based on a previously published journal article, reprinted with permission from the *Journal of Japanese Studies* 44, no. 1 (2018): 1–23, © the Society for Japanese Studies. I thank the coeditors for allowing this.

This book would not have been even remotely possible without the loving support of family and friends. Simon Forsyth, Hilary Lustick, and Winter Jade Werner have always been generous with their wisdom and time. David Dudley, in addition to being my first Japanese teacher, has been a superstar friend of the family. My dad, Franz, took me on my first trip to Japan when I was in high school; at some point, tired of being a tourist, I blurted out something like, "I'm sick of going to all these temples and shrines!" Well, look at me now, Dad. Thanks for expanding my horizons. Every time I talk to my brother, Justin, I am awed by his thoughtfulness, breadth of knowledge, and unrivaled sense of humor. *Carpe!* Emma, Grace, Nikki, Angel, Lily, David, Laurie, and all my aunts, uncles, and cousins—thank you so much for your kindness and encouragement. My wife, Ash, is the fiercest advocate one could possibly imagine; thanks to her I was able to take the time I needed to finish this book. Our daughter, Maeve, chief transgressor and queen of the realm, brings excitement and joy to every single day. Life would be unbearably dull without both of them.

Lastly I would like to thank my mom, Paula, who passed away in December 2023, not long after I signed the contract for this book. It is difficult to accept that she will never hold the finished product in her hands. My only hope is that I have succeeded in engaging even a shred of the curiosity she had about the world, as demonstrated by her lifelong interest in reading, learning languages, traveling, and thinking about other places. Thanks, Mom.

Abbreviations

Ch.	Chinese
DNK	*Dai Nihon kokiroku*, ed. Tokyo Daigaku Shiryō Hensanjo
J.	Japanese
NG	*Nihon geinōshi*, ed. Nihon Geinōshi Kenkyūkai
NKBT	*Nihon koten bungaku taikei*
NST	*Nihon shisō taikei*
SNKBT	*Shin Nihon koten bungaku taikei*
SNKBZ	*Shinpen Nihon koten bungaku zenshū*
SNKS	*Shin Nihon koten shūsei*
SZKT	*Shintei zōho Kokushi taikei*, ed. Kuroita Katsumi
ZST	*Zōho shiryō taisei*

Note to the Reader

Premodern dates appear in the following format: year/month/day (era-name year). For example, the twelfth day of the seventh month of 1096 is rendered as 1096/7/12 (Eichō 1). I include the Japanese era names (*nengō*) in parentheses to help readers locate passages in the primary sources, which sometimes, especially in the case of courtier diaries (*kokiroku*), do not list the corresponding Gregorian year. In premodern Japan, intercalary months were added once every few years to keep the seasons synchronized with the calendar. I indicate these months by placing an "i" before the month: for example, "866/i3/1." Birth and death dates, if known, are given parenthetically after the first appearance of a name. Unless otherwise specified, all dates refer to the Common Era (CE).

When referring to a story in a large collection like *Konjaku monogatari shū*, I make note of the scroll (*maki*) and the story's position within that scroll. For example, the parenthetical notation in "'The Story of Governor of Izu Ono no Itsutomo's Deputy' (28:27)" means that this story is the twenty-seventh story in the twenty-eighth scroll.

For translations of court positions, the names of buildings and structures, and other historical terms, I frequently referenced the University of Tokyo Historiographical Institute's "Online Glossary of Japanese Historical Terms," accessible at https://www.hi.u-tokyo.ac.jp/collection/digitalgallery/glossary/. I thank the countless scholars whose meticulous work populates the database's thousands of entries.

Many of the literary Sinitic texts I use throughout the book are published alongside renderings into classical Japanese (*yomikudashibun*). For ease of reference, I cite the location of both whenever possible. A typical citation looks as follows: "'Shin sarugaku ki,' 301 (CJ:

134)," where the first page number refers to the location of the literary Sinitic and the second refers to the location of the classical Japanese (CJ) *yomikudashi.*

When romanizing literary Japanese (*bungotai*), I follow the Hepburn system but use historical orthography (*rekishiteki kanazukai*) to approximate more closely the orthography of premodern texts. For the sake of readability, though, I use modern orthography for particles (e.g., *wa* and *o* instead of *ha* and *wo*) and when referring to literary Japanese words in my analysis (e.g., *zōgei* instead of *zafugei*).

When translating primary source material, I aim for a balance of readability and fidelity. I generally use brackets to insert words or phrases not in the original, unless the additions are already heavily implied by the language. All translations are my own unless otherwise noted.

INTRODUCTION

Performance, Order, and Transgression in Heian Japan

> Prohibitions imply their transgression. Order implies disruption; reason implies irrationality, sensibility intelligibility, past present. This is how we know: in the discovery of one in the other. We experience the meaning of the objective past in the transgression of its limits, in it becoming something other, in it changing.
>
> —Michael Shanks, *Experiencing the Past*

Experience, like transgression, is an act of boundary crossing that brings about change. But what does it mean to experience the past? David Lowenthal has written that "past and future are alike inaccessible. But though beyond physical reach, they are integral to our imagination."[1] The past is necessary to our imagination despite the impossibility of our experiencing it directly and sensorially. We cannot *only* think within the parameters of the vanishing present, even if we cannot *actually* grasp the vanished past. Lowenthal's paradox anticipates Michael Shanks's understanding of how past and present constitute one another: past implies present in the same way that

1. Lowenthal, *The Past Is a Foreign Country*, 23.

prohibition implies transgression, because the past emerges out of the present, again and again. Experiencing the past means apprehending the present and past as fundamentally intertwined.

In this book, I reach out from the present toward a specific vanished past: the embodied practices of non-elite performance as they existed during the Heian period (794–1185). The high degree of mediation and transposition involved in working backward through the visual and textual sources that preserve (however imperfectly) these practices necessitates an initial engagement with the meaning of absence. This will be familiar territory for scholars of performance, music, and other forms of "intangible culture" (*mukei bunka*). William Malm, for example, once wrote that "it is worth reflecting for a moment that beyond the capital there must have been a great body of folk music that floated unnoticed and unrecorded over the muddy rice fields."[2] Malm suffuses his musical landscape with subjunctive likelihood instead of certainty, with a temperate "must have been" that signifies the limitations of the archive and the wider project of documentary history. With its reflexive assumption of loss, this evocation of folk music rehearses familiar assumptions about the distant past: all we have are traces, and what the traces stand for is gone. At the same time it gestures toward a lingering ambient presence, similar to Lowenthal's "imagination" and Shanks's idea of relational experience—something that *must have been* there even if it cannot be fully grasped. With his comment, Malm ignores the traces that do, in fact, remain—the histories, diaries, poetry collections, essays, picture scrolls, and contemporary performances that record, represent, document, and otherwise transmit aspects of non-elite performance—but he does so in a way that leaves room for a historiographical practice that is not based

2. Malm, *Japanese Music*, 35. More than forty years after Malm wrote these words, Hugh De Ferranti appealed to a similar sense of loss by stating that "comparatively little is known of music in ancient Japan apart from the élite traditions," before describing records related to *sangaku*—the literary Sinitic text *Shin sarugaku ki* and the *sumie no dankyū* drawings—as exceptions. De Ferranti, *Japanese Musical Instruments*, 8.

solely on positivism.[3] As Marc Bloch once observed, "it is only for the sake of simplification that we sometimes speak of evidence rather than probabilities."[4] History can never be strictly objective because it is ceaselessly reborn through acts of interpretation in the present, and as a result, it "requires us to join the study of the dead and of the living."[5]

I therefore trade Malm's invitation to reflect momentarily for an extended contemplation of historiography, the absent presence of past performances, and the social dynamics of transgression and identification that records of these performances illuminate. Doing so raises a series of methodological questions. How can we reconstruct the vanished past? What tools are necessary? Where do evidence, imagination, and positionality intersect within interpretation? These in turn prompt social questions. Was folk music, and non-elite performance more broadly, actually unnoticed and unrecorded? What vectors of contact existed between elites and non-elites, between urban and rural populations? What sorts of boundaries did performers, farmers, courtiers, and emperors transgress, and why? And finally, the ontological questions: What is performance and how is it transmitted? How does language transpose sound and movement? In what ways can performance survive between the archive and the repertoire?[6]

I argue that non-elite culture takes on a more definite shape if we amplify its lingering fragments and expand the archive beyond the disciplinary boundaries that have kept it circumscribed. This means approaching a variety of texts not as closed, self-referential systems but instead as sites in which representation and narrative are indivisible from social, political, and sensorial aspects of the phenomenal world. Non-elite performance in the archive is always hybrid, multiple: its kinetic energy and sensorial appeal reverberate throughout the language employed to fix it in writing.

3. For a critique of the positivist approach to unearthing the past, see Shanks, *Experiencing the Past*, 25–27.

4. Bloch, *The Historian's Craft*, 133.

5. Bloch, *The Historian's Craft*, 47.

6. See Taylor, *The Archive and the Repertoire*, 16–33.

Non-elite performance in the Heian period encompasses a diverse repertoire of song, dance, and music. This book focuses in particular on the noisy rhythms and raucous dances of *dengaku* ("paddy music") and the humorous antics and captivating acrobatics of *sangaku* (Ch. *sanyue*, "diverse music"; later known as *sarugaku* or "monkey music"). *Dengaku*, *sangaku*, and other forms comprise different repertoires of kinetic and musical practice, but they are united by their ontological instability, their ambivalent reception by elites, and the potency of their political and cultural impact—their ability to break into symbolically central spaces.

Due to its capacity to both attract and repel, non-elite performance is fertile ground for examining the mechanics of transgression and identification during a time of rapid political, social, and cultural change. Prior to the tenth century, performance was one of many non-elite cultural practices appropriated by the centralized state (*ritsuryō kokka*) to shore up authority and legitimate claims on territories near and far. However, a series of changes throughout the tenth and eleventh centuries—including the weakening of the centralized state at the hands of the Fujiwara regents, the new politics of culture formulated within the emergent cloistered emperor system (*insei*), and demographic shifts in the capital resulting in increased competition among aristocrats—ensured a new function for non-elite performance. No longer choreographed by and for the state, it became a medium in which high and low mixed, asserted, and protested. The last 150 years of the Heian period were a time when these performances flourished amid the shifting of sociopolitical boundaries.

In this book, I use documentation related to non-elite performance to better understand its political and cultural significance, focusing especially on performances that transgress the borders of social order. I focus on *performance* because it was performance in its many forms—music, dance, acrobatics, ritual—that constituted the primary medium through which acts of transgression and identification materialized.[7] And I focus particularly on *non-elite* performance because

7. I use the word "performance" throughout this book not only due to its breadth of signification but also for its conceptual difference from theater, which, especially when centered around stage and auditoria, tends to involve an institutionalization of

it was the comparatively unsanctioned forms of expressive culture belonging to non-elites that produced spaces in which confrontation, contestation, and negotiation flourished.

From the viewpoint of most Heian-period aristocrats, non-elite performance was inferior to orthodox cultural pursuits such as *gagaku* ("refined music," instrumental music from the continent) and *bugaku* ("dance and music," stately dances set to *gagaku* music). Nonetheless, the distinction between official and unofficial performance was not absolute and often shifted depending on local circumstances. There was also a porousness between the forms of non-elite performance, with performers of one set of practices freely drawing on the skills and techniques of others. This malleability contributed to non-elite performance's capacity to channel a range of impulses and desires, modulated through flexible repertoires of bodily techniques.

Non-elite performance can be accessed through different types of sources: texts, images, material objects (instruments, clothing, structures related to performance), and repertoires of embodied transmissions (modern and contemporary folk performance). Modern scholarship on non-elite performance tends to follow one of two disciplinary approaches: history or ethnology.[8] Historians have focused primarily on texts and visual materials, ethnologists have emphasized embodied transmission, and both groups have made use of material objects. Historians have conventionally stressed the broader environment (*kankyō*) and significance (*igi*) of performance; ethnologists have been more concerned with form (*geitai*) and the dynamics of transmission (*denju*). Historians have tended to view performances as dynamic components within a larger network of cultural, political, and religious currents; ethnologists have typically sought to better understand the formal characteristics of performances and how they relate to earlier and later formations. These two approaches need not be mutually exclusive, and it is indeed only by combining methodologies from both disciplines that a more comprehensive understanding of

---

shared and even private cultures. See Pearson and Shanks, *Theatre/Archaeology*, 108–10.

8. For an introduction to these two approaches, see Kumakura, "Joron 2: Geinōshi no shiten," 73–86.

non-elite performance—both its contexts and its contours—becomes possible.[9] This book hence unites historical and ethnological methodologies into an approach tailored to the study of past performances, wherein form becomes meaningful only through a consideration of environment, and environment remains meaningless without an awareness of the specific movements and practices that delineate its contours.[10]

Non-elite performance in the Heian period was often transgressive, blurring the boundaries between high and low, culture and politics, and writing and orality. In this sense it bears a genealogical relationship to later medieval performance cultures, including the noh and *kyōgen* theaters, the potlach-like *basara* entertainments of the fourteenth century, and certain kinds of tea ceremony. But *dengaku* and *sangaku* have received comparatively little attention, perhaps due to the relative lack of documentation. Literary scholars interpret texts and historians construct narratives based on identifiable facts and evidence (or "probabilities," as Bloch would have it), but scholars of performance must grapple with the ephemeral nature of their objects of study, especially in the case of past performances, which we access as either two-dimensional textual or visual records, three-dimensional objects, or embodied encounters with transmitted forms. Engaging with past performances may be an exercise in sparring with various kinds of distance, but how these performances unfolded *in the moment* could not have been more different: they were immediate, intense, and direct in their sensorial appeals. The work of the performance historian, then, is to take the skeletal remains of performance's presence in the archive and restore some of the fleshy vigor that characterized its existence in the phenomenal world.

By tracking the interplay of representation and experience, language and performance, and bones and flesh, this book seeks to blur

9. Hayashiya Tatsusaburō places such a combined methodology at the center of his "new performance history" (*shin geinōshi*). Hayashiya, *Chūsei geinōshi no kenkyū*, 31–33.

10. Though I draw on both methodologies throughout this book, I focus my analyses on documents from the archive. The one major exception is the conclusion, where I devote space to considering my embodied experience of several folk performances in the 2010s.

disciplinary and terminological boundaries and thereby present a more holistic view of non-elite performance. These performances emerged through the media of body and voice, spread via the embodied transmission of patterned movements, and found their way into textual and visual archives. Today we are accustomed to documenting performances using reproducible media like digital video and photography, but historically performance lived on through the analog, nonmechanized techniques of embodiment and inscription. And though such modalities of transmission—from performance to representation, representation to performance, performance to performance—might naturally prompt narratives of loss and appropriation, it is worth considering how the "gap between disappearance and reappearance [. . .] may not be entirely as untrustworthy as we are habituated to assume."[11] Peggy Phelan famously argues that performance is defined above all else by its own disappearance. "Performance's only life," she writes, "is in the present. Performance cannot be saved, recorded, documented, or otherwise participate in the circulation of representations *of* representations: once it does so, it becomes something other than performance."[12] Here Phelan delineates a firm boundary between performance as it unfolds in the present moment and its other lives in the pasts and futures that bracket it. This presentist approach to performance reminds us of the importance of being in a particular place at a particular time, and of experiencing with our own sensing bodies. The demarcation of performance as such, however, is not always tenable, and equating performance with the present detracts from performance's relationship with other forms of media. For example, Philip Auslander shows that much of what we consider to be live performance is in fact actively shaped by recorded media and documentation, those elements Phelan considers to be "something other."[13] In a more general sense, performance tends to move beyond the boundaries placed around it. It is not simply that anything can be studied *as*

11. Schneider, *Theatre and History*, 68.
12. Phelan, *Unmarked*, 146 (emphasis in the original).
13. Auslander, *Liveness*.

performance regardless of whether or not it *is* performance.[14] Even those bounded events considered to be performance based on convention, context, and tradition—plays, poetry slams, dance recitals—exceed the span of their appearance and disappearance. Performance lingers and haunts; it summons past, present, and future bodies into motion; and it generates traces in viewing eyes, recalled emotion, and sore muscles. This book likewise approaches performance not only as a series of bounded events but as a continuum of practices that links disparate times and places and lays bare the sociopolitical dynamics of transgression and identification.

Transgression and Identification

Throughout this book, "transgression" refers to actions that prompt shifts in the boundaries between order (that which is licensed or sanctioned by an authority) and disorder (that which is not). I view transgression as neither a revolution nor a safety valve but instead as an act that initiates the process of reimagining political, social, and cultural norms.[15] I borrow this idea from Barbara A. Babcock, who, drawing on the work of Victor Turner and others, rejects the "functionalist steam-valve explanation" of rites of reversal and other expressions of inversion or negation, instead arguing that "what is socially peripheral is often symbolically central, and if we ignore or minimize inversion and other forms of cultural negation we often fail to understand the dynamics of symbolic processes generally."[16] In Heian Japan, non-elite

14. Richard Schechner has long written about the differences between "'as' performance" and "'is' performance," the boundary between which is becoming increasingly blurred in the contemporary world, he believes. See Schechner, *Performance Studies*, 22–23.

15. This reimagining is rarely consistent or systematic. As Janet R. Goodwin notes in her study of female sexual entertainment in the Heian and Kamakura periods, the notion of sexual transgression certainly existed but remained ambiguous and unevenly defined (even in a given text or political community) through the fourteenth century. "Forming concepts of orthodoxy and transgression," she writes, "was not a neat linear process." Goodwin, *Selling Songs and Smiles*, 81.

16. Babcock, introduction to *The Reversible World*, ed. Babcock, 22, 32. For Turner's related idea of *communitas*, which refers to the set of nonhierarchical bonds

performance became a medium for transgression because its noisy musicality and rapidity of movement contravened the ordered harmonies and scripted patterns of court ritual. But why did non-elite performance matter to literate elites to begin with? Why did courtiers and scholars record, respond to, and even participate in what were thought to be transgressive acts? The answer has to do with identification, with how "the act of identifying something as taboo [. . .] thereby invests it with enormous magnetic power."[17] This magnetic power resulted in elites performing unorthodox feats in spectacles of excess. It also enabled non-elite performance to take on a potent symbolic status in texts and picture scrolls, where it could signify supernatural possession, the downfall of political regimes, and various other threats to the social order. The way non-elite performance simultaneously attracted and repelled reveals the close link between transgression and identification.

In their study of transgression in early modern Europe, Peter Stallybrass and Allon White emphasize the recurrence of this dynamic throughout European history, describing it more specifically as the mutual dependency of the symbolically central and the socially peripheral.[18] The fair and the pig, the grotesque body, the sewer and the slum—these socially peripheral topoi of medieval and early modern Europe become symbolically central due to the elite's absorption of, and ultimate dependence on, "low" cultural forms. For elites, they write, there is "a mobile, conflictual fusion of power, fear, and desire in the construction of subjectivity: a psychological dependence upon precisely those Others which are being rigorously opposed and excluded at the social level."[19] In this economy of transgression, elite culture identifies with that which has been rendered taboo, preserving symbolically what it excludes socially and destabilizing the boundaries

formed in liminal spaces between those existing beyond the normative social structure, see Turner, *The Ritual Process*.

17. Partridge, *The Lyre of Orpheus*, 64.

18. Stallybrass and White, *The Politics and Poetics of Transgression*. In formulating this central idea, the two authors depend on Babcock's notion of the interrelation between socially peripheral and symbolically central. See Babcock, introduction to *The Reversible World*, 13–36.

19. Stallybrass and White, *The Politics and Poetics of Transgression*, 5–6.

between high and low.[20] Even when it is met with the reimposition of order, transgression continues to generate the conditions for opening up spaces of movement and change.[21]

In early, classical, and medieval Japan, the relationship between the socially peripheral and the symbolically central underwent a broad diachronic change. The Confucian-style central state of the seventh and eighth centuries sought to absorb the socially peripheral as symbolically central, whereas starting in the early medieval period a destabilized center allowed for a greater degree of "independence" for the socially peripheral. When the central state initially took shape, it appropriated non-elite practices and products as part of a broader attempt to consolidate political legitimacy. For example, Emperor Tenmu (r. 673–686) issued an imperial decree on 675/2/9 to thirteen provinces ordering each to "select and offer as tribute dwarf dancers [*shuju*], ritual performers [*wazahito*], and men and women skilled in singing."[22] Later, at the beginning of the eighth century, the state claimed lands in southern Kyushu belonging to the Hayato—tribes of culturally and linguistically distinct hunter-gatherers—and demanded tribute.[23] Along with other peripheral peoples (including mountain

20. Mikhail Bakhtin's study of carnival in medieval Europe is frequently cited in scholarship on transgression and constitutes one of the fundamental texts on which Stallybrass and White base their analysis. Bakhtin differentiates between two worlds: the serious and exclusive world of officialdom, ecclesiastical authority, and politics; and the comic and inclusive world of carnival. He argues that these two worlds seem to have been equal before the development of the hierarchical, consolidated state. Once this unity dissolves, carnival enters into the realm of folk culture and no longer constitutes a general form of social and political order, instead supporting the institutionalization of a "second life" that temporarily inverts hierarchies. Bakhtin, *Rabelais and His World*, 6, 10. For Bakhtin, dualities such as high and low are mutually exclusive, with periodic spaces of inversion serving only to strengthen the boundaries between them. But in my view, transgression ultimately weakens such boundaries by rendering them legible and thus contestable.

21. Partridge, *The Lyre of Orpheus*, 102.

22. *Nihon shoki*, SNKBZ 2:358 (CJ: 359). Ten years later, on 685/9/15, Tenmu issued a decree specifying these men and women singers and flute players should transmit their skills to their descendants. *Nihon shoki*, SNKBZ 2:448 (CJ: 449–50). See Ishii, *"Monomane" no rekishi*, 41–42, for a brief discussion of these and other performers commissioned by Tenmu.

23. Batten, *To the Ends of Japan*, 32, 69.

dwellers known as the Kume and native inhabitants of Yoshino known as the Kuzu), Hayato were summoned to the capital to perform dances and songs, attend state functions, and provide the court with local goods.[24] The court viewed socially peripheral peoples as culturally distinct and used the mechanism of tribute to symbolically incorporate them.

In terms of legal definitions, the Taihō Code (Taihō ritsuryō, 701) developed a tripartite schema of social status: the venerable (*ki*, the imperial family), the good (*ryō*, anyone belonging to a tribute-paying household, both aristocrats and commoners), and the base (*sen*, slaves, guards of imperial tombs, servants and menials, laborers, and sustenance households).[25] According to Yamaguchi Masao, whereas the good constituted the largest and most materially productive category, the venerable and the base were linked together by their comparative dearth of material production and their mutual involvement in various purification rituals. He argues that "the venerable needed the good as producers of their food and the base as supporters of their religious and ritual activities."[26] Yamaguchi mischaracterizes the category of the good—as Herman Ooms notes, both commoners and nobility were perceived as belonging to the good so long as they were members of a tribute-paying household—leading him to claim that peasants, as the sole representatives of the good, were in fact socially superior to the elites that ruled over them. Nonetheless, the close ties Yamaguchi identifies between the imperial family and the base are a useful point of departure for considering the typological background that structures many acts of transgression. Those with the least amount of status and wealth were in certain ways integrated into the rarified spaces of the imperial family and the state that supported it.

By the late eleventh century, the state had largely relinquished its policies of cultural tribute and assimilation, leading to significant shifts in how elites viewed non-elite performance. The increased

24. Ueda, "Kodai geinō no keisei," 217–19.

25. Ooms, *Imperial Politics and Symbolics*, 262. In his discussion of *senmin*, Ooms relies almost exclusively on Jinno, *Ritsuryō kokka to senmin*.

26. Yamaguchi, "The Dual Structure of Japanese Emperorship," S8. For a sampling of Yamaguchi's writings on the emperor system, see Yamaguchi, *Tennōsei no bunka jinruigaku*.

visibility of these performances in and around the capital prompted various forms of identification. On the one hand, since it often appeared with eruptive force, court elites typically perceived non-elite performance to be categorically violent and a threat to the very foundations of social order.[27] On the other hand, elites were no strangers to festivities, and the carnivalesque spaces forged by *dengaku* and other kinds of performance also attracted displays of aristocratic extravagance. For example, although several scholars have emphasized the difference between "attendant" and "courtier" performers during the Great Dengaku of 1096 (discussed in chapter 3), Kataoka Kōhei has perceptively observed that the two groups acted in parallel fashion by staging performances of excess outside the purview of imperial authority.[28] The elite encounter with non-elite performance was not a situation in which effete courtiers, knowing nothing but poetry and blossoms and the stirrings of the heart, were uniformly shocked and repelled by the raucous performances unfolding in the streets around them. The movement of performances across class and status divides instead suggests that phenomena customarily associated with non-elite culture—festivity, embodiment, violence, and excess—also had a role to play in the practices of court culture.[29] As a result, records of non-elite performances can be used to better understand the role of transgression in mediating relationships between high and low.

This broad shift in the court's relationship with the periphery is an important context for understanding the new forms of culture that emerged by the end of the Heian period. In short, the shift encapsulates the ongoing decentralization and privatization of the state. By the twelfth century, the bureaucratic apparatus designed to absorb non-elite culture, transform it into symbolic capital, and contribute to the creation of a unified realm had deteriorated through successive waves

27. Hashimoto, *Engi no seishinshi*, 19.

28. Kataoka, "Eichō no daidengaku no dōkō," 50.

29. Courtier diaries written between the tenth and twelfth century, which tell quite a different story about elites' everyday lives than do works of literature, have over the past several decades received more attention from scholars. See, for example, Shigeta, *Naguriau kizokutachi*; and Kuramoto, *Fujiwara Michinaga no nichijō seikatsu*. Additionally, Francine Hérail has written a brief but helpful overview of courtier criminality that details specific examples. See Hérail, *Emperor and Aristocracy*, 170–77.

of structural change. These included the domination of court politics by the Fujiwara regency in the tenth and eleventh centuries, the reassertion of imperial power through the establishment of cloistered governments in the eleventh and twelfth centuries, and the mounting influence of monastic institutions and warrior families in the twelfth century. The historical moment was one in which performance, formerly "part and parcel of ritual, began to break away from a unilateral allegiance to imperial authority and the state."[30] As this "ritual state" (*girei kokka*) fell apart, non-elite performance gained a new social and territorial mobility, leading to unscripted mass performances in the capital and the development of temple- and shrine-affiliated performance troupes. *Dengaku* and *sangaku/sarugaku* are main characters in this story.

Dengaku: Transgressive Crowds

Dengaku, which can be translated simply as "paddy music," encompasses a broad range of performance practices, from the songs sung by farmers to coordinate manual labor and summon divine favor to a form of imitative drama (*monomane*) that played no small role in the development of noh theater.[31] Emerging in rural spaces sometime before the Heian period, by the eleventh century, *dengaku* was performed in the capital, where it constituted one of several "others" through and against which urban elites understood themselves.[32] In this way, although the material specifics of *dengaku* performance varied significantly with wider cultural and political shifts, there is a kind of rhythm by which *dengaku* and its signifieds—rural, productive,

30. Sakurai, "Geinō to bungaku," 107–8.

31. For a lively English-language overview of *dengaku*, see Lancashire, *An Introduction to Japanese Folk Performing Arts*, 39–46.

32. A lack of documentation about the early history of *dengaku* means that its provenance remains a matter of conjecture. Some scholars, such as Yamaji Kōzō, stress its connections with other archipelagic rites and performances related to wet-rice agriculture, whereas Arai Tsuneyasu emphasizes its formal similarities with *sanyue* and other continental performances, arguing that both *dengaku* and *sarugaku* are generic descendants of *sangaku*. Arai, *Nihon no matsuri to geinō*, 142.

ritualistic, itinerant, antagonistic, supernatural, unpredictable—became objects of elite identification.

The earliest recorded performance of *dengaku* dates to 922, and from then until the end of the Heian period, the documentary archive consists of more than thirty additional performances, most from the late eleventh and twelfth centuries. (See appendix 1 for a timeline of selected performances.) Closely related to wet-rice agriculture, *dengaku* bears a generic relationship to *taue* (rice-planting) festivals and *ta-asobi* (rice-related rites performed in the new year).[33] But unlike rites and festivals tied to agricultural production, by the eleventh century *dengaku* was performed in spaces that had no direct link to agriculture.

Dengaku in fact denotes a range of musical practices that shifted over time and as it spread to different places. Yamaji Kōzō identifies three types of *dengaku*, which I describe here to introduce *dengaku*'s basic forms and contexts. There was (1) "rice-planting *dengaku*" (*taue o hayasu dengaku*); (2) "professionalized *dengaku*" (*sengyō dengaku hōshi ni yoru dengaku*), which incorporated *sangaku* techniques and was performed by musicians who dressed as monks; and (3) extravagant *dengaku* (*furyū dengaku*), which was performed by aristocrats and their attendants.[34] Yamaji sees the first two forms as enduring, and the third, which consisted mostly of amateurs combining elements of the first two, as an ephemeral product of the late Heian period.[35]

The first type, "rice-planting *dengaku*," emerged from the broader context of ritualized rice planting. These rituals consisted of women (*saotome*) taking seedlings thought to be divine manifestations (*yorishiro*) and planting them while singing; meanwhile, men (*saotoko*) played drums (both the smaller *tsuzumi* and the larger *koshitsuzumi* or *kaketsuzumi*), flutes, and *sasara* nearby as rhythmic and melodic

33. For an ethnological overview of *taue* and *ta-asobi*, see Arai, *Nihon no matsuri to geinō*, 67–87, 110–20, respectively. For a description in English, see Raz, *Audience and Actors*, 16–20.

34. Yamaji, "Nōfu, denpu no gaku," 273–82.

35. Yamaji, "Nōfu, denpu no gaku," 281.

accompaniment.[36] Fig. I.1 is an early-modern woodblock illustration of rice-planting *dengaku* that took place during a planting ritual described in the historical tale *Eiga monogatari* (Tale of flowering fortunes; ca. 1030s). (See chapter 2 for a full analysis of the passage.) The left side shows five *dengaku* performers gathered before the rice fields. Some dance (*odori*, "stomping," as indicated by their alternately raised legs) and play instruments, while others gesture with fans. Meanwhile, courtiers and a retinue of aristocratic women (indicated only by their colorful robes) look on. The performer on the right plays the *sasara*, also known as the *surizasara*, a scraper that produces a rasping sound when the bundle of tightly bound bamboo strips (in his right hand) is moved across a longer serrated pole (in his left).[37] The performer in front of him plays the transverse flute, while the one to their right plays what the text identifies as a "crude-looking drum," which has been fastened to his hip.[38] Immediately to the left, two figures crouch grasping open fans; one is gesturing, mouth open, toward the performers, while the other is looking off to his left, perhaps at the courtiers assembled on the veranda. Other spectators stand behind these performers, one of them pointing toward the action. As demonstrated by the illustration, this type of *dengaku* retained a deep connection with rice-planting rites even when staged in more urban environments.

36. Yamaji, "Nōfu, denpu no gaku," 271. *Koshitsuzumi* and *kaketsuzumi* can be translated respectively as "hip drum" and "attached drum." Early medieval picture scrolls often depict *dengaku* performers with large drums fastened to their hips, so it seems likely that these were large, resonant drums. For more on the types of drums used in *dengaku* performance, see Itō, *Dengaku shi no kenkyū*, 7–9.

37. The *sasara*, along with the related *binzasara*, is an idiophone and the quintessential *dengaku* instrument. The *binzasara* consists of several small wooden planks strung together and is played by grasping the curved wooden handles at either end and causing the planks to clatter together in succession by moving one's hands. The *sasara* in particular was associated with excess and transgression, likely due to the noise it produced. For example, the picture scroll *Tengu zōshi* (The tengu scrolls; ca. late thirteenth century) shows Jinen Koji, the Zen monk known for his "singing and dancing sermons" (*kabu sekkyō*), striking a *sasara*, one of his many unusual actions ridiculed in the scroll's text. See Matsuoka, *Chūsei geinō*, 36–37.

38. *Eiga monogatari*, SNKBZ 32:346.

FIGURE I.1. *Dengaku* is performed (left) as part of a rice-planting rite held for Fujiwara no Michinaga's daughter Shōshi. Though the scene is a later reimagination of a description from an eleventh-century text, it visualizes several aspects of Yamaji's first *dengaku* type. Note in particular the figure clad in light blue playing the *surizasara* and the planting women (*saotome*) on the right. *Eiga monogatari*, n.d., vol. 6. Courtesy of Waseda University Library.

The second type, "professionalized *dengaku*," took shape not in rice fields but in shrines and urban spaces, where groups of fourteen or fifteen performers formed circles and performed one by one. The performers were not farmers but instead unranked commoners who shaved their heads and dressed like monks, despite not being affiliated with any religious institution. The instruments they used were subtly different from those of rice-planting *dengaku*: their *koshitsuzumi* were smaller and presumably less loud, and instead of the *surizasara* they used the more elegant *binzasara*. Professionalized *dengaku* also incorporated *sangaku* techniques, including swallowing knives (fig. I.2). This type of *dengaku* frequently appeared in the urban festivals discussed in chapter 1.

Lastly, "extravagant *dengaku*" receives particular attention in this book (see chapter 3), because it emerges in a contact zone (a space

FIGURE 1.2. A troupe of professional *dengaku* musicians perform in the courtyard of a shrine. Three play the *binzasara*, two play the large *koshitsuzumi*, and the figure in the center seems to be preparing to swallow knives. The undulating motion of the *binzasara* echoes the wider kinetic energy that swirls around the courtyard, as a throng of spectators looks on in delight. *Nenjū gyōji emaki*, scroll 4. Courtesy of National Diet Library.

where elites interfaced with non-elite culture) and therefore enables a deeper examination of transgression and identification.[39] As Yamaji notes, this type of *dengaku* combined techniques, instruments, and customs from the other two types into a hybrid form performed not by farmers or professional musicians but by amateur (*shirōto*) aristocrats and their attendants.[40]

39. Pratt, "Arts of the Contact Zone," 34–37.
40. Yamaji, "Nōfu, denpu no gaku," 281.

Yamaji's schema is useful not only because it separates *dengaku* into three distinct types, each with its own unique forms and contexts, but also because it shows the breadth of practices that *dengaku* encompasses. There have been attempts to construe *dengaku* more narrowly. For example, some early twentieth-century intellectuals attempted to purge *dengaku*'s historical incorporation of *sangaku* elements to strengthen its agrarian associations amid the rise of fascism and ultranationalist fervor.[41] More recently, Marxist scholars in the early 1970s, when the Anpo protests and student uprisings led to renewed historical interest in crowd formations and mass movements, emphasized *dengaku*'s ability to function as a medium of protest and self-expression for the lower classes.[42] Building on Yamaji's broader view, I see *dengaku* as a medium that enabled acts of resistance *and* appropriation, an occasion for both the articulation and the contestation of authority.

Dengaku has visual, bodily, and sonic aspects, but the role of verbal language is negligible. Though it had incorporated aspects of imitative drama by the Kamakura period (1185–1333), it was *sarugaku*, not *dengaku*, that underwent the fusion of courtly poetics and ritual performance that eventually produced the noh plays (*yōkyoku*) that are still performed today. Although *sarugaku* became legible to and consumed by an elite audience (and eventually a public), *dengaku* declined and drifted toward disappearance. But *dengaku* lives on, in both the archive and the repertoire. Accounts of it can be found throughout most of written Japanese history, and a modern version of it is regularly performed today in rural and urban spaces throughout Japan. From very early on, the relationship between this rural kinetic performance and its representation by urban sedentary elites has been fraught with ambivalence. More often than not, *dengaku* involved (or was thought to involve) an itinerant kind of movement that transgressed both geographical and social boundaries. *Dengaku* movement threatened the sedentary topography of court elites even as it appealed as a strange and numinous other. The tension between the conflicting

41. Hashimoto, *Engi no seishinshi*, 166–67.

42. See, for example, Toda, "Shōen taisei kakuritsu ki"; and Inoue, "Eichō gannen no dengaku sōdō."

characteristics conveyed by this otherness—the other as simultaneously inspiring centripetal and centrifugal acts of identification—powered the discourse on *dengaku.*

Dengaku has been interpreted as a metaphor for the medieval period writ large, imitating as it does the rise and fall of now-vanished forms of culture and politics.[43] But with its divergent movements that transgressed social, bodily, and political boundaries, and furthermore haunted the archive, *dengaku* resists the simplicity of a schematized parabola. Unfixed and fugitive, *dengaku* keeps moving, largely excluded from conventional accounts of theater history, which typically consider the building of permanent stages to be the crucial point in theater's development into increasingly complex forms.[44] In this narrative, theater emerges within a structure of sedentism, political stability, and teleological development. In pivoting to performance, I am instead interested in those practices that thrive in a variety of spaces and situations, central and marginal alike. *Dengaku,* as performance, tells a different history of sociopolitical change.

Sangaku and *Sarugaku*: Transgressive Bodies

Sangaku refers to a range of acrobatic techniques and other bodily arts that expanded the boundaries of what bodies could achieve. It initially took shape in China, likely through waves of influence from western locations along the Silk Road, including Persia.[45] Records such as the *Jiu Tang shu* (The old book of Tang; 945) and the *Tang huiyao* (The institutional history of Tang; 961) describe *sanyue* as a repertoire of games, skills, and performing arts that was heterodox in relation to the orthodoxy of "refined music" (Ch. *yayue*, J. *gagaku*) or "proper music" (Ch. *zhengyue*, J. *seigaku*). According to these records, *sanyue* included acts like sword juggling and swallowing, puppetry, pole

43. Moriya, *Chūsei geinō no genzō*, 39.

44. Ortolani, *The Japanese Theater*, 11.

45. For a brief overview of early Chinese performance, including *sanyue* and related forms, see Dolby, *A History of Chinese Drama*, 1–13. For an account of the development of *sanyue* with reference to related currents in Japan, see Hama, *Nihon geinō no genryū*, 11–55.

climbing, fire breathing, wrestling, stilt walking, and tumbling, in addition to imitative drama and dance sketches.[46]

The range of performances and entertainments designated by the term *sanyue* shifted over time. One of the earliest and most evocative descriptions can be found in Zhang Pingzi's (78–139) *Xijingfu* (Western metropolis rhapsody), which was anthologized in Xiao Tong's *Wenxuan* (Selections of refined literature; ca. 526). In this lengthy piece, Zhang delineates the splendors of Chang'an, the Western Han capital, in graceful and erudite language. He devotes a passage to the assorted entertainments that take place within the capital, and although he does not use the term *sanyue*, many of the acts described can be found in later accounts of *sanyue* performances.[47] The passage describes the emperor viewing an assortment of virtuosic feats: cauldron hoisting, pole climbing, diving, balancing one's body on the sharp tip of a spear, ball juggling, sword juggling, and tightrope walking (fig. I.3). Next a troupe of performers manipulates animals and meteorological processes. Then comes the *manyan* (J. *man'en*), a kind of dance tableau involving a giant beast carrying performers dressed as bears, tigers, gibbons, and monkeys.[48] Also present are

46. Iwahashi, *Geinōshi sōsetsu*, 128–29. The organization of these practices under the label of *sanyue* happened centuries after they first appeared in documents. Terms like *zaxi* (J. *zatsugi*, "miscellaneous acts") and *zaji* (J. *zatsugi*, "miscellaneous skills") signified a similar range of practices in texts from the Three Kingdoms period (ca. 220–280), though the generic term *baixi* (J. *hyakugi*, "one hundred acts") was also frequently used. The passage from *Wenxuan* discussed below was written long before the dichotomous grouping of music into orthodox and heterodox, and it therefore lacks the appeal to categorical organization. For more on the history of these terms, see Hirama, *Kodai Nihon no girei*, 99–105.

47. For David Knechtges's translation, see *Wen xuan*, 227–35. For the original, see *Monzen*, 153–56.

48. In *Rakuyō dengaku ki* (An account of the dengaku in the capital; ca. 1100), Ōe no Masafusa writes that an official in the Documents Bureau performed the *manyan* dance as part of the Great Dengaku. But given the official's "wizened body" (*rōmō no mi*), Masafusa's conception of the *manyan* dance must have been different from what Zhang Pingzi describes here. Masafusa was undoubtedly familiar with *Wenxuan*, but perhaps this is evidence of the *manyan*'s status as part of a living repertoire, inevitably different from what Zhang had written hundreds of years earlier in a different place. "Rakuyō dengaku ki," NST 23:219 (CJ: 218).

FIGURE I.3. Two acrobatic *sangaku* feats. On the right, three children perform "stacked standing." On the left, a man performs a handstand on the shoulders of his partner, his sash and feet momentarily resisting the downward pull of gravity. *Shinzei kogaku zu*. Courtesy of Tokyo Geijutsu Daigaku.

illusionists (Ch. *qihuan*, J. *kigen*) who impress their audience by disfiguring themselves, swallowing swords, and breathing fire (fig. I.4). The episode ends with more acrobats performing amazing feats: coordinated glides and flips, sprints, and poses executed while teetering on poles.

In Japan, *sangaku* was institutionalized during the Nara period (710–784) in the form of the Sangaku Division (Sangakuko) of the

FIGURE 1.4. A *sangaku* performer breathes fire, his knees bent unevenly in movement and his left arm mimicking the trajectory of the flame. *Shinzei kogaku zu*. Courtesy of Tokyo Geijutsu Daigaku.

Gagaku Bureau (Gagakuryō), but the division was abolished in 782.[49] During the early Heian period, it maintained a semiregular presence at various state ceremonies and rituals, especially the annual wrestling ceremony (*sumahi no sechi*). By the mid-Heian period, performances increasingly highlighted comic antics. This newer form was generally, but not always, treated with a certain amount of wariness by elites, as when Fujiwara no Michinaga (966–1027) complained that a sutra reading he attended turned out to be more "like a performance of *sangaku*."[50] Pejorative uses of the words *sangaku* and the related *sarugaku* are found elsewhere in writings from the tenth and eleventh

49. For more on this and other music divisions, see Yamaji, "'Gakuko' no denryū," 55–78.

50. According to an entry in Fujiwara no Sanesuke's (957–1046) diary dated 1012/12/4 (Chōwa 1), "the grand minister said, 'Yesterday was the final day of the sutra

centuries, suggesting an ambiguous status: increasingly distanced from aristocratic culture and yet still retained by aristocratic discourse. As state patronage of *sangaku* declined, performers affiliated with shrines and temples demonstrated their techniques during shrine rituals and urban festivals.

Sangaku was also one of several influences on the noh theater, which was shaped by the playwriting and performances of Kan'ami (1333–1384) and his son Zeami (1363–1443?). Zeami in particular endeavored to elevate his troupe's art by ensuring the patronage of elite audiences, resulting in a theater that adhered to the social and cultural norms of those for whom it was staged.[51] Although I occasionally refer to these later developments, my focus is mostly on traces of the acts that made up the pre-noh repertoire, including historical records, literary and encyclopedic texts, and visual representations. In particular, I explore several entries in histories and courtier diaries, Fujiwara no Akihira's (d. 1066) *Shin sarugaku ki* (An account of the new monkey music; ca. early 1060s), and *Shinzei kogaku zu* (Shinzei's images of old music; ca. mid-twelfth century). In these representations, Heian-period *sangaku* emerges as both a vibrant carnival culture that embodied the palpable energy of the streets and a figure of fantastical difference.

Terminology and Typology

One of the difficulties of writing about *dengaku* and *sangaku* is making sense of the social status of performers, who were mostly unable to represent themselves in writing. There is the *ritsuryō* tripartite schema discussed earlier in this introduction—*ki*, *ryō*, and *sen*—but performance often destabilized this hierarchy, as when *dengaku* quickly spread from the *ryō* (farmers) to the *sen* (urban commoners) and then

reading. Major Counselor Lord Tadanobu was in charge, but the proceedings were like a *sangaku* performance.'" *Shōyūki*, ZST 47:294.

51. Lim, "They Came to Party," 114. Lim goes on to argue that the later integration of *sarugaku* noh into elite diversion and cultural practices led to the creation of a "temporary social space, [within which] performers and spectators often transgressed the boundaries of their social identities" (129).

to the *ki* (the imperial family) during the Great Dengaku of 1096. In contemporary scholarship, the term used most often by performance historians to signify non-elites—including farmers, low-ranking functionaries, low-ranking guards or warriors, laborers, merchants, performers, mountain dwellers, and fishermen—is *shomin*, which might be translated as "common people."[52] *Shomin* appears in documents as early as the tenth century, so unlike neologisms like Yanagita Kunio's (1875–1962) *jōmin* (abiding folk), the term is not anachronistic.[53] But it is also not as prevalent as other terms, most notably *hyakushō*, which scholars formerly glossed as "farmer" or "peasant," until Amino Yoshihiko resuscitated the broader range of nonagricultural identities and professions it signified.[54]

My use of "non-elite" throughout this book is intended as a translation of *shomin* that better emphasizes the diversity of status and profession designated by the word. "Elite" and "non-elite" signify the two constitutive extremes of the sociopolitical hierarchy as established by the laws and codes of the central state. In my previously published work, I have used "commoner" and "folk" to indicate the same social terrain.[55] "Folk," of course, has its origins in the discourse of nineteenth-century nationalism, a context that is in many ways far removed from Heian Japan.[56] Throughout this book, I have decided not to use "folk" in reference to Heian and early-medieval performances to avoid

52. The related term *minshū* (masses) has a more Marxist connotation and was widely used by historians earlier in the postwar period.

53. "Abiding folk" is Harry Harootunian's apt translation of the term. Reading its emergence as a nativist reaction against the rapid development of modern urban subjectivities in the 1920s and 1930s, he writes, "in a certain sense, it is precisely this difference and heterogeneity of class, gender, and sexuality that marked the streets that Yanagita tried to efface with his conception of *jōmin*, the indefinite and unmarked 'ordinary and abiding folk.'" Harootunian, *Overcome by Modernity*, 21.

54. See, for example, Amino, *Nihon chūsei no hinōgyōmin to tennō*. Redefining words like *hyakushō* is part of Amino's wider critique of the agrarian fundamentalist ideology on which, he argues, ruling classes had sought to establish their legitimacy from the time of the centralized *ritsuryō* state through the early modern period. Amino, *Rethinking Japanese History*, 25.

55. For the former, see Lazarus, "Performing Culture"; for the latter, see Lazarus, "Folk Performance as Transgression."

56. On the problem of approaching Heian Japan through the lens of the nation, see LaMarre, *Uncovering Heian Japan*, 1–10.

conjuring a timeless, classless subject (along the lines of Yanagita's *jōmin*).[57] I also avoid using "commoner," because it implies a certain homogeneity of social status or identity that does not accurately reflect the diversity of different actors. "Non-elite" gestures to this diversity; furthermore, because the word consists of a negation of its opposing term ("elite"), it suggests the dialectical relationship between the two. "Non-elite" may strike some readers as overly abstract (it certainly does not appear in any primary sources), but the perfect word simply does not exist—a point worth bearing in mind. Despite the central state's investment in establishing hierarchies, including employing language to codify and stratify, transgressive performance favored the social margin, where a broad range of practices, statuses, and occupations mixed and thrived.

In addition to conveying certain assumptions about the subject matter of this book, my use of the term "non-elite" enables a referential shorthand. This does not mean, however, that documents do not contain more localized terms that convey social status and specify lines of relationality. Recent historical scholarship has done much to elucidate this more granular language. For example, Kuramoto Kazuhiro's book on "low-ranking functionaries" (*kakyū kannin*) examines the range of non-elites living and working in the Heian capital from the late ninth through the mid-eleventh century. Kuramoto makes a basic distinction between those who possessed a rank (sixth rank and below constituted the "low" portion of the hierarchy) and were therefore officially part of the court bureaucracy, and those who did not possess a rank. (See table I.1 for the hierarchy of ranks and offices in the Heian court bureaucracy.) The former (*geshū*, *shimobe*) performed defined duties in bureaus and households, and the latter (*zōnin*, *genin*) were what I refer to as "unranked attendants": temporary workers who were summoned when needed.[58] My analyses of performances in the following chapters use Kuramoto's distinction to further contextualize the vectors of transmission and contact.

57. For more on the academic impact of Yanagita's problematic attempt to give voice to the voiceless, see Law, *Puppets of Nostalgia*, 13–16.

58. Kuramoto, *Heiankyō no kakyū kannin*, 29.

Table I.1. Ranks and offices in the Heian period

Social division		Rank (*i*)	#	Example of office (*kan*)
Nobility (*kizoku*) < 130	Senior nobility (*kugyō*, *kandachime*) < 30	Senior first	1	Grand minister (*daijō daijin*)
		Junior first	2	
		Senior second	3	Minister of the Left (*sadaijin*)
		Junior second	4	Minister of the Right (*udaijin*)
		Senior third	5	Grand counselor (*dainagon*)
		Junior third	6	Middle counselor (*chūnagon*)
	Middle nobility (*tenjōbito*, *unkaku*) < 100	Senior fourth upper	7	Head of a bureau (*kyō*)
		Senior fourth lower	8	Advisor to the emperor (*sangi*)
		Junior fourth upper	9	Controller of the Left (*sadaiben*)
		Junior fourth lower	10	Controller of the Right (*udaiben*), middle captain (*chūjō*)
		Senior fifth upper	11	Middle controller of the Left (*sachūben*)
		Senior fifth lower	12	Middle controller of the Right (*uchūben*)
		Junior fifth upper	13	Assistant head (*shō*)
		Junior fifth lower	14	Lower counselor (*shōnagon*)
Lower officials (*jige*, *kakyū kannin*) < 1,000		Senior sixth upper	15	Secretary of the controller (*taish*
		Senior sixth lower	16	
		Junior sixth upper	17	
		Junior sixth lower	18	
		Senior seventh upper	19	
		Senior seventh lower	20	
		Junior seventh upper	21	
		Junior seventh lower	22	
		Senior eighth upper	23	
		Senior eighth lower	24	
		Junior eighth upper	25	
		Junior eighth lower	26	
		Greater initial rank upper	27	
		Greater initial rank lower	28	
		Lesser initial rank upper	29	
		Lesser initial rank lower	30	

NOTE: The numbers underneath each social division indicate the approximate number of members at any given time. Shigeta Shin'ichi notes that by the latter half of the tenth century, those of senior sixth rank upper were considered part of the nobility (*kizoku*). By this time, hardly anyone received a lower rank, such that the population of the capital was divided into two sectors: those of senior sixth rank upper and above, and those effectively without rank.

SOURCE: Adapted from Shigeta, *Kakyū kizokutachi no ōchō jidai*, 14.

The most wide-ranging recent work on Heian-period non-elites has been done by Shigeta Shin'ichi. Unlike Kuramoto, who restricts his study to courtier diaries (*kokiroku*) due to their entries' proximity to the events they describe, Shigeta typically draws on a range of historical documents, literary works, and visual representations to construct a multifaceted view.[59] In *Shomintachi no Heiankyō*, he discusses a variety of aspects and practices of non-elite life, including causing mayhem at court ceremonies and urban festivals, telling stories, appealing for justice when wronged, working as a servant in a household, the social status of beggars, the everyday circumstances of servants who took care of oxen (*ushikai warawa*), and gambling.[60]

Both studies are valuable resources for surveying what we know about non-elites in the Heian period and how we know it. And yet, notwithstanding a few passages and references, there is little attention paid specifically to performance. Kuramoto includes a chapter that briefly describes several professions held by residents of the Heian capital (scholar, wrestler, horse racer, ceremonial archer, dancer, *sarugaku* performer, doctor, *asobi*, and glutton), which begins with a brief discussion of *Shin sarugaku ki*.[61] And Shigeta's monograph includes a chapter on the famous "Hitachi no suke" episode from *Makura no sōshi* (The pillow book; ca. 1000), in which Sei Shōnagon (ca. 966–ca. 1020) narrates several encounters with a beggar nun who sings bawdy songs and composes *waka* (traditional court poetry).[62] But neither monograph contains a sustained treatment of the role of performance in the broader culture of non-elites. This book seeks to remedy that.

Geinō as Performance

The performances discussed in this book are, in modern and contemporary Japanese scholarship, treated as *geinō*, a word often translated as "performance" or "performing arts." Since the Taishō period

59. Kuramoto, *Heiankyō no kakyū kannin*, 9.
60. Shigeta, *Shomintachi no Heiankyō*.
61. Kuramoto, *Heiankyō no kakyū kannin*, 214–15.
62. Shigeta, *Shomintachi no Heiankyō*, 158–91.

(1912–1926), *geinō* has been used to refer to a broad range of cultural practices, including film, theater, music, dance, and storytelling, although in more recent times its meaning has moved closer to what is meant by the English term "the performing arts."[63] And unlike the more restricted term *engeki* (theater), which appeared in the Edo period (1600–1868) to refer to stage performances, the word *geinō* has a history that stretches across millennia and continents.[64]

In early Japan *geinō* signified learning and cultivation in a broad sense, as per Confucian ideals from the continent, but by the medieval period the word was also used to refer to some of the performances discussed in this book.[65] For example, *Futsū shōdōshū* (Standard anthology for preaching; early fourteenth century), which consists of catalogues of classes and professions as well as explanatory verses on Buddhist sutras, contains a list entitled "Two Types of Performances: The Religious and the Worldly." The "worldly" (*seken*) section enumerates several non-elite performers, including *miko* (female shamans), *yūjo* (female entertainers, also called *asobi*), *shirabyōshi* (women who danced and sang *imayō* [popular songs]), *tsuzumi uchi* (drum players), *dengaku* and *sarugaku* actors, and *biwa hōshi* (blind lute-playing priests). Also on the list are several figures that would not be considered performers in the narrower modern sense: gamblers, merchants, doctors, and smiths.[66] The *geinō* of *Futsū shōdōshū* hence blurs the boundary between the broad and narrow definitions of the word: there are actors, singers, musicians, and dancers but also those who practice various crafts and trades. This heterogeneity demonstrates that in the medieval period *geinō* broadly signified the development and

63. One indication of this shift can be seen in the development of the academic journal *Geinōshi kenkyū* (Journal of performance history). The first volume was published in the spring of 1963 and included both academic articles on performance history as well as a "Performance Journal" section consisting of reviews of traditional performances, television shows, and films. In the fall 1964 issue, however, the TV and film columns were cut, and by the winter 1968 issue, the entirety of the "Performance Journal" was dropped.

64. On the shifting meaning of the word *geinō*, see Moriya, "Geinō to wa nani ka," 19–34.

65. Moriya, "Geinō to wa nani ka," 21–22.

66. *Futsū shōdōshū*, 6.

possession of skills that drew on bodily capacities and were aligned with non-elite status or professions.

This passage does not discuss the social spaces in which *geinō* took place, but its categorization of such activities into "religious" (*shusse*) and "worldly" suggests an investment in distinguishing between practices that propagate the Buddhist teachings (*buppō*) and those that do not. The construction of boundaries—between religious and worldly, sacred and profane, high and low, us and them—is a fundamental characteristic of writings about non-elite performance. Of particular interest here is not the mere textual presence of such boundaries but rather the regularity with which they were crossed in the phenomenal world, rendering typologies—be they textual, bureaucratic, or philosophical—both provisional and recurrent. In the end, non-elite performance's capacity for transgression has less to do with some essentialized notion of the practices themselves than with their relationship to elite culture.

Transgression, ordering, and reordering are social processes found within non-elite and elite cultures alike. But the culture of Heian Japan was one in which elites absorbed, experienced, and experimented with cultural forms that had hitherto been deemed "low" or "other," especially within the field of *geinō*. The transposition of these embodied cultural forms into writing constitutes a rich site for untangling the politics of culture and gaining insight into how different forms of relationality were constructed.

Chapter Summaries

This book consists of two parts. Part 1 ("Crowds," chapters 1–4) explores festivals, *dengaku*, the shifting status of rural practices, and audiences through the figure of the crowd. Part 2 ("Bodies," chapters 5–7) considers the corporeality of the *sangaku*, *sarugaku*, and *imayō* repertoires, the transposition of dynamic embodied practices into discourse, and persistent metaphors of illness and contagion in writings on performance.

Chapter 1 ("Transgressive Spaces: Open Festivals in the Heian Capital") traces the eleventh-century emergence of boisterous festivals in the capital. I argue that these "open festivals" indicate a shift in the politics of culture whereby the central state's symbolic focus became trained more narrowly on the body of the emperor, resulting in a decentralization of a variety of rites and rituals. Once a cosmologically central place, the capital took on a heterogeneous texture as parades, especially those related to the Inari Festival and *goryōe* (spirit pacification ceremonies, the most important of which is the one centered around Gion Shrine), forged a variety of new transgressive spaces. The second half of the chapter uses the visual depictions of festivals in *Nenjū gyōji emaki* (The picture scrolls of annual events; ca. 1170s), associated with GoShirakawa (1127–1192), to consider how open festivals crossed boundaries and destabilized distinctions of status and rank.

Chapters 2 and 3 approach *dengaku* as a crowd-activating performance that excelled in moving between rural and urban spaces. Chapter 2 ("Working the Land: *Dengaku*, Agriculture, and Rural Practices") places *dengaku* within a broader set of performance practices related to agriculture—*taue* and *ta-asobi*, in particular—and shows how records of *dengaku* frequently make use of a rhetoric of otherness to imbue it with meaning.

Chapter 3 ("From the Ground Up: The Great Dengaku of 1096") reads the variety of records of one of the most spectacular performance events of the Heian period, including Fujiwara no Munetada's (1062–1141) diary entries and Ōe no Masafusa's (1041–1111) retrospective account. I argue that *dengaku* exerted not only a symbolic force on elites but a social one as well. By occupying the capital with its rhythms, melodies, and movements, *dengaku* demonstrated its capacity to trigger transgressive acts of identification.

Chapter 4 ("Audience as Crowd: *Shin sarugaku ki*, Social Typology, and Urban Life") turns to Fujiwara no Akihira's *Shin sarugaku ki* (An account of the new monkey music; ca. 1060s), which briefly describes a performance of *sarugaku* and, at much greater length, the many members of a large family present in the audience. I argue that Akihira uses *sarugaku* as an occasion to catalogue the capital's social topography in encyclopedic fashion, generating an administrative tableau that transposes the exuberance of non-elite performance into a source of ordered knowledge. In *Shin sarugaku ki*, a large crowd of spectators narratively encloses the performances, a structure that demonstrates how performers (and their associated acts) and spectators (and their associated behaviors and vocations) were momentarily integrated in the same urban space.

Part 2 probes transgression on the more localized scale of bodies. Chapter 5 ("Transgressive Bodies: *Sangaku*, *Sarugaku*, and *Zōgei*") considers the repertoire of *sangaku* heterodox entertainment and its relationship to an assortment of "miscellaneous" performances (*zōgei*). Initially referring to a range of performances and entertainments in China, *sangaku* in early and medieval Japan encompassed a range of spectacular feats: sword juggling, fire breathing, stilt walking, human pyramids, and sleight-of-hand magic. The virtuosic performing body was a source of both awe and anxiety for assembled audiences, and it prompted both acclamation and censure.

Chapter 6 ("Bracketed Bodies, Vanished Voices: *Imayō*, Abstraction, and the Archive") explores the twelfth-century case of *imayō* to analyze similar tensions in the transposition of embodied practices, especially vocal arts, into archival texts. I consider how GoShirakawa, through his collection of *imayō* (*Ryōjin hishō* [Secret selection of the dancing dust; ca. 1150–1180]) and his accompanying treatise on *imayō* practice, history, and genealogy (*Ryōjin hishō kudenshū* [Collection of oral transmissions about the secret selection of the dancing dust; ca. 1150–1180]), appropriated the resonance and virtuosity of *imayō* and other female performance practices for his own textual gain.

Chapter 7 ("Between Bodies: Performance, Identification, Illness, and Contagion") takes up in greater detail two bodily tropes found throughout writings on non-elite performance: illness and contagion. By revisiting some of the performances already discussed, tracking their fate in the later medieval period, and expanding the focus to new terrain (epidemic illness and *kugutsu* puppetry), I explore the persistence of appeals to otherness in the discourse on non-elite performance. Having teased out the modes of elite identification suggested by these records, I end by considering two stories that depict identification and transgression from the embodied viewpoint of non-elites.

The book ends with a conclusion, "The Performance in the Document," in which I consider recent scholarship on performance documentation and reflect on what my study of non-elite performance in

Heian Japan can contribute to the broader field of performance historiography. By focusing on the pragmatic utility of documents, be they visual or textual, I conclude the monograph with an appeal to historiographical practice that situates the past within the present and transgresses the border between scholarly subject and studied object.

PART I

CROWDS

CHAPTER ONE

Transgressive Spaces

Open Festivals in the Heian Capital

The history of non-elite performance in Heian Japan is in many ways the history of crowds. From collective performances in agricultural communities, to throngs of revelers at urban festivals, to erratic performances of *dengaku* troupes, crowds often made up the basic units of action. Part 1 of this book explores the role of crowds in urban festivals (chapter 1), a range of rural crowd performances (chapter 2), a particularly raucous mass performance of *dengaku* (chapter 3), and a fictionalized crowd of festival spectators (chapter 4). Taken together, the four chapters show how urban festivals in the capital ushered in a range of non-elite performances and ritual practices, with *dengaku* emerging in the eleventh century as an especially effective medium for this transgressive development. Part 1 is therefore structured around the history of *dengaku* in particular, but I also emphasize the fluidity with which *dengaku* interfaced with other performance types, both rural and urban. *Dengaku*'s ability to spread depended on this fluidity and on the centripetal nature of both its structure and its appeal.

Always shifting and absorbing, *dengaku* was a crowd-performance phenomenon. But it was not alone in this; vigorous crowd movements were an integral part not only of Heian society but of premodern Japan in general. Consider the protesting monks who periodically infiltrated the capital from the surrounding hills with petitions and grievances (*gōso*); the picture scrolls (*emaki*) that depict the streets of the capital teeming with crowds of hungry ghosts or ill bodies; and the phenomenon of the Amida *raigō*, in which Amida Buddha jolts into the human realm flanked by a crowd of attendants, ready to transport a devout believer to be reborn in the Pure Land.[1]

Like the tip of an iceberg, the word "crowd" sits atop a deep history of ideas related to social organization, social psychology, and social order. In researching different conceptual understandings of crowds, I have been particularly struck by Elias Canetti's historiographic approach and the relevance of his ideas to a premodern society like Heian Japan. In *Crowds and Power* (1960), Canetti writes a global history of the figure of the crowd, which he breaks down into several different typologies, the most useful of which is the dyad of closed crowds and open crowds. Closed crowds, he explains, renounce growth, stress permanence, and emphasize uniqueness.[2] Open crowds, on the other hand, are popular, peripheral, fast moving, short-lived, politically charged, and prone to disappearance; they also transgress class boundaries, occupy central spaces, collaborate with or contribute to a dominant culture, and leave traces behind in elite records. In the open crowd, Canetti writes,

> [One] has a sense of relief, for the distances are removed which used to throw him back on himself and shut him in. With the lifting of these burdens of distance he feels free; his freedom is the crossing of these boundaries. He wants what is happening to him to happen to others too; and he expects it to happen to them. An earthen pot irritates him, for it is all boundaries. The closed doors of a house irritate him. Rites and ceremonies, anything which preserves distances, threaten him and seem unbearable.[3]

1. On *gōso*, see Adolphson, *The Gates of Power*, 240–87. For a recent discussion of *Yamai no sōshi* (The illustrated scrolls of illness; ca. 1171–1177), a picture scroll that depicts crowds of suffering bodies, see Watanabe, "Reexamining the *Yamai no Sōshi*." On visual depictions of the Amida *raigō*, see Lee, *A History of Far Eastern Art*, 326–46.

2. Canetti, *Crowds and Power*, 17.

3. Canetti, *Crowds and Power*, 20.

Open crowds push beyond boundaries, and boundedness more generally—not only closed doors but also the fixed codes of rites and ceremonies. Open crowds encompass a range of social actors and contexts, and the moments of their emergence and articulation highlight specific tensions between non-elite and elite, center and periphery, stasis and movement, politics and culture, and writing and orality. Open crowds have no time for theater, if theater is understood as the scripted presentation of embodied practices in defined places. The open crowd has no place, no itinerary, no script. The open crowd is fundamentally a performance phenomenon.

Writing in the late 1950s, Canetti drew on the fields of structural anthropology and its offshoots in history and literary studies to formulate his concepts. More generally, the idea of the crowd loomed large from the time of the Industrial Revolution (ca. 1760–1840), be it as a symbol of revolutionary potential or as a space in which subjectivities dissolved into a collective mind. This latter understanding was in vogue at the turn of the twentieth century, when the social sciences first took shape. It is particularly well-known in the form of Gustave LeBon's *The Crowd: A Study of the Popular Mind* (1895), the pioneering study of crowd psychology. According to LeBon, in a crowd, an individual "is no longer himself, but has become an automaton who has ceased to be guided by his will."[4] In this influential take, crowds enable mob rule and are nothing more than the submission of the individual to the collective will.

More nuanced approaches to interpreting crowds began to appear post–World War II amid the rise of labor history and new sociological analyses of collective behavior. Although some still emphasized the fundamental irrationality and homogeneity of the crowd, by the 1990s, sociologists had started to question this view based on empirical research into crowd dynamics.[5] Canetti anticipated this: in his study, crowds are not perversions but instead fundamental and dynamic units of social organization, an examination of which enables new approaches to human history. Instead of parroting the paranoid

4. LeBon, *The Crowd*, 32.

5. See McPhail, *The Myth of the Madding Crowd*, esp. 149–90. McPhail favors the term "gathering" over "crowd."

anti-communalism that characterizes much of the earlier work on the topic, his book takes crowds seriously and through them seeks to better understand the complex relationship between interpersonal networks and broader social, political, and religious forces. Part 1 of this book follows a similar historiographical (with nods to the psychological and sociological) approach, seeking to demonstrate how crowds and the anxieties they generated were a central feature of the spread of *dengaku* and related performances.

Performance, Ritual, and the State in Heian Japan

In premodern Japan, political shifts had a decisive impact on the relationship between performance, ritual, and the state. The transition from ancient to early medieval forms of governance involved, broadly speaking, a trajectory of decentralization. The Confucian-style statutory government (seventh through eighth centuries) gave way to an increasingly decentralized regency dominated by the Fujiwara family (tenth through eleventh centuries), which was then followed by a reassertion of imperial authority in the form of the retired emperor system, which was in turn supplanted by mounting warrior influence and the eventual establishment of the Kamakura shogunate (eleventh through thirteenth centuries). Though ritual had played an important legitimizing role in what Herman Ooms calls the "liturgical state" of ancient Japan, subsequent political and economic privatization led to a decentralization of ritual activity across multiple power blocs.[6]

Given the changes in the statutory government that emerged by the tenth century, the capital was no longer solely a site for the symbolic centering of imperial power. There instead emerged multiple loci of political, economic, and cultural activity beyond the imperial palace and its theater-state choreography: the proliferation of sumptuous

6. Ooms, *Imperial Politics*, 105–31. Kōnoshi Takamitsu also emphasizes the role of festivals in legitimizing the *ritsuryō* state, writing that they "served as prayers for a prosperous and peaceful year and to guarantee the orderly functioning of the cosmos; by presiding over these rituals, the emperor became the ruler of the world, with the festivals guaranteeing the legitimacy of the emperor." Kōnoshi, "Constructing Imperial Mythology," 55.

aristocratic compounds to the east of the palace enclosure, residences for low-ranking functionaries and temporary workers throughout the city (especially to the west of the palace enclosure and in the southeastern quadrant), robust marketplaces (particularly the Eastern Market at Shichijō and Ōmiya), and shrine complexes beyond the city limits that grew ever more vibrant.[7] This diversification of resources and networks marked the beginning of what Matthew Stavros describes as "the transformation of Heian-kyō from an inert realm of imperial statecraft—a 'capital' in an austere sense—into an infinitely more diverse and undoubtedly more interesting social milieu, a medieval 'city.'"[8] Joan Piggott similarly portrays the transformation as a shift from a "closed capital" to an "open capital," a process she deems well underway by the twelfth century.[9] These were fertile conditions for the growth of urban festivals: as stasis turned to dynamism and closed became open, scripted theater gave way to spontaneous performance.

Meanwhile, the imperially sanctioned rituals intended to bind together emperor, realm, and populace were reimagined to accommodate what Asuka Sango refers to as a "politics of affinity [. . .] where in addition to one's official position within the Ritsuryō bureaucracy, one's close relationship with the emperor became an important ground of legitimacy."[10] Sango argues that this new politics of affinity did not replace the politics of *ritsuryō* bureaucracy but rather supplemented it, such that "the emperor was Janus faced, relying on both of these principles to legitimize his authority."[11] This is a useful challenge to simplistic narratives of bureaucratic decline, which interpret ritualistic and ideological changes as moments of structural rupture. There was, Sango reminds us, plenty of creative continuity in the changes in how rulership was conceived and implemented.

7. For more on how the Fujiwara elite's grasp of power fundamentally changed the economy and, by extension, decentered the symbolic position of the imperial palace, see Teeuwen, *Kyoto's Gion Festival*, 17–18.

8. Stavros, *Kyoto*, 55.

9. Piggott, "Mō hitotsu no Heiankyō," 223–25.

10. Sango, *The Halo of Golden Light*, 61.

11. Sango, *The Halo of Golden Light*, 65.

An example of the tension between change and continuity is how the Great Purification Rite (Ōharae), initially conducted twice a year to purify both the emperor and the people of their transgressions, was redesigned to manage a narrower symbolic space around the emperor's body and living quarters.[12] By this point, the rite's function had shifted to maintaining the symbolic purity of the emperor's body, in line with the emergent centrality of purification as a political ideology.[13] The reach of this formerly commanding rite was taken over by a multitude of rites organized by several increasingly wealthy and powerful shrines. In this new ecosystem of "public rites" (*kōsai*), the emperor was no longer the sole linchpin that held the ritual economy together but instead one of the many petitioners of divine favor.[14] With this privatization of the ritual base came new opportunities for non-elite residents of Kyoto to participate in the festive superstructure.

From Ritual Place to Festive Space

Amid these changes, the festival or *matsuri* became a significant presence in the quickly urbanizing capital. Helen Hardacre succinctly describes how these spaces function: "During the *matsuri*, society's rules are suspended and overturned. Unrestrained feasting, singing, dancing, violence, and sexual license are permitted—even expected. All these elements are regarded as contributing to the rebirth of the Kami, the community, and the life force of the individual. Society returns to primitive chaos, making possible a complete communication with a different world, with the Kami."[15] This description does not refer to a particular festival held at a specific time or place but rather to the general capacity of traditional festivals. Her summary nevertheless highlights many of the elements that made festive space in the Heian

12. Hardacre, *Shinto*, 32, 110; Piggott, "Mō hitotsu no Heiankyō," 220.

13. Burns, *Kingdom of the Sick*, 23. Burns cites Niunoya Tetsuichi's compelling study of this new "pollution ideology" and the decisive role of the *kebiishi* (capital police) in implementing it. See Niunoya, *Zōho Kebiishi*, esp. 44–67.

14. Hardacre, *Shinto*, 109.

15. Hardacre, *Shinto*, 476.

period so dynamic: the excess it encouraged, the inversions it dramatized, and the *communitas* it built.

By the tenth century, urban festivals had started to draw capital residents into the streets to perform spectacular acts of devotion, celebration, and protest. This was especially the case during the chaotic "festival season" of the third through sixth months, when temperatures warmed and the monsoon came and went.[16] These festivals were organized by several nearby shrines, including Matsu-no-o (third month), Inari (fourth month), Imamiya (fifth month), Hino (fifth month), and Gion (sixth month), and, depending on prevailing social and economic conditions, could turn into raucous affairs that attracted large swaths of the city's residents—laborers, craftsmen, peasants, servants, aristocrats, nobles, and members of the imperial family alike. Two prime examples of how festivals mediated performative excess are the Great Dengaku of 1096 (discussed at length in chapter 3), which took place during the Gion *goryōe*, and the *sarugaku* described in Akihira's *Shin sarugaku ki* (discussed at length in chapter 4), introduced as taking place during the Inari Festival.

Boisterous festivals like these were alternately included with and excluded from the annual rites and celebrations that structured court life. By the eleventh century, court protocol had been ritualized and elevated to the same level as pilgrimages, celebrations, and Shinto and Buddhist rites. Performing everyday actions according to the minute etiquette of precedent became one of the court's primary foci, and courtiers compiled exquisitely detailed protocol manuals to preserve this knowledge.[17] The codification of all aspects of serving the emperor resulted in highly formalized relationships and practices, detailed discussions of which permeate courtier diaries. Festivals, on the other hand, were spaces where this obsession with status and protocol could be momentarily suspended. As a result, records of festivals, when viewed collectively, display a fundamental ambivalence: some aristocrats were shocked by the carnival, while others participated in it. The emergence of two major urban festivals in the capital—the Inari

16. Gomi, *Inseiki shakai no kenkyū*, 365.
17. Hérail, *Emperor and Aristocracy*, 45.

Festival and the Gion *goryōe*—enable a closer examination of these dynamics of identification.

The Fourth Month: The Inari Festival

Inari Shrine was one of the sixteen shrines designated for imperial offerings in 966, and furthermore one of the "Upper Seven Shrines" codified in the list of twenty-two shrines promulgated in 1039.[18] Located a few kilometers southeast of Kyoto, in Yamashiro Province, it was a common pilgrimage destination for courtiers throughout the Heian period, with Emperor GoSanjō (r. 1068–1072) making the first imperial pilgrimage to the shrine in 1072.[19] The shrine organized an annual festival, starting in the third month and ending in the fourth, during which a group of deities (three at first and five by the twelfth century) were transported via *mikoshi* (divine palanquins) to two *tabisho* (temporary enshrinement sites) within the city. There they stayed for twenty days before returning to Inari Shrine. The return parade proceeded along Shichijō Avenue, in the southeastern sector of the city, and drew large crowds to see the *mikoshi* and the performers that accompanied them: court musicians and dancers, *dengaku* musicians, lion dancers, puppeteers, *sangaku* performers, and extravagantly dressed boys riding horses (*umaosa*).[20] Surrounding the action were men and women, boys and girls, and monks and nuns, while courtiers and ladies-in-waiting watched from ox-drawn carriages. In the eleventh century, the Inari Festival (along with the Gion *goryōe*) transformed into an inversion of the Kamo Festival: it belonged to the capital in general instead of the aristocracy and the imperial family, and it was more raucous than refined.[21]

Akihira, the author of *Shin sarugaku ki*, included two descriptions of the Inari Festival in *Meigō ōrai* (Akihira's epistolary textbook; ca.

18. Hardacre, *Shinto*, 113.

19. Sekiguchi, "Inari matsuri to shiten shōnin," 467.

20. These boys were often the sons of nobles' retainers, making them objects of elite fascination. See Teeuwen, *Kyoto's Gion Festival*, 34–35.

21. Okimoto, *Ranmai no chūsei*, 10–11.

1060s), an epistolary collection (*ōraimono*) containing 213 model letters.[22] Collections like this started circulating in the eighth century, but it was not until the eleventh that there appeared collections that "introduced young students to the ritual calendar, social etiquette, and a local idiom of epistolary prose that broke from literary Sinitic models to incorporate Japanese-language-based usage."[23] Akihira's text covers a wide variety of topics, from the extraordinary to the mundane: gift giving, requests to borrow various items (books, food containers, oxen), invitations, descriptions of poetry competitions, attending festivals and banquets, thanking colleagues after being promoted, and preparations for Buddhist rituals. Most of the model letters are part of a two-letter exchange between aristocrats or monks, allowing readers to learn how to both initiate and respond to social discourse.

Several letters concern festivals. Some demonstrate how to invite a friend to watch, and others model how to report on what one saw and heard. The author of letter 19 describes how he received a visit from a friend who asked him to go see the Inari Festival. He reports:

> I hastily agreed and rode with him to Shichijō Avenue. As chamberlains from the palace and the regency formed groups and challenged one another, the situation became extremely disorderly. The secretary captain's attendant boys [*kotoneri waraha*] ran out ahead, and a massive group of followers brought up the rear. On one side were the attendants Seita, Kuro, and Kansu. Hoping for a fight with the other side, Seita and company screwed up their eyes and roared. The foes fell back with their horses, demonstrating that they were no match. The behavior of the *umaosa* boys was extremely unusual. Some whipped their horses maliciously without taking up the reins, while others rode fast steeds and paid no attention to their bodies. Galloping hooves were everywhere. Which way was south and which way was north? The riders were also decked out in gold- and silver-studded clothing. Silk and embroidery had been cut and sewn onto their collars and sleeves. Truly, it took the wealth of ten households to outfit just one person. What an extremely wasteful thing. There were also performances of *sangaku*. Actors temporarily took on the appearance of husband and wife. Studying a wizened old

22. The text is also known as *Unshū shōsoku* and *Unshū ōrai*.
23. Steininger, *Chinese Literary Forms*, 166.

man, one actor became the husband; mimicking a young lady, another became the wife. First they spoke lustrous words; later they engaged in bawdy exchanges. The capital dwellers—the gentlemen and the ladies in the audience—laughed so hard they dislocated their jaws and split their bellies. It was all exceedingly indiscreet. The events ended at dusk, the carriage poles came out, and I returned home. Observing this festival has two benefits. First, one witnesses the gravity of the divine ritual, and second, one cultivates a feeling of quiet enjoyment. Tomorrow I have business at the palace. Make sure you are also in attendance. I'd like to calmly tell you all my thoughts. With respect.[24]

The letter writer lingers on three moments during the festival: the fight between two groups of attendants, the extravagantly dressed *umaosa* boys (fig. 1.1), and a performance of *sangaku*. Though he describes the first of these with a neutral voice, the latter two receive a critical treatment: the mounted procession behaves in an "extremely unusual" manner, and their costumes are "extremely wasteful"; and the bawdy *sangaku* drama is "exceedingly indiscreet." These rebukes furthermore contrast with the letter's conclusion, which briefly describes the virtues of attending the festival. This contradiction speaks to the tension between the festival's nominal function, which is to entertain the gods as they are transported from the *tabisho* back to Inari Shrine, and the carnivalesque space forged by the procession. The letter begins and ends with formulaic greetings and sentiments, but its middle section reverberates with the unscripted bodies of revelers.

In his response, the recipient of the letter explains that he was unable to attend the festival this year but goes on to describe his observations of last year's festival:

Last year I was invited by a certain person to watch the Inari Festival in secret. It was most interesting, especially the solemnity of offerings made as the *mikoshi* passed by—truly, veneration inspired by the gods. How praiseworthy. I don't know how many tens of thousands of attendants

24. "Unshū shōsoku," 191–92. When preparing my translation, I consulted Shigematsu Akihisa's rendition of the text into Classical Japanese. See *Shin sarugakuki, Unshū shōsoku*, 89–91.

FIGURE 1.1. "Truly, it took the wealth of ten households to outfit just one person." An *umaosa* boy impresses with his extravagant outfit. *Nenjū gyōji emaki*, scroll 12. Courtesy of National Diet Library.

[*zōnin*] were there, but they boisterously presented various kinds of performances in carrying out the gods' wishes. Naitōta's transverse flute, the blind lute priest's *biwa*, Kuroosamaru's puppetry, Hakutōta's *sarugaku*—it was impossible to count the number of entertainers present. There were also several groups here and there. As they fought over front and back to determine who won and who lost, some became strong like tigers and others hid like mice. The strong and the weak stood out. There were also groups of *umaosa* boys who acted as though they'd gone mad. Their clothes were beautiful: white robes from Qi and cloth from Echigo. Their horses had the bravery of King Mu of Zhou's swift steed. There were various other sights to see. How could I possibly detail it all? It was the greatest spectacle of all.[25]

25. "Unshū shōsoku," 192–93. For a Classical Japanese rendering, see *Shin sarugaku ki, Unshū shōsoku*, 91–92.

The response echoes much of what was written in the first letter: the streets were alive with boisterous performances (in this case, *biwa* playing, puppetry, and *sarugaku*), fierce competition, and extravagantly dressed boys promenading on horses.

Like all the letters in the collection, these two are intended to be conventional. By reading them, courtiers learned how to navigate the social dynamics of court life, with its emphasis on etiquette and protocol. The fact that an exchange about the Inari Festival (along with additional exchanges about festivals at Kamo and Iwashimizu) appears in the collection suggests that by the mid-eleventh century it had become one of several civic gatherings that attracted courtiers, which in turn indexes the continued decentralization of imperial ritual in the capital.

The Sixth Month: *Goryōe*

Taking place during the sixth month, when the monsoon gave way to hotter and drier weather, *goryōe* (spirit pacification ceremonies) can be traced back to rites that sought to protect the capital from disease deities (*ekijin*), the appearance of which accompanied the rapid spread of epidemics starting in the eighth century.[26] Identifying the eighth, ninth, and tenth centuries as "an age of pestilence in Japan," Mark Teeuwen explains that "increased contacts with the continent, combined with the founding of imperial capitals as centres of national administration, gave microbes unprecedented opportunities to multiply and spread."[27] In the late ninth century, the function of *goryōe* expanded to include the pacification of the vengeful spirits (*goryō*) of those killed or banished in political disturbances. *Goryōe* were regularly held throughout the tenth century in response to the outbreak of epidemics, and in the 970s they coalesced into an annual event, based at Gion Shrine to the east of the Kamo River, that lasted several days

26. Teeuwen, *Kyoto's Gion Festival*, 23.
27. Teeuwen, *Kyoto's Gion Festival*, 21.

and involved *mikoshi* being paraded through the city.[28] Like the Inari Festival, these parades featured a variety of entertainments for the gods: wrestling, archery, dancing, horse racing, *dengaku*, and *sangaku*.

The earliest record of a *goryōe* is found in *Nihon sandai jitsuroku* (A true record of the three reigns; 901), the last of the six national histories, in an entry dated 863/5/20 (Jōgan 5).[29] According to the entry, a pacification ceremony was held at Shinsen'en garden, south of the palace enclosure, to enshrine the *goryō* of six figures that had been executed or exiled following political disputes. Offerings included readings of the Golden Light Sutra and the Heart Sutra, musical performances by *gagaku* musicians, dances performed by the children of the emperor's attendants and high-ranking families, and competitions featuring *sangaku* and other assorted techniques. The four gates of the garden were opened so that residents of the capital could enter freely and watch.

The entry then names the six lingering spirits (Prince Sawara [posthumously Emperor Sudō]; Prince Iyo and his mother, Fujiwara no Yoshiko; Fujiwara no Nakanari; Tachibana no Hayanari; and Funya no Miyatamaro) and, shifting from description to interpretation, explains that these spirits were the cause of recent outbreaks of disease (*gaibyō* or *sekiyami*, possibly influenza) that had claimed many lives.[30] The disease, visible only through its devastating effect on human

28. Before becoming an annual event, the ceremonies were prevalent in the capital's surrounding areas, especially near cemeteries like Toribeno and Murasakino. Wakita, *Chūsei Kyoto to Gion matsuri*, 15. On the emergence of the Gion *goryōe* in the 970s, see Teeuwen, *Kyoto's Gion Festival*, 27–28. Teeuwen also notes that the Gion complex was a *miyadera*, "a Buddhist temple enshrining deities to whom the monks directed rites of pacification," and was referred to as both a temple and a shrine in documentation (25).

29. *Nihon sandai jitsuroku*, SZKT 4:112–13. This final national history chronicles the reigns of three ninth-century emperors: Seiwa (r. 858–876), Yōzei (r. 876–884), and Kōkō (r. 884–887). The text is a detailed and valuable source of information about annual events, court protocol, and the various petitions and proclamations that constituted court governance. Given that it is a long chronicle (fifty-one scrolls) that recounts a relatively short period of time (thirty years), the level of detail is generally much higher compared to works that attempted to situate the present within a broader sweep of history.

30. The entry dated 863/4/3 (Jōgan 5) relates that this disease had been spreading throughout the spring, resulting in many deaths. *Nihon sandai jitsuroku*, SZKT 4:110.

life, was hence rendered tangible through its connection with the summoned spirits, which were entertained, pacified, and sent away. Through these actions, the court sought to establish a "ritual system" that rendered the invisible visible and enabled control over the uncontrollable.[31]

Next the entry relates how *goryōe* held during the summer and autumn had spread from the capital region to outlying provinces (*gaikoku*). Like the one organized by the court, these well-attended ceremonies included revering buddhas and expounding sutras, performing music and dance, and entertaining the spirits with a range of competitions, including wrestling, horse racing, and archery. The entry concludes by connecting the exceptional scope of the ceremonies with the large number of people who had recently perished.

This entry, along with the early history of *goryōe*, highlights the importance of inversion in festive space: suffering is transformed into exuberance. The choreography of transmuting disease into deity was intended to parry the threat to human life, but the specific means of doing so expanded participation from specialists in court ritual to residents and performers who had no official connection to the court. The attempt by the court to appropriate and institutionalize a ceremony that arose organically in response to the ravages of epidemics was, however, problematic. As Teeuwen argues, the officially sanctioned ceremony in 863 "may well have been designed to offer an alternative to [spontaneously occurring ceremonies], which could easily trigger riots."[32] Two years later, the court indeed banned such pacification ceremonies. An entry in *Nihon sandai jitsuroku* explains that the ceremonies were being used as pretexts for horse racing and archery competitions, and it also cites the unrestrained mischief of children.[33]

But the ceremonies continued to take place, thriving as attempts to contain drought and disease, and they became routinized into an annual event by the late tenth century. It was at this point that some

31. Komine, *Inseiki bungaku ron*, 871.

32. Teeuwen, "Kyoto's Gion Festival," 7.

33. *Nihon sandai jitsuroku*, SZKT 4:159. The entry is dated 865/6/14 (Jōgan 7).

of the elements still observable in the modern incarnation of the festival (the Gion *matsuri*) slid into place, including the procession of three *mikoshi* from Gion Shrine to the Ōmandokoro *tabisho* on the seventh day of the six month, and their return one week later, on the fourteenth day. There was one *mikoshi* for each of the three deities (or constellations of deities) that were by then associated with the festival: Gozu Tennō (also known as Tenjin), his consort Harisaijo, and their eight children known collectively as Hachiōji.[34] The return parade drew particularly large crowds and all manner of energetic entertainments, including *dengaku*.[35] Every year, across several days of the sixth month, the Gion *goryōe* brought residents from all corners of the capital together into the sunbaked streets, where they clamored for the gods to relieve them of drought, sickness, and suffering. The growth of this festival, along with others, reveals an increasingly open city composed of multiple nodes of power: the imperial family, nobles, religious authorities, warriors, and a range of non-elites.

Although other festivals, including the Inari Festival, also drew spectators from low and high, the Gion *goryōe* did so to an exceptional degree. Unlike the Inari Festival, which involved a raucous procession along Shichijō in the southeastern quadrant of the city, the *goryōe* processions took place in the northeast, along Sanjō and Gojō, an area populated by a large number of aristocrats and situated much closer to the greater palace compound.[36] As a result, the action unfolded closer to the symbolic center of the realm and made the emperor's involvement, in one way or another, inevitable. Wakita Haruko describes how in the twelfth century retired emperors (*in*) and their powerful daughters (*nyoin*) routinely set up viewing galleries along Sanjō from which to observe the procession.[37] The emperor, on the other hand, customarily avoided the *mikoshi* as they were carried

34. For a detailed analysis of the history, iconography, and cultic anchoring of Gozu Tennō and his entourage, see Faure, *Gods of Medieval Japan*, 107–49. Faure notes that, based on historic records, the association of Gozu Tennō with Gion Shrine likely took shape between the late eleventh century and the mid-twelfth century (125).

35. Teeuwen, "Kyoto's Gion Festival," 3.

36. Wakita, *Chūsei Kyoto to Gion matsuri*, 33–38. See p. 35 for a map of the route taken by the *mikoshi*.

37. Wakita, *Chūsei Kyoto to Gion matsuri*, 36–37.

along the streets, due to an incident in 1085 when Emperor Shirakawa's (r. 1072–1086) wife died shortly after a *mikoshi* passed by their temporary residence. This avoidance is not explained outright in contemporary sources, but the event seems to have triggered anxiety about contact between the emperor and the disease deities temporarily enshrined in the *mikoshi*.[38] As discussed at length in chapter 3, the aristocrats who documented the Great Dengaku of 1096, which took place during the Gion *goryōe*, used a similar logic to make sense of the sudden death of the *nyoin* Ikuhōmon'in following her enthusiastic participation in organizing the performances. More so than other urban festivals of the time, the Gion *goryōe* excelled in dismantling boundaries between classes and ontological orders, creating liminal spaces that sometimes resulted in crises of containment.

Visualizing Festive Space: Orders of Space in *Nenjū gyōji emaki*

By the latter half of the twelfth century, urban festivals had long become routinized. This did not mean that festivals no longer embodied the festive energy described by Hardacre, as discussed earlier in this chapter, but they did constitute an essential part of the court's annual calendar, along with court ceremonies and other Shinto and Buddhist rites. As a result, urban festivals occupied an ambiguous position: they were both volatile spaces of transgression and stabilizing waypoints in the cosmological oscillation of court-centered order.

The ambiguity of festive space is on full display in *Nenjū gyōji emaki*, which depicts several festivals, events, and court ceremonies that took place in the Heian capital. Commissioned by Retired Emperor GoShirakawa, it is thought to have originally encompassed some sixty scrolls. Only a fraction of these remains, in the form of an early seventeenth-century copy, and it is unclear if the ordering of scenes in the copy is the same as that of the original. This lack of clarity has led historians to question whether the copy can function as a reliable source of knowledge about the events it portrays, but given its rich

38. Wakita, *Chūsei Kyoto to Gion matsuri*, 37–38.

representations of public events during the late Heian period, it remains an important work to consider.

The scrolls often juxtapose two kinds of social space: the geometric and regimented space of court ceremony and the decentered, multidirectional space of festive crowds. Although there are other picture scrolls that depict annual events, created both before and after *Nenjū gyōji emaki*, the degree to which GoShirakawa's scrolls exhibit both kinds of space is unparalleled.[39] The two are not mutually exclusive and at times bleed into one another, suggesting the proximity of high and low in the increasingly urbanized capital. As a transgressive yet ultimately ordered assemblage commissioned by a powerful retired emperor, the scrolls depict scenes in which elites as well as ordinary residents of the capital—attendants, servants, and entertainers—participate in spaces of collective exuberance.[40]

The scrolls' two kinds of social space recall the notions of "smooth space" and "striated space" developed by Gilles Deleuze and Félix Guattari: smooth space is nomadic and heterogeneous, striated space is sedentary and homogeneous. Building on this, the space of festivals appears "smooth," since it consists of fibrous, heterogeneous entanglements; the space of court ceremony, on the other hand, appears "striated," because it exhibits a more homogenous structure. But just as Deleuze and Guattari question "the principles of the mixture, which are not at all symmetrical, sometimes causing a passage from the smooth to the striated, sometimes from the striated to the smooth, according to entirely different movements," so too do the two spaces in the scrolls interact in complex and asymmetrical ways.[41] The space of court ceremony impinges on festival space, bending smooth toward striated, but the crowds linger and sometimes transgress these newly imposed boundaries, thereby inflecting the striated with the smooth.

39. Nagai, "Hizō sareta 'toshizu,'" 153.

40. My readings of the scrolls follow the reproduction found in Komatsu Shigemi's *Nihon emaki taisei* series, which consists of the sixteen scrolls of the *Sumiyoshi-ke mohon*—the first seven are in color, while the latter nine are in black and white—as well as three black-and-white "separate scrolls" (*betsu hon*). The height of each scroll is between 45.3 and 47.4 centimeters, while their length varies widely, from 4.181 to 15.933 meters. See *Nenjū gyōji emaki*, front matter.

41. Deleuze and Guattari, *A Thousand Plateaus*, 475.

GoShirakawa: Vision, Exposure, Concealment

The interlaced sociospatial perspectives found in *Nenjū gyōji emaki* evoke GoShirakawa's wide range of cultural practices, which were often spectacular and frequently involved contact with non-elites. He was a devoted student of *imayō* vocal performance, which was practiced and transmitted primarily by unranked women.[42] His contemporary Jien (1155–1225) once referred derisively to "those unranked people [*gerō*] GoShirakawa kept close by: the crazy people [*kuruhimono*] of the world, including female spirit mediums [*miko*], itinerant *miko* [*kaunagi*], dancers [*mai*], *sarugaku* actors, and also—what can one say?—coppersmiths [*akaganezaiku*] and the like."[43] GoShirakawa also made the difficult pilgrimage to the shrines of Kumano more than thirty times, contributed to the construction of nearby replicas of distant shrines (e.g., Imagumano Shrine and Shin Hiyoshi Shrine), and had his attendants act out lavish warrior processions for his viewing pleasure. These are all, according to Komine Kazuaki, part of a broader cultural project of "making things visible" (*kashika suru*).[44] And with visibility comes exposure—to unfamiliar ideas, practices, and people, but also to critique.

For all his interest in spectacle, GoShirakawa simultaneously indulged in concealment, especially the stockpiling of precious objects like picture scrolls in his treasure vault (*hōzō*) at Rengeōin.[45] Two anecdotes in the tale collection *Kokon chomonjū* (A collection of notable tales

42. Kawashima, *Writing Margins*, 73–119. See chapter 6 for a discussion of the tension between this embodied vocal practice and GoShirakawa's textualization of it.

43. *Gukanshō*, NKBT 86:292. Jien makes a similar observation elsewhere, writing that GoShirakawa had a "natural predilection for dancers and *sarugaku* actors" (*tsune wa mai, sarugaku o konomi*) (278). For a catalogue and analysis of GoShirakawa's interactions with a variety of unranked urban residents, see Tsuji, *Chūsei no yūjo*, 98–106. Akiyama Kiyoko has furthermore demonstrated the extent to which GoShirakawa was an avid organizer of private performances of *sarugaku*. See Akiyama, *Chūsei kuge shakai*, 131–49.

44. Komine, "Inseiki no bunka to jidai," 25.

45. On GoShirakawa's treasure vault, see Abe, "Geinō ō no tōjō," 124–30. Contemporary records contain references to eighty different scrolls likely kept in the vault, and more than half of these were depiction of various annual events. Komatsu, "*Nenjū gyōji emaki* tanjō," 119.

old and new; 1254) give glimpses of how and why *Nenjū gyōji emaki* ended up in this vault. The first establishes a link between the scrolls' documentary function and GoShirakawa's admiration for them:

ON FUJIWARA NO MOTOFUSA [1144–1230] ATTACHING CORRECTIONS TO THE PICTURES OF ANNUAL EVENTS WHEN GOSHIRAKAWA WAS RETIRED EMPEROR

> When GoShirakawa was retired emperor, he commissioned pictures of annual events. He enjoyed them so much that he sent them to Motofusa. Motofusa analyzed them in depth, attaching slips of paper where errors had been made. He made note of the mistakes with his own hand and returned the pictures with the slips. The Dharma King [GoShirakawa] looked at the pictures, thinking he would have them corrected, but [instead] issued a statement: "Given the brilliance of Motofusa's corrections, how could I possibly dispose of the originals? As a result of his additions, these pictures have already become treasures." He then had them placed into the treasure vault at Rengeōin. The slips survive to this day. How remarkable![46]

We do not learn anything specific from the story about the content of the scrolls or GoShirakawa's precise motivations for commissioning them. But the idea that Motofusa would suggest corrections, and furthermore that those corrections would win GoShirakawa's admiration, indicates that *Nenjū gyōji emaki* was valued according to its verisimilitude to the events it represented. The exchange of pictures and information between the two suggests a documentary function for the scrolls. Having received corrections from an authority on the subject, GoShirakawa realizes that nothing more can be added and subsequently has the scrolls stored in his treasure vault. But if the scrolls were valuable insofar as they documented the rites and festivals of the court and the capital, why would he lock them away? The story introduces a tension between the potential utility of the scrolls and their treatment as precious objects. If the scrolls enabled a visualization of the ceremonial calendar, which in many ways provided the

46. *Kokon chomonjū*, SNKS 76:40–41.

court with its basic structure, perhaps GoShirakawa, as a retired emperor, sought to demonstrate mastery of this calendar by claiming sole possession of them.

The second story about the scrolls also highlights their value, but in this case the interlocutor is not a noble but rather the newly appointed shogun, Minamoto no Yoritomo (1147–1199):[47]

HOW THE GENERAL OF THE RIGHT MINAMOTO NO YORITOMO DID NOT LOOK AT THE PICTURES FROM THE TREASURE VAULT

> The Kamakura general of the Right once came to the capital for an offerings ceremony held at Tōdaiji. He said that he wanted to see the Dharma King's [GoShirakawa's] pictures from the treasure vault, since such things were truly hard to come by in Kantō. Yet Yoritomo [also] said, "How could I possibly fix my eyes on items from my lord's secret vault?" And so he abstained, looking at the pictures not even once, and had them sent back to the capital. It was unexpected, but the Dharma King was thoroughly entertained by this turn of events.[48]

In this case, Yoritomo's abstention from viewing serves to reinforce the notion that the scrolls are valuable precisely because they have been locked up and hidden from view. So powerful is this valence of the unseen that Yoritomo cannot bring himself to look at the scrolls even after they have been brought out specifically for his eyes alone.

These two stories show how in the generations after GoShirakawa's death, the scrolls were idealized as secret documentations of rites, ceremonies, and festivals, precious objects that retained value to the extent that they remained hidden from view. Seen in this way, *Nenjū gyōji emaki* becomes a panoramic and encyclopedic representation of the spatiotemporal flow of annual events in the capital, albeit one tethered to the latent vision of a single spectator: GoShirakawa.

47. The story does not specifically mention *Nenjū gyōji emaki*, but rather the more general "pictures from [GoShirakawa's] treasure vault," which most likely included but were not limited to the scrolls. *Kokon chomonjū*, SNKS 76:43.

48. *Kokon chomonjū*, SNKS 76:43.

The Structure of *Nenjū gyōji emaki*

The breadth of GoShirakawa's visualization project is on full display in *Nenjū gyōji emaki*, which covers some thirty-two annual events in its extant form.[49] The events include processions, banquets, diversions like kickball and archery competitions, purification rites, promotion ceremonies, and festivals. Some sections depict the monumental space and ordered choreography of elite events; others show a throng of festive bodies moving in multiple directions.

As a compendium of annual events, *Nenjū gyōji emaki* naturally begins with one of the ceremonies of the new year: the emperor's procession to the residence of his parents (*chōkin gyokō*). The procession unfolds from right to left, in the typical narrative grammar of picture scrolls. At the beginning of the scroll, the emperor emerges from the Shishinden outfitted in his ceremonial ochre robes, flanked by two female attendants, one holding the sacred jewel and the other the sacred sword, their faces obscured with fans. A black-robed figure, likely the regent, sits off to one side. Moving to the left, the viewer's gaze descends a steep staircase and encounters an ordered group of red-robed attendants who bear the phoenix-capped palanquin that the emperor will soon board. The attendants are in turn surrounded by several dark-robed palace guards outfitted with bows and quivers full of arrows. Further unfurling the scroll reveals more guards and attendants dallying between Shōmeimon and Kenreimon gates—the latter marking the boundary between the inner palace and the greater palace compound—and next a larger patchwork of groups preparing for the procession. The viewer eventually reaches Taikenmon gate, which provides passage between the greater palace compound and the city proper (at the intersection of Ōmiya and Nakamikado) and is overrun with crowds who have come to catch a glimpse of the procession.

When one peers at the aperture linking the palace with the wider city (fig. 1.2), it is difficult not to be struck by the diverse tangle of officials and attendants, women and men, children, animals, and

49. Fukuyama, "*Nenjū gyōji emaki* ni tsuite," 10. Based on the content of the scrolls, the term "event" (*gyōji*) signifies a range of ritual practices, including rites, ceremonies, and festivals.

FIGURE 1.2. A multidirectional, interclass, interspecies crowd surges around Taikenmon Gate as the emperor embarks on a New Year's outing. *Nenjū gyōji emaki*, scroll 1. Courtesy of National Diet Library.

objects, all charged with kinetic energy. The effect is heightened by the fact that *Nenjū gyōji emaki* does not often make use of *iji dōzu hō*, a stylistic technique whereby multiple temporalities are suggested by the appearance of the same figure(s) at different locations within the same frame.[50] As a result, unfurling the scroll does not enable the imperial procession to be tracked as it moves through the crowd, which would create the illusion of the passage of time. Instead, the scroll fixes in space and time the moment when crowds excitedly await the appearance of the procession. This fixing brings the differences between the two kinds of space—elite and non-elite, striated and smooth—into greater relief, as the hierarchical spatial arrangement of

50. The textbook example is found in *Ban Dainagon ekotoba* (The picture-tale of Grand Counselor Ban; late twelfth century), in a scene showing successive stages of a fight. *Ban Dainagon ekotoba*, 56.

the procession at the outset is quickly supplanted by the crowded multidirectionality of the greater imperial palace and beyond. Instead of depicting one central figure against an ever-changing ground (e.g., the emperor's palanquin as it moves through the avenues of the capital), the scene depicts a stable ground (the gates and avenues of the capital) teeming with countless figures.

Festive Space in *Nenjū gyōji emaki*

The two festivals discussed earlier in this chapter, the Inari Festival and the Gion *goryōe*, both receive sustained attention in the scrolls. These depictions not only enable us to visualize the two festivals' material and kinetic details around 1170, but they also prompt a consideration of the function of smooth space within the scrolls' broader form. The crowds that circulate through both scenes bring the festival to life for viewing eyes, even as they cause those same eyes to dart haphazardly from one disordered tangle of performing bodies to another. The depictions simultaneously attract and repel—they provide information about an external reality even as their multidirectional counterflow throws off the conventional narrative movement from right to left—and in this respect they share a sensibility with other treatments of non-elite practices.

As mentioned, the visual narrative of a picture scroll generally flows from right to left. To read a scroll, one places it on a flat surface, unties and unravels its clasp, and unfurls it leftwards a few feet at a time. To follow the narrative, one allows the right side to curl in on itself toward the left until it is about to contact the furled cylinder of paper, before unfurling another length. Through fluid repetition of this process, the passage from one scene to the next is interrupted only momentarily, resulting in something akin to a moving picture.[51]

It is therefore significant when action in picture scrolls tracks other vectors. The depiction of the Inari Festival and the Gion *goryōe* in *Nenjū gyōji emaki* are examples of such alternate movements. Instead

51. For more on the stakes of our physical engagement with picture scrolls, see Jackson, *Textures of Mourning*, 52–54.

of moving from right to left, the crowds generally progress from left to right: both scenes depict the part of the festival during which the *mikoshi* are transported from the capital back to the shrines, from west to east along the avenues. This eastward, rightward movement cuts against the grain of conventional narrative grammar, and as a result, unfurling the scrolls means beginning in a peripheral location and moving through masses of processing performers and revelers before arriving at a more central location where *mikoshi* are carried by groups of shrine attendants and watched by exuberant crowds lining the streets.

This countermovement immediately signals difference: the eye is not guided seamlessly, as it is in the case of the striated space of regimented ceremony, but it is rather left to wander among the smooth space of festivity. The depiction of the Inari Festival, for example, begins with a dense gathering of ox-drawn carriages, from which aristocrats lean out to get a better look at the horse-mounted *miko* balancing large umbrellas bedecked with sumptuous models of cranes, pines, and other auspicious symbols.[52] Tracing the movement leads the viewer to the Kamo River and the crowds gathered there. As shown in figure 1.3, the curved line in the upper left corner of the image is the eastern bank of the river, which means these participants have just crossed it (apparently on foot) and left the capital. This crossing evokes the general countermovement from left to right, but multiple spatial trajectories compete for attention. The action coalesces into four main zones. The bottom-right corner of the image shows a circle of several mounted *dengaku* musicians wearing wide-brimmed *ayaigasa* hats and playing their characteristic instruments: the transverse flute, the small *tsuzumi* drum, a larger *koshitsuzumi* drum, and the *binzasara*.

52. The festival constitutes the last third of the scroll. For a reproduction of the entire scroll, see *Nenjū gyōji emaki*, 56–65. The middle third of the scroll also depicts a festival. There is a shrine populated by revelers, followed by rice fields and a temporary stage, where spectators have gathered to watch *bugaku* dances and listen to music. Next there is a procession of *umaosa* boys, lion dancers, and attendants wearing extravagant clothing. The festival is not identified in the scroll, but based on the appearance of the shrine and the sorts of entertainments present, Gomi Fumihiko interprets it as the Imamiya Festival. Gomi, *Inseiki shakai no kenkyū*, 348–49.

FIGURE 1.3. A variety of boisterous performances during the Inari Festival, including *dengaku*, lion dances, and stone throwing, take place as the procession crosses the Kamo River on its way back to Inari Shrine. *Nenjū gyōji emaki*, scroll 11. Courtesy of National Diet Library.

A circular space fashioned by bodies is typical of a performance of *dengaku*; here the geometry not only indexes this convention but also diverts the rightward and leftward flows of action into an eddy, further differentiating space and inviting the eye to linger. Behind them follows a group of lion dancers, whose undulating costumes convey the jaunty music animating their progress. The upper half of the image, meanwhile, is dominated by leftward movement. Three stone throwers (*inji-uchi*) fling stones across the river at a rival group and are cheered on by a throng of supporters while below them an extravagantly dressed mounted guard, surrounded by warrior attendants, moves toward the bank.[53]

Continuing to the left, the viewer crosses the Kamo River at the same time as several attendants who carry poles outfitted with cascading paper streamers (*gohei*) that flutter in the wind. Above them can be seen the opposing group of stone throwers, gleefully preparing to fire their ammunition, and below them a man tugs on the arm of a woman who appears to have momentarily lost her footing while crossing the river. The pole-bearing attendants precede a group of five *mikoshi*, which is announced by a large *taiko* drum and a *bugaku* dancer. Groups of male attendants wearing hats and sandals carry the *mikoshi*, and they are joined by horse-mounted musicians and more pole-bearing attendants.

As the viewer's gaze crosses into the capital and spies the first *mikoshi*, several groups of spectators form a zone above and parallel to the main procession. Some onlookers peer out from row houses (*nagaya*) lining the avenue; others sit out front with their hands clasped and heads tilted toward the ground in reverence (fig. 1.4).[54] This zone of spectatorship (*mimono*) extends horizontally for the remainder of the scroll, culminating in three ox-drawn carriages jostling to win their aristocratic cargo a better view of the procession. The zone's horizontal sweep mirrors the linear unfolding of the procession, establishing a formal connection between viewing and being viewed that is held together by the negative space of the avenue. But though the spectators do not avert their gaze from the procession, the mobile crowd pays them little notice and instead looks elsewhere: mostly in front at the parade extending before them but also behind, toward the ground, and sometimes directly at the viewer. The

53. Also known as *tsubute*, the organized violence of stone throwing was a common occurrence at shrine festivals as early as the eleventh century. Amino Yoshihiko argues that stone throwing constituted an extrajudicial space of "haven" (*muen*) that was both feared and respected by elites. Amino, *Igyō no ōken*, 154–96.

54. My analysis of this and other images in *Nenjū gyōji emaki* was aided by Kurata Minoru's reproductions, which are painstakingly labeled and annotated. See Kurata, *Zukan Mono kara yomitoku ōchō emaki* 3:18–27. I thank Haruko Wakabayashi for telling me about this helpful resource when it was initially only available online.

FIGURE 1.4. A line of seated spectators parallel attendants carrying the first two *mikoshi* during the Inari Festival. *Nenjū gyōji emaki*, scroll 11. Courtesy of National Diet Library.

spectators' gaze gravitates centripetally toward the action, but the participants' gaze scatters centrifugally throughout the boisterous procession. Regardless of whether the viewer of the scroll enters the scene through the spectators or the participants, one is inevitably drawn toward the crowd and pulled this way and that by its multidirectional energy.

Nenjū gyōji emaki's depiction of the Gion *goryōe* also flows from left to right, features several discrete groups of performers, and makes use of negative space to suggest kinetic action and lines of sight.[55] Some scholars have questioned whether the festival depicted in the

55. For a reproduction of the scroll, see *Nenjū gyōji emaki*, 44–48.

scrolls is not a different festival altogether. Gomi Fumihiko, for example, argues that details like the inclusion of a performance of *seinō* and what appears to be one of the *tabisho* being dismantled suggest instead the Imamiya Festival.[56] Wakita, though agreeing that *seinō* is rarely mentioned in records of the Gion *goryōe*, notes that it is nonetheless found in records of other *goryōe*. Moreover, she argues that the structure being dismantled is a temporary viewing hut (*akusha*) and not one of the three permanent *tabisho* used during the Gion *goryōe*. Because three *mikoshi* are depicted, one for each of the Gion deities, Wakita instead posits that the scrolls visualize the festival from the viewpoint of the Sanjō *tabisho*, at the intersection of Sanjō and Ōmiya, since this is where the *mikoshi* assembled after being carried along two different routes.[57] Wakita's reading is convincing. The Sanjō *tabisho* is where the two crowds converged and prepared to charge east along Sanjō in a climactic return to Gion Shrine, a fitting moment to depict. Furthermore, showing the procession from the viewpoint of the *tabisho* aligns the viewer's eyes with GoShirakawa's, allowing viewers to see the same smooth space that elites did.[58]

The scroll begins with two groups of spectators jostling to get a look at a performance of *dengaku*. *Dengaku* was not simply one of the many performances included in *goryōe* as entertainment for the gods. Commencing the depiction of the *goryōe* with *dengaku* is a nod to what had become a conventional association by the 1170s. As the first thing to appear upon unfurling the scroll, the *dengaku* performance arrests the viewer's gaze and encourages an exploration of a dense, smooth performance space that vibrates with kinetic energy

56. Gomi, *Inseiki shakai no kenkyū*, 346–48. *Seinō* (literally "thin man" or "man of ability," depending on which sinographs are used) is an ancient form of dance that, according to Heian-period records, consisted of a group of six performers dressed in white robes and masks, two playing flutes, two drumming, and two dancing. In the twelfth century it was associated with *goryōe* as well as the Kasuga Wakamiya Festival (Onmatsuri). See "Seinō."

57. Wakita, *Chūsei Kyoto to Gion matsuri*, 52–53.

58. GoShirakawa was also materially involved. *Hyakurenshō* (One hundred tempered selections; thirteenth century), a compilation of records, contains an entry dated 1172/6/14 (Jōan 2) stating that GoShirakawa donated three *mikoshi* and seven lion-dance costumes for the 1172 Gion *goryōe*. *Hyakurenshō*, SZKT 11:87.

FIGURE 1.5. *Dengaku* musicians perform during the Gion *goryōe*. *Nenjū gyōji emaki*, scroll 6. Courtesy of National Diet Library.

(fig. 1.5).[59] The musician in the middle of the semicircle flings his drum into the air. He tilts his head skyward, his mouth opens wide in song, and his outstretched hands anticipate the drum's rapid descent. This midair suspension is mirrored by the surrounding musicians' arched *binzasara* and wide, uneven stances. Nothing is stationary. To the left of the semicircle kneels a bald man, hat around his waist, holding a pole fitted with two horizontal pegs and waiting for his turn to perform. He is a practitioner of *takaashi* (also *kōsoku*), a feat of balance

59. For labels and analysis, see Kurata, *Zukan Mono kara yomitoku ōchō emaki* 3:36–45.

similar to stilt walking but making use of only one pole.[60] This dynamic scene communicates the corporeal intensity that *dengaku* radiated by the end of the twelfth century, when it had integrated the music of rural agricultural festivals with the urban acrobatics of *sangaku*.

Moving on from the *dengaku*, the viewer next encounters a flurry of activity: one horse has fallen and bucked its rider, another rears out of control and causes the *umaosa* boy riding it to hold on for dear life. Attendants caper around, their eyes fixed on the scene and their mouths agape with excitement. The scene recalls the description of the out-of-control *umaosa* procession during the Inari Festival discussed by Akihira's nameless letter writer. Farther to the left, the procession increases in density: attendants carry sacred sticks and poles outfitted with paper streamers, a *miko* riding on a horse displays a decorated parasol, and a *bugaku* dancer lifts his knee and thrusts his hand out in a performance of the dance Sanju. Several shrine attendants march in front of the first *mikoshi* (bearing Gozu Tennō) and carry the spears (*hoko*) that would eventually come to typify the Gion *goryōe*. The three *mikoshi* are surrounded by a tangle of lion dancers, mounted *dengaku* musicians, *miko*, street urchins (*kyōwarawa*), and a line of spectators. Bringing up the rear of the procession is another bucking horse (and attendants scattered around it), some stragglers, and finally several men dismantling a viewing hut and a few stray groups of conversing spectators. As the end of the scroll approaches, the boisterous procession breaks into pockets of activity before fading into negative space.

Nenjū gyōji emaki depicts not only the many events that constituted the court's ceremonial calendar but also the entanglement of these events with public space and its unscripted energies. Unlike the manuals of events written by courtiers, it looks beyond the panoply of ceremonial details and situates events in their wider urban contexts. Even depictions of imperial processions inevitably include crowds of unaffiliated spectators hoping to catch a glimpse. The scrolls hence situate the gestures, spatial arrangements, objects, and costumes that

60. Hama Kazue associates *kōsoku* and the related *issoku* (literally "one-footing") with a form of Chinese pole balancing called *gaoqiao*. Hama, *Nihon geinō no genryū*, 285–91.

made up annual events within the real spaces of the capital, where smooth and striated interlaced and transgression came and went. It is in this sense that *Nenjū gyōji emaki* documents: it does not present exemplary types to be emulated but rather contingent formations that momentarily arrest the fluidity of time and space.

Contingency and fluidity—these two words epitomize the broader shift away from the older model of a sage emperor ruling the realm through centripetal ritual. The emergence and formalization of urban festivals over the course of the Heian period embodies this shift: the capital went from being the "inert realm" of a theater state invested above all in the bureaucratic management of symbolic purity to a vibrant, diverse, uneven, and contested space harboring multiple power blocs and spheres of influence. Festivals, incorporated but not wholly integrated, epitomize this emergent order.

CHAPTER TWO

Working the Land

Dengaku, Agriculture, and Rural Practices

In this chapter, I situate the emergence of *dengaku* within a broader constellation of agricultural rituals and performances, using a variety of historical records and literary texts to explore the textures of elite identification triggered by these practices. In the Heian period, the cultivation of cereals was symbolically central to how the state imagined and expressed itself, and this importance was broadly attested by a range of cultural nodes, from enduring myths about agricultural deities in *Kojiki* (An account of ancient matters; 712) and *Nihon shoki* (The chronicles of Japan; 720) to rituals like harvest festivals (*niinamesai*), the Great Thanksgiving Festival (Daijōsai) performed as part of an emperor's enthronement, and local *taue* planting rites. Though many of these have long been interpreted as heightening the value of rice in particular—and thereby creating a sacred bond between rice, the state, and society—more recent scholarship shows how the polycultural reality of agricultural production throughout the premodern period signifies a lack of any "conceptual particularity" or "distinctive symbolism" for rice.[1]

A less intuitive but no less interesting complication of the "agricultural fundamentalist ideology" that perpetuates this "rizicentric argument" inheres in the history of *dengaku*, a repertoire that possessed

1. Von Verschuer, *Rice, Agriculture, and the Food Supply*, 290.

strong links with wet-rice agriculture and the technique of divine appeal, yet still produced ambivalent reactions among elites.[2] As *dengaku* moved into the urban spaces of the capital, the anxieties it provoked—about crowds, rurality, and otherness—demonstrated the lack of any straightforward veneration of rice and the rites that supported its cultivation. Elites, of course, depended on the cultivation of cereals and pulses for food, but as residents of an urban enclave, they were not farmers and were therefore often distanced, materially and psychologically, from the production of these crops. Agriculture and the labor it necessitated signified ambiguity, pulling some in and pushing others away.

I begin with Sei Shōnagon's two encounters with farmers laboring in the fields just outside the capital, examining how the first experience inspires repulsion and the second attraction. Next, I discuss a series of rice-planting rites (*kōden no rei*, related to *taue*) performed by nonelites for Emperor Seiwa in the 860s, arguing that they are attempts to stage open crowds as closed—that is, efforts to choreograph the festive performances that support agricultural labor as elite observational pleasure. I then describe the Shidarajin Incident of 945, in which tens of thousands of provincial revelers marched—singing, dancing, pounding on drums, and playing flutes—toward the capital carrying shrines devoted to a trio of deities. In terms of its crowd dynamics and trajectory (moving from the periphery toward the center), this incident can be seen as a precursor to the Great Dengaku of 1096, discussed at length in chapter 3. Lastly, I examine literary and historical representations of *dengaku* in the eleventh century, which were typically embedded in othering discourses of violence, the strange, and humor.

Sei Shōnagon's Rural Encounters

Sei Shōnagon's *Makura no sōshi* is a multisensory account of aristocratic life in the capital consisting of things seen, heard, felt, experienced, and remembered. As a member of Empress Teishi's (976–1000)

2. Amino, *Rethinking Japanese History*, 25; and Von Verschuer, *Rice, Agriculture, and the Food Supply*, 265.

salon, she had access to the highest levels of court society, and her miscellany reads as a distillation of mid-Heian aristocratic values and aesthetics. *Makura no sōshi* has often been read as an account of the elite's self-absorption and inwardness, yet there is much in the text that gestures beyond the rarefied boundaries of the court. Sei in fact interacts with and comments on a variety of social others. For example, she mentions the inappropriate appearance of a hemp palm in an "inferior" (*waruki*) dwelling (section 38, "Nonflowering Trees") and the unsuitability of snow falling on a "lowly" (*gesu*) home (section 43, "Unsuitable Things").[3] In general, Sei distances herself from non-elites by describing them as rough, repulsive, and ignorant, but due to the dialectical nature of her acts of identification, the text retains a detailed account of non-elite culture.

Jeffrey Angles, in an article analyzing the range of depictions of commoners in *Makura no sōshi*, argues that Sei's seemingly pejorative treatment of commoners cannot be taken at face value, as had been the case in previous scholarship. Angles instead shows how her disparaging attitude and remarks are related to a more nuanced intentionality. First, Sei sometimes includes scenes in which her patron, Empress Teishi, behaves sympathetically toward non-elites, likely a calculated rhetorical move designed to bolster the empress's reputation, especially in those accounts written after the death of her father and subsequent loss of political backing.[4] And second, Sei's negative treatment of non-elites often seems to stem from a distaste for social transgression in general, as she also criticizes her fellow elites for acting in ways not in line with their rank and status.[5] In this section, I explore Sei's situational and performative invocation of non-elites, arguing that their representation embodies a transgressive excess that

3. Section numbers refer to the edited version of the Sankanbon text found in *Makura no sōshi*, SNKBZ 18. For a brief overview of the text's manuscript lineages, see Midorikawa, "Reading a Heian Blog," 144–45. The hemp palm is unsuitable in non-elite dwellings because it has a "Chinese appearance" (*kara mekite*), making it more suitable for the gardens of aristocrats. The second example implies that the beautiful and poetic scene of snow falling on a house is at odds with the image of a non-elite dwelling. *Makura no sōshi*, SNKBZ 18:94, 100.

4. Angles, "Watching Commoners, Performing Class," 43–49.

5. Angles, "Watching Commoners, Performing Class," 53–55.

activates the simultaneous attraction and repulsion characteristic of the many acts of elite identification examined throughout this book.

Representing the variety of sounds experienced in and around the court is one of the ways Sei demonstrates her membership in court society. As Nakagawa Shin argues, Sei uses sound to map the boundaries between the rarefied world of the court (both its real and discursive spaces) and the world beyond—the boundaries that demarcate inside from outside, high from low.[6] Such social geographies materialize when, for example, Sei deplores the absence of the call of the *uguisu* (bush warbler) among the palace grounds (section 39, "Birds"): "The *uguisu* is described as a wonderful bird in Chinese poems. Its song and appearance as well are so beautiful that it's very untoward [*ito waroki*] for it not to come onto the palace grounds and sing. [. . .] But if you go out, you'll hear them chattering away in a nondescript plum tree near some lowly dwelling [*ayashiki ie*]."[7] Sei bemoans the fact that the *uguisu*, with its charming song and poetic significance, was never heard at the palace, its proper place according to court aesthetics. Her complaint serves to anthropomorphize the bird, who transgresses the ideal social order of space. Sei further chastises the bird in section 206, "Spectacles," where she describes how thrilling it is to hear the call of the *hototogisu* (lesser cuckoo) during a procession but also registers her mild annoyance at an *uguisu* that "mimics" (*nisemu to*) the call with its own "old song" (*oitaru koe*).[8] These episodes introduce the crux of Sei's perspective on social standing and identity: certain sounds belong to certain social spaces, and an act of mimicry that transgresses the boundaries between these spaces, even momentarily, is unseemly.

Sei again transforms birdsong into a contested social space when she records her encounter with rice-planting women while on a pilgrimage to Kamo Shrine (section 210):

> When on a pilgrimage to Kamo Shrine, I came upon several women who were planting rice [*ta uu to te*] while singing songs and wearing what looked like new serving trays as hats. They were hunched over so I

6. Nakagawa, *Heiankyō*, 78–80.
7. *Makura no sōshi*, SNKBZ 18:96.
8. *Makura no sōshi*, SNKBZ 18:343.

couldn't quite make out what they were doing [*nanigoto suru tomo miede*], but they moved backward. *I wonder why*, I thought, and looked on in fascination [*wokashi to miyuru*], at which point I heard them sing a horrible song about the *hototogisu*. It was so unpleasant. It went:

Hey you there, *hototogisu*, all of you!	*hototogisu, ore, kayatsu ya*
It's all thanks to your song	*ore nakite koso*
that our planting moves along!	*ware wa ta uure*

Hearing it made me think of the poem—whose was it?—that goes, "Don't sing so loud!"[9]

Kamo Shrine was only a few kilometers north of the palace, but Sei's encounter with the women in the liminal space between the two dramatizes its symbolic distance from the aristocratic center. The women are visually confounding: Sei seems unfamiliar with the broad hats they wear and summons the image of a serving tray to describe them. Furthermore, she cannot quite make out what they are doing. They appear to be hunched over, moving backward through the field—an entirely natural posture for the labor-intensive act of planting rice. But their song reaches her ears with perfect clarity, despite the unrefined language (*ore*, *kayatsu*) they use. Sei's fascination with the women dissipates when her aesthetic sensibilities are offended, causing her to quickly transition from their folk song to the more familiar territory of *waka*.

The following section, 211, develops in parallel fashion but with notable differences. It is now the eighth month (early autumn), and Sei is on pilgrimage to Kōryūji in Uzumasa, west of the capital. Instead of women planting rice and singing folk songs, she encounters men cutting the rice stalks that have grown during the intervening months. She first quotes a poem from *Kokin wakashū* (Collection of ancient and modern waka; ca. 913), reflecting on the rapid passage of time, and then proceeds to detail her fascination with the men's labor: "They cut the base

9. *Makura no sōshi*, SNKBZ 18:348. A handful of poems begin with the phrase "*Hototogisu*, don't sing so loud!," so it is not possible to know which one Sei refers to here.

[of the rice stalks] using something or other. It looked easy, like something I might want to try. For some reason they laid out the ears of rice and crouched around them, and this too was interesting."[10]

As in the previous section, Sei's attention is captured by the seasonal labor demanded by wet-rice agriculture, but in this case her fascination is not immediately diverted into aristocratic frames of meaning. The autumnal colors (the rice ears have turned red), the ease with which the men slice the stalks, and the interesting (*wokashi*) way they lay them down and crouch around them—these details draw her in and produce a desire to perform the same kind of labor (*semahoshige ni miyuru ya*). Although planting and culling rice are both physically demanding, performing the latter does not involve getting one's hands dirty in the same way, due to the availability of a sickle (*kama*), the likely referent of the "something or other" (*nanika aramu*) used by the men. On this fall pilgrimage to a famous Buddhist temple, Sei does not deride or reject the unfamiliar practices she encounters but rather identifies them as things that she too might want to do. In an act of imagined commonality, Sei projects herself into the position of the laboring men she watches and considers what it would be like to do something she has never done before, something she perhaps has no way of doing given the nature of the Confucian society in which she lived. She does not cross the boundary between imagined desire and experienced reality, but in this passage, at least, she does not deny the desire to do so.[11]

Rice-Planting Rites in the Capital: Staging Symbolic Authority

Sections 210 and 211 in *Makura no sōshi* play on the tension between repulsion and attraction that characterizes many acts of elite identification. Elites often viewed agricultural labor and its attendant culture

10. *Makura no sōshi*, SNKBZ 18:349.

11. Angles perceptively notes that the text uses the word *hito* or "person" to refer to the men, which "by not semantically marking them as peasants and thus dividing herself from them [. . .] opens up a possible channel of identification." Angles, "Watching Commoners, Performing Class," 57.

with ambivalence—it happened largely out of sight, in other places, and yet it was integral to life, both real and symbolic. Even though aristocrats did not typically work the land with their own hands, it was not uncommon for them to sponsor rites that sought to ensure abundance, especially when affected by drought, epidemic, or resource depletion.

To consider how the state attempted to integrate such non-elite performances into its ritual economy, I first examine two ninth-century rice-planting rites (*kōden no rei*) in the capital, as described by entries in *Nihon sandai jitsuroku*.[12] The rites themselves are not treated in depth but instead constitute one element in a multifaceted celebratory ritual that placed Emperor Seiwa at the center of several auspicious activities, including the appreciation of cherry blossoms, musical performance, poetry composition, archery demonstrations, and the giving of alms and emoluments. The events took place at the Somedono, the residence of Grand Minister Fujiwara no Yoshifusa (804–872), but unlike the other activities, the rice-planting rites were situated just outside the eastern gate of the residence, a liminal zone due to its proximity to but strict exclusion from the space of imperial diversion.[13] This spatial configuration indicates the ambiguous position of non-elite agricultural performance in one of its earliest

12. *Kōden* denotes the practice of cultivating a field for wet-rice agriculture. *Kōden no rei* thus refers to the ritual practice that generally accompanied that labor. Rural *dengaku* (*nōson dengaku*) can be classified as one permutation of this practice; others are the field dances (*tamai*) and field songs (*tauta, taue uta*) that were included in Daijōe (ceremonies held after the accession of a new emperor) and shrine festivals. See Ushio, *Ōtaue to taue uta*. A description of a similar event can be found in an earlier entry in *Nihon kiryaku*, copied from *Nihon kōki* (A later account of Japan; 840), which, as the third national history, covers the years 792–833. The entry, dated 832/4/14 (Tenchō 9), states that Fujiwara no Junshi (809–871), the principal wife of Emperor Ninmyō (r. 833–50), "went to the Urin Pavilion to observe the customs of farming." *Nihon kiryaku zenpen*, SZKT 10:333.

13. According to *Nihon sandai jitsuroku*, Yoshifusa officially assumed the position of grand minister (*daijō daijin*) on 866/8/19 (Jōgan 8). *Nihon sandai jitsuroku*, SZKT 4:193. But later texts, such as *Ōkagami uragaki* and *Kugyō bunin*, push this development back to 858. Regardless of the exact date, Yoshifusa's appointment—the first non-imperial recipient of the position—is often situated as an important moment in the Fujiwara family's consolidation of political power and the inauguration of the regency system. See Mezaki, "Fujiwara no Yoshifusa."

documented moments of contact with the center of imperial power. The encounter does not pit capital against countryside in any categorical way but instead indicates the uneasy but inevitable connections between the multiple centers and peripheries that constituted the segmented political and economic environment of Heian Japan, despite the chroniclers' attempt to idealize relationships between these different groups as seamless and productive.[14]

The account of the first rice-planting rite appears in the entry dated 864/2/25 (Jōgan 6), which describes Emperor Seiwa's visit to Yoshifusa's Somedono residence:

> Emperor Seiwa traveled by palanquin to the grand minister's residence, in the eastern section of the capital, to admire the cherry blossoms. On the way he stopped at Ichijō Mansion, for this is where he was born. The grand minister had drink brought to the various attendants, bureaucrats and officers, and the imperial entourage. Prizes were gathered in the courtyard as the emperor watched. All received various amounts. He then entered the Flower Pavilion.[15] The crown princes and chamberlains were all arrayed in waiting. The grand minister had court musicians perform from the instructional repertoire. He then summoned ten exceptionally skilled poets, fifth rank and above; ten sixth-rank bureaucrats from the various ministries; and twenty students of letters. He ordered music played and poems composed. Wine was served and all rejoiced. The emperor then moved from the Flower Pavilion to the archery field. He drew his bow and arrow and felled a swan with a single shot. His entourage cried out in applause. Next up were the crown princes, who took turns shooting. The governor of Yamashiro, Ki no Imamori, lower senior fourth rank, arrived at the eastern fence with a group of district officials and farmers [*hyakushō*].[16] They proceeded to perform the rice-planting rite. [Imamori] wanted the emperor to watch

14. See Adolphson and Kamens, "Between and Beyond," 2–3.

15. "Flower Pavilion" is a literal translation of "Katei," which appears to have been one of the buildings that made up the larger Somedono compound.

16. Although the Modern Japanese term *hyakushō* refers specifically to farmers, this was not always the case. Amino Yoshihiko notes that this particular meaning did not emerge until the early modern period; during the medieval period and earlier, *hyakushō* signified—in addition to farmers—mountain dwellers, ocean dwellers, and even merchants and artisans who lived in cities. See Amino, *Nihon chūsei no minshū*

> in order to learn about the farmers [*nōmin kore o shiru*]. They reveled from dawn till dusk and then retired.[17]

Here Emperor Seiwa is described enjoying various kinds of entertainment at Yoshifusa's residence. The highlight of the passage for present purposes is the appearance of farmers conducting a rice-planting rite for the eyes of the emperor. That provincial governor Imamori considers this an opportunity for the emperor to learn about farmers and their labor implies that the emperor was indeed cut off from such people and practices. Furthermore, as Inoue Mitsurō notes, it is significant that the farmers do not arrive on their own but are led to the Somedono by Imamori.[18] This means that the emperor's act of viewing the rite is mediated by the presence of this provincial official and, in a more general sense, by the increasingly complex set of relationships between central and provincial authorities.[19] The triangulation of emperor, non-elite performers, and governor further highlights the theatrical nature of the occasion: not only does the emperor witness an agricultural rite deprived of its primary productive context, but he also does so through the mediating presence of a provincial governor, who, it can be surmised, wished to parlay the occasion into political capital.

A description of another rice-planting rite appears two years later, in an entry dated 866/i3/1 (Jōgan 8), and it too indicates a concern with notions of proximity and observation. In addition to the usual diversions, "the emperor went to the eastern gate to watch the farmer men and women [*nōfu denpu*] as they cultivated a rice field, performing miscellaneous music all the while."[20] "Miscellaneous music" trans-

---

zō, 20. In this case, *hyakushō* most certainly signifies farmers, but it is important to note the term's breadth when used in premodern documents.

17. *Nihon sandai jitsuroku*, SZKT 4:132.

18. Inoue, "Eichō gannen no dengaku sōdō," 4–5.

19. The growing friction between these two groups, and the accompanying rise of regional bands of warriors, is vividly illustrated by the rebellions that erupted during the Shōhei and Tengyō periods (931–947). For narratives of these rebellions, see "Shōmonki," NST 8:315–26 (CJ: 186–227), and the entry dated 940/11/21 (Tengyō 3) in *Fusō ryakki*, SZKT 12:218–19.

20. *Nihon sandai jitsuroku*, SZKT 4:179.

lates *zōgaku*, a term signifying a broad range of musical practices and, along with *sangaku*, often used in opposition to court music (*gagaku*). (See chapter 5.) As with the previous entry, the work of the men and women is situated as an object of imperial observation. The festive and felicitous tone is also similar, but an intriguing divergence brings the entry to an end. Instead of listing the promotions awarded, the entry concludes by calling attention to the plight of the poor: "Today the poor and struggling of the capital gathered along the Kamo River. Fifty thousand *mon* of newly minted coins and 2,500 bundles of rice were distributed, and recitations of the Diamond and Heart Sutras were carried out at thirty-three temples in the vicinity of the capital."[21] The careful articulation of a benevolent sage emperor is certainly in line with the operative *ritsuryō* ideology, but the presence of these abject figures also indexes the recurring economic and epidemiological crises faced by the court in an age of depopulation—a reminder of the fragility of the social order.

These imperial rice-planting rites belong to a strategy of peripheral assimilation that was moribund by the 860s. Along with poetry, music, and archery, here agricultural labor becomes an object of the imperial gaze, but unlike the other performances, the activities of the farmers are presented as political pedagogy. Seiwa's act of observing these farmers and their labor attempts to stage a unity between the sage emperor and the rural workers that make up the vast majority of the populace: to see is to know, and to know is to rule. Of course, the choreographed nature of this encounter belies the sincerity of such a unity. As William Wayne Farris has shown, the stretch of time between 800 and 1050 was marked above all by depopulation and labor shortages caused by epidemics, ecological degradation, and crop failure.[22] With increasing numbers of rice fields falling fallow, many farmers retreated to the mountains and the ocean for sustenance, a trend that prompted estate managers and provincial officials to counter with attempts to "encourage agriculture." Farris notes the "highly ritualized" nature of this endeavor, which "included a ceremonial offering of rice wine on the first day of the year, 'playing in the fields' [*ta-asobi*]

21. *Nihon sandai jitsuroku*, SZKT 4:180.
22. Farris, *Japan to 1600*, 59–60.

to soothe the spirit of the lands with dance and song, and a petition to family gods to protect the household from disaster."[23] The appearance of rice-planting rites within the space of imperial diversion shows how this policy of encouraging agriculture was a central concern of the court as well. By having Emperor Seiwa view groups of performing farmers, what would over time become codified as an agrarian fundamentalist ideology obtained an early expression.

The hierarchical act of viewing depicted in the account of these rites accords with the general orientation of closed crowds, which renounce growth and stress permanence. Open crowds, as will be discussed further in the next several sections and in chapter 3, facilitate transgressions of boundaries—between spectators and performers, elites and non-elites. The fear of the open crowd betrays the anxieties of identity: contact stimulates fantasies of separation and containment, prompting a reinvention of both self and other through the festive crucible of performance. Whereas the emperor's observation of rice-planting rites was one of the many acts that defined his cosmologically central position in a closed system, the greater degree of participation by the imperial family and courtiers in the Great Dengaku of 1096, for example, gave rise to reactionary discourses of otherness. By tracing the transition from the closed crowd of the ninth century to the open crowd that had emerged in central spaces by the eleventh century, I argue that these events demonstrate a significant shift in the politics of culture across the Heian period.

The Shidarajin Incident: Religion, Agriculture, and Rural Protest

In the fall of 945, nearly a century after Emperor Seiwa viewed the rice-planting rites, tens of thousands of revelers paraded behind portable shrines carrying an obscure triad of deities. This is one of the earliest examples of a wide-ranging open crowd in the early medieval archive, and it subsequently became known as the Shidarajin Incident, in reference to one of these deities. The sources for the event are several

23. Farris, *Japan to 1600*, 66.

lengthy entries from *Honchō seiki* (The eras of our realm; begun ca. 1150) and a brief entry from *Ribu ōki*, the diary of Prince Shigeakira (906–954).[24]

Not much is known about the three deities depicted as the focal point of religious activity during the disturbance: Shidarajin, Koigasagami, and Hachimengami. The appearance and disappearance of these deities has prompted much speculation among scholars, but barring the discovery of additional materials, questions about their nature and function will remain a matter of speculation.[25] On the other hand, the extant descriptions reveal quite a lot about the Shidarajin Incident itself—where it began, its geographical and crowd trajectory, and even the songs performed by the revelers. Broad parallels between this event and the Great Dengaku of 1096 can be drawn in terms of size, trajectory, and the centrality of performance to each movement's functioning. In contrast to court-sponsored invitations of non-elites to temporarily perform in the capital, as with the rice-planting rites, open-crowd formations like the Shidarajin movement arose in a more spontaneous fashion, from the bottom up. In this sense, the Shidarajin Incident marks an important moment in the history of relations between rural performers and elites in the capital.

The incident unfolded during the fall of the eighth year of the Tengyō era (945). Spanning from 938 to 947, this era witnessed several important political developments, including the continued

24. *Honchō seiki* is a work of history encompassing more than two hundred years, from 935 to 1153, and was compiled by Fujiwara no Michinori (also known by his Buddhist name, Shinzei, 1106–1159), an influential scholar and supporter of GoShirakawa who was executed during the Heiji Disturbance. The text begins where *Nihon sandai jitsuroku*, now deemed to be the last of the six national histories, left off, but many sections were never completed due to the author's untimely death. The reigns of emperors Horikawa (r. 1086–1107) and Konoe (r. 1141–1155) receive by far the most detailed coverage, but the text also preserves valuable records from earlier time periods. Prince Shigeakira was the fourth son of Emperor Daigo (r. 897–930); his diary is also known as *Rihō ōki*.

25. According to later records, Shidarajin worshippers made another pilgrimage to the capital in the early eleventh century. The chronicle *Hyakurenshō* records in an entry dated 1012/2/8 (Chōwa 1) that "Shidarajin [worshippers] came to the capital from Chinzei [Kyushu]. Today they arrived in Mt. Funaoka and Murasakino." *Hyakurenshō*, SZKT 11:14.

consolidation of the regency system by the northern branch of the Fujiwara family and the vigorous rebellions of Taira no Masakado (quelled in 940) and Fujiwara no Sumitomo (quelled in 941). There were also several noteworthy natural disasters: flooding and a large earthquake in 938, downpours in 941, famine in 942, and typhoons and flooding in 943 and 944. As Yamagami Izumo argues, the Shidarajin Incident in many ways reveals the regency government's inability to effectively manage the natural and political disasters that beset the realm.[26] In this sense a parallel can be drawn between the crowds that populated the Shidarajin movement and the bands of warriors that launched the two regional rebellions. The two groups are even depicted as following some of the same deities.[27]

The earliest description of the Shidarajin Incident is found in *Honchō seiki*, in an entry dated 945/7/28 (Tengyō 8). A full translation follows:

> As of late rumors [*kagen*] have been circulating throughout the capital that various deities have arrived in the capital from the provinces to the east and west. They are called Shidarajin, Koigasagami, and Hachimengami. The report submitted today from Settsu Province follows.

A REPORT CONCERNING THREE PORTABLE SHRINES BEING CARRIED TO THE EAST

> As mentioned, a report was acquired from an official of Teshima District on the twenty-sixth day of this month, according to which there were three portable shrines bearing the name Shidarajin. On the twenty-fifth, at the Hour of the Dragon [8:00 a.m.], three portable shrines venerating Shidarajin [arrived] from the direction of Kawabe District. The three shrines were carried by hundreds, who displayed offerings, struck small drums, and performed songs and dances. Arriving in this district, men and women, monks and laypeople, high and low, old and young all

26. Yamagami, "'Shidarajin' shinkō," 22.

27. Uejima Susumu points out that Hachiman and Tenjin—two of the deities supported by the Shidarajin movement—were at the time incorporated into the devotional activities of those who resisted state authority. Uejima, *Nihon chūsei shakai*, 236–37.

> gathered from dawn till dusk in groups and moved mountains with their songs and dances. On the twenty-sixth, at the Hour of the Dragon, they hoisted up the shrines and made offerings, performing songs and dances in this way. The offerings included fruit as well as numerous types of miscellaneous goods. They [next] departed for Shimashimo District. Upon inquiring, [it was discovered that] one shrine was covered with cypress bark and a *torii* dedicated to Fumie Jizai Tenjin. The two other shrines were covered with cypress leaves but no *torii*. Today Eishun came at the Hour of the Snake [10:00 a.m.] and said, "Those carrying the three shrines again performed songs and dances. This morning they brought them to Jiyadera in Kawabe District."
>
> Here ends the report. It cannot go unheeded, so it appears here in full. Seventh month, twenty-eighth day, Tengyō 8 [945].
>
> Senior Sixth Upper Rank Senior Clerk Lord Ikehara no Yasu . . .[28]
> Junior Fifth Lower Rank Lord Governor Fujiwara no Fuminori[29]

The entry consists mostly of a report from Settsu Province that describes the incident but begins by noting the circulation of rumors (*kagen*) throughout the capital. Unlike the Great Dengaku, which inspired descriptions in courtier diaries only after it had spread throughout the real spaces of the capital, the Shidarajin Incident first reached the political center as transient verbal echoes of a spectacle unfolding elsewhere. The speaker takes these rumors seriously, as indicated by the concluding entreaty that "the district's report cannot go unheeded" (*gunge no mune wa mōsazu bekarazu*). *Kagen*—groundless or false (*ka*) words (*gen*)—threaten not by virtue of their misrepresentation of a particular reality but rather due to their ability to circulate widely and inspire action.

The belief that words can function performatively to bring about certain effects (*kotodama*), both auspicious and inauspicious, was an important component of early Japanese thought and has implications for how we understand reactions to exogenous events like the

28. There is a lacuna in the text here.
29. *Honchō seiki*, SZKT 9:109.

Shidarajin Incident.[30] Descriptions of such events were often accompanied by parallel concerns about an intangible yet ritualistically manageable force at work, one that demanded just as much attention as the "actual" event. This is one reason why those who recorded events like the Shidarajin Incident frequently referred to figures like rumors, "strange words" (*yōgen*), songs thought to foreshadow and in some cases provoke events (*wazauta*), and a range of invisible, supernatural beings.[31] Making sense of strange phenomena unfolding in the world involved a system of belief centered on the ability of words to perform actions and address potential threats.

It is unclear whether the three names of deities given—Shidarajin, Koigasagami, and Hachimengami—refer to three discrete deities. It is possible that they simply signify three different names for the same deity. Despite this ambiguity, the movement was in many ways organized around Shidarajin, whether one or many. Although its provenance remains unknown, the name seems to be phonetically associated with rhythmic percussion. For example, in the songs performed by the Shidarajin followers, discussed at the end of this section, the phonetic recurrence of *shidara* with the verb *utsu* (to strike) supports this interpretation, as does a note from *Kōtai jingū nenjū gyōji* (Inner shrine annual events; 1192) that refers to "*shidara* being struck and hands being clapped" (*shidara o uchi, te o tataku nari*).[32]

Rhythm is again highlighted in the report from the local government of Settsu Province. It describes a large and diverse group of revelers moving east across the province, from Kawabe through Teshima to Shimashimo, toward Yamashiro Province and the capital. They sing and dance and, significantly, strike the *tsuzumi* (small drum),

30. On *kotodama* in early Japan, see Ebersole, *Ritual Poetry*, 19–23.

31. References to *wazauta* are not uncommon in early Japanese literature. For example, the penultimate story (3:38) in *Nihon ryōiki* (*Record of Miraculous Events in Japan*; ca. 822) discusses several cases of *wazauta* circulating during the eighth century. It begins, "It is said that when good or evil omens are about to appear, they are preceded by songs that spread through the land. The people of the time in the lands throughout the country hear the songs, sing them, and thus communicate their message." *Record of Miraculous Events*, 189. For the original, see *Nihon ryōiki*, SNKBZ 10:362 (CJ: 351).

32. Quoted in Yamagami, "'Shidarajin' shinkō," 22–23.

which has nearly unparalleled musical and ritual significance in the medieval period. The *tsuzumi* is the primary instrument that regulates rhythm in a noh play, and as seen in early records of *dengaku* performance, the sound it produces is often described as particularly loud and disruptive. As Matsumoto Shinpachirō puts it, "In opposition to the reed and string instruments of courtly aristocrats, the adoption of percussion instruments by farmers constituted a revolution."[33] The Shidarajin Incident represents the emergence of a new kind of culture, not only because it was a non-elite production that transgressed borders around the capital but also because it sounded a musicality unfamiliar to most elites.

By 945/8/1, the revelers had arrived at Iwashimizu Hachiman Shrine, on the border of Yamashiro and Settsu provinces. Details about their progress are conveyed in a report from temple administrators at the complex and are included in the second and final related entry in *Honchō seiki*, dated 945/8/3:

> Today, reports of a letter from Hachiman Shrine concerning the arrival of the six portable shrines reported in Settsu Province on the twenty-eighth day of the previous month. (Copied in full below.)
>
> Submitted by the administrative council of Iwashimizu Hachimangū Temple.[34]
>
>> On the first day of this month during the Hour of the Dragon [8:00 a.m.], a letter . . . called Usa Bodhisattva.[35] One gave the name of the Shrine of the Great Bodhisattva of Usa Hachiman. The names of the other five shrines were not noted.
>
> Additionally submitted was the following draft, attached to a platform made of *sakaki* wood.[36]

33. Matsumoto, "Chūsei no shisō," 216.

34. The words for "administrative council" literally mean "the three classes." This refers to the main administrators of a monastic complex, specifically the head monk (*jōza*), the temple master (*jishu*), and the temple administrator (*tsuina*). The three names given at the end of the report correspond to these positions.

35. The ellipsis stands in for five missing or corrupted characters.

36. Wood from the flowering evergreen *Cleyera japonica* was often used in shrine rituals.

> The first day of the present month. It was decided that the monks' rites for the Liberation of Living Beings Festival would take place as per usual on the fifteenth at the temple. While the administrative council was convened with shrine attendants to develop a policy regarding this, the previously mentioned portable shrines suddenly arrived from the village of Yamazaki, displaying offerings. There were multitudes of people, surrounded in front and behind by groups of singers. Surprised and suspicious, the three temple administrators approached. They summoned the group's leaders, the heads of Yamazaki village, and asked for an explanation. They replied, "Around the Hour of the Rooster [6:00 p.m.] on the twenty-ninth of the previous month, multitudes of people suddenly came from Shimakami District in Settsu Province, transporting the deity in this way—a strange and frightening sight. At the Hour of the Boar [10:00 p.m.] on the same day, a certain woman voiced a message from the gods: 'I hasten to Iwashimizu Shrine.' In several villages people high and low, venerable and base assembled without prompting. This is why the deity has been transported here." Things similar to what has just occurred at this shrine must not continue to take place. This must be reported. We request the court's advice. Humbly submitted.

Eighth month, third day, Tengyō 8

Temple Administrator Senior Priest[37]
Temple Master Senior Priest En'ei
Head Monk Senior Priest Keinen[38]

One of the most interesting details of this report is the leader's description of the role played by a female shaman or *miko*—literally a "certain woman" (*aru onna*)—through whom a deity had voiced (*takusen*) directions for followers to "hasten to Iwashimizu Shrine." This moment of vocal expression is presented as a mixture of *kana* and *kanbun* (literary Sinitic) and begins with the declarative "I" (*are*) characteristic of oracular proclamations. It is not that the narrative somehow preserves an unmediated (or less mediated) voice, which would give us access to

37. No name given.
38. *Honchō seiki*, SZKT 9:109–10.

a more immediate understanding of what was happening on the ground. Rather, the narrative performs a stylistic directness to emphasize the importance of what was said at a particularly dramatic moment.

The three officials making up the shrine's administrative council respond with "surprise and suspicion" to the sudden appearance of revelers. Their report describes the presence of "multitudes" (*sū senman nin*, literally "some ten million people," but *senman* was often used figuratively to mean "an extremely large number"), but beyond this we have no way of knowing the actual size of the group that converged on the shrine. As in the report reproduced in the first entry, the Shidarajin worshippers are described here as people with geographically and socially diverse backgrounds, an indication that the attractive sweep of the movement had absorbed all in its path, prompting the village heads from nearby Yamazaki to criticize the movement as a "strange and frightening sight." As an open crowd, the Shidarajin movement transgressed geographic and social boundaries with seeming ease as it strove for more density, increase, and range. Although there are undoubtedly social and economic issues at play—especially rural discontent with rough and exploitative economic conditions—the discharge of energy that propels the movement forward exceeds these. The crowd, in other words, is not a symptom of underlying forces but rather its own condition, which, once formed, proceeds according to its own internal forces and desires.

Prince Shigeakira's entry in his diary *Ribu ōki* adds a few important details to our understanding of the Shidarajin Incident. He writes:

> Eighth month, second day. The governor of Settsu Lord Fujiwara no Fuminori visited the grand minister [Fujiwara no Tadahira (880–949)] and presented him with a report from the province. It said that portable shrines from Tsukushi had arrived in Kawabe District, all three of which were roofed with cypress bark. One had a *torii* with a placard inscribed "Jizai Tenjin"—that is, the spirit of the former minister of the Right Kankō. Of the two remaining shrines, one was called Usa Haruō Sanshi and the other Sumiyoshigami.[39]

39. *Ribu ōki*, 130–31. No manuscript copies of the diary exist, although a modern typeset edition has been created based on excerpts found in a wide array of later texts. The entry translated here is from a work entitled *Gyokuruishō*.

This brief entry supplements some interesting details. Shigeakira refers to a "report from the province" (*kokuge*), which is probably the same document reproduced in the *Honchō seiki* entry from 945/7/28. Shigeakira does not mention the performance activities of the amassed revelers, but he notes that the three shrines have been carried all the way from Tsukushi (Kyushu), a journey of nearly four hundred miles (assuming a departure from Usa Hachiman Shrine). In addition, he lingers on Tenjin, explaining that this deity is "the spirit of the former minister of the Right Kankō," that is, Sugawara no Michizane (845–903), whose manifestation as an *onryō* (vengeful spirit) was in the process of becoming ritually contained as the Tenman Jizaiten *goryō* (venerable spirit). Prince Shigeakira's explicit invocation of Michizane is noteworthy because Michizane was seen not only as a "tragic" victim of political rivalries within the court but also as an active enabler of rebellion, as in the case of Masakado's insurgency.[40]

These details speak to the Shidarajin movement's range and its oppositional valence. The movement furthermore had a deep connection to wet-rice agriculture, as made most explicit by the lyrics of the songs performed by revelers. *Honchō seiki* records a total of six songs, at the end of the final entry concerning the incident. Elsewhere in the text they are referred to as *uta*, but here the compilers specify *wazauta*, prophetic songs thought to give voice to the populace and herald future events:[41]

The moon wears a misty shroud[42]
Hachiman sows the seeds
Now let us cultivate the fallow fields!

40. For more on Michizane's deification, see Borgen, *Sugawara no Michizane*, 307–36.

41. Kuroda Hideo has translated the songs into a more intelligible classical Japanese. My translation depends largely on his interpretations. See Kuroda, *Nihon chūsei kaihatsushi no kenkyū*, 412.

42. I follow Kuroda's suggestion that *kasa* 笠 (literally, "conical hat") evokes the halo (*kasa* 暈) produced when the moon is shrouded by the mists of early spring. Kuroda, *Nihon chūsei kaihatsushi no kenkyū*, 441.

"Strike the *shidara*!" proclaims the deity
We strike it, so that we may live for a thousand years—
The *shidara* rice!
If sake flows from the quick river
That sake is the beginning of our abundance!

If you strike the *shidara*
The oxen will come to your side
Make a saddle, spread it out
Now let's load it with rice!

Envoys

The shadows have spread since morning
But if it is to rain
Then let it rain rice!

We are filled with abundance
We are linked together, filled with abundance
Throw up the houses, let loose the smoke!
Now we will flourish for a thousand years.[43]

With the repetition of the words *shidara* and *utsu* (to strike), these songs create a forceful impression. The lyrics parallel what the authors of the petition describe as the music's performative capacity to move mountains, clamorously appealing for abundance through a range of images related to wet-rice agriculture: fallow fields sown with seeds, flowing sake, saddles loaded with rice, and rice falling from the heavens. Presiding over this ideal of agricultural abundance and communal endeavor are Hachiman and Shidarajin, which establishes that the calls for divine assistance have been heard.

The Shidarajin Incident can be read, following David T. Bialock, as a case in which "nomadic speech and wandering movement that are initially perceived as a threat are subsequently captured by being enshrined in a specific locality."[44] Once the shrines cease their movement, the open crowd can no longer grow and soon disintegrates, with

43. *Honchō seiki*, SZKT 9:110–11.
44. Bialock, *Eccentric Spaces, Hidden Histories*, 140.

the threats it posed now subsumed by the wider ritual economy. In the end, the Shidarajin Incident demonstrates both the vigor and the transience of open crowds—the remarkable way in which masses of performing bodies appeared, discharged, and then vanished.[45]

Dengaku and Violence

Originating in the same nexus of agriculture, rural community, and performance as the rice-planting rites and the Shidarajin movement, *dengaku*, by the eleventh century, encompassed a range of different forms and expressions, from mass crowd movements to commissioned troupe performances. It had one foot, so to speak, in rural communities and another in the urban avenues of the capital, and this capacity to move across a variety of spaces was undoubtedly part of the ambivalence of its reception by elites. The remainder of this chapter explores three of *dengaku*'s most persistent associations: violence, the strange, and humor.

As an open-crowd performance that mediated transgression, *dengaku* inevitably developed a link to violent acts, from fighting and flinging stones to arson and killing. One early record of a *dengaku* performance during the annual festival at Matsu-no-o Shrine, in the foothills to the west of the capital, on 999/4/10 (Chōhō 1), reveals nothing about the content of the performance but several details about its violent impact. According to the account, "people from the port of Yamazaki performed *dengaku*, during which fights broke out among unranked attendants [*zōnin*] and several residents of the capital [*kyaubito*] were killed. Furthermore, these men set fire to more than thirty dwellings, completely destroying them."[46] In his reading of this passage,

45. In 988, a thirty-one–article petition (*gebumi*) detailing the excesses and malfeasance of Fujiwara no Motonaga, the provincial governor of Owari, was submitted to the court by local notables. This well-known document embodies a different form of protest, one that sought to work within the order imposed by the court to achieve justice. For an overview of the document, its context, and what it reveals about communication, taxation, and transportation between the provinces and the capital, see Von Verschuer, "Life of Commoners."

46. *Nihon kiryaku kōhen*, SZKT 11:191.

Moriya Takeshi highlights the prevalence of words like "brawl," "killed," "fire," and "destroying," concluding that "we are made to forget that this is an entry about the performing arts [*geinō*]."[47] But the way violence subsumes musicking here is, I argue, very much part of *dengaku*'s status as an open-crowd performance. As a result, the violence described as emerging from a performance of *dengaku* should not be bracketed as extrinsic but instead be considered an intrinsic element of how it animated crowds. Whether or not this disqualifies it from the category of *geinō* is beside the point, since, like most non-elite performance in the Heian period, *dengaku* morphed according to its transgressive movement across different orders of social space.

Nearly one hundred years later, another account of *dengaku* highlights its links with physical violence. The account is found in Fujiwara no Munetada's diary *Chūyūki* (1087–1138), in an entry dated 1094/5/20 (Kahō 1), which describes an encounter between two rival groups of aristocrats on the streets of the capital. The conflict is between two courtiers, Minamoto no Ietoshi and the regent Fujiwara no Moromichi (1062–1099).[48] Ietoshi has been traversing the avenues of the capital with a crowd of raucous *dengaku* performers who attack Moromichi and his entourage as they perform music. In the account, Munetada juxtaposes the chaos of *dengaku* with the refined performance of song and flute (*uta fue*). The former features bold and captivating movements along the streets of the capital; the latter is marked by the sedentary pursuit of artistic diversion. He writes:

> Tonight Minor Counselor Minamoto no Ietoshi assembled some ten functionary guards [*aozamurai*], and before long they were roaming around the capital performing *dengaku*.[49] Some of the attendants were

47. Moriya, *Chūsei geinō no genzō*, 17–18.

48. Ietoshi's birth and death dates are unknown. Minor counselor at the time.

49. The term *aozamurai*, also read *aosaburai*, likely refers to low-ranking guards attached to aristocratic families. Inoue Mitsurō notes another possible meaning for the word: provincial warriors who were brought into the capital to serve and protect nobles. He argues that provincial warriors aware of their relatively low status in the capital would have been eager to make a show of their discontent through *dengaku*, and he therefore prefers this meaning based on the context. Inoue, "Eichō gannen no dengaku sōdō," 9–10.

naked and others were without their caps: it was strange and bizarre [*itei kii*], and they resembled a nocturnal procession of demons [*hyakki yagyō*] to those who encountered them on the street. They eventually passed by the gate in front of the regent Fujiwara no Moromichi's residence (facing Takakura Street) and came out onto Nijō Avenue. On the northern side of the residence was the dwelling of Assistant Secretary of the Offerings Office Sugawara no Arizane.[50] The regent had gathered several members of the Chamberlains' Office there, and they were pleasantly diverting themselves with song and flute. Because Ietoshi believed Moromichi had slighted him, he turned to his functionary guards and had each of them pick up tiles and stones and throw them [at Moromichi's group].[51] As they fell like rain on Arizane's house, the members of Moromichi's group ran around in a panic. As he left the house to inquire into what was happening, Presented Scholar Minamoto no Arikane (an official who worked for the regent) was struck and he collapsed on the spot.[52]

The lot of *dengaku* performers dispersed in all directions, and although the regent's attendants chased them to the north, they apprehended only one, whom they brought back to his residence. Moromichi took a close look at him [and saw that he was] a member of the palace guards. (Apparently it was such-and-such-*maru*, Ietoshi's flute teacher.) He was immediately entrusted to the capital police, who questioned him about the cause of the disturbance. The man stated the details one by one. Moromichi informed the retired emperor through the controller,

50. Arizane was a scholar and mid-ranking courtier who eventually served as one of the academy's two professors of law (*myōhō hakase*).

51. *Gareki* literally means "tiles and stones" but can connote "debris" in a more general sense. Ietoshi's group may be using whatever ammunition they can find around them, but the flinging of tiles and stones recalls the more structured practice of *inji-uchi*, discussed in chapter 1.

52. "Presented scholar" translates *shinshi*, which originally referred to a particular civil service examination, but by the Heian period it was also used to denote those who had passed this exam. According to Robert Borgen, the *shinshi* was "one of the four civil service examinations. Others were *shūsai* ('flourishing talent'), *myōgyō* (classics), and *myōhō* (law). The *shinshi* examination consisted of two essay questions on 'the essential business of governing the nation' and a test of the candidates' memorization of two Chinese texts—Wen-hsuan and Erh-ya, the former being the then popular literary anthology and the latter an early lexicographic work." Borgen, *Sugawara no Michizane*, 76.

and sent a letter explaining what had happened to the chamberlain of the guards.

> This is a strange event [*koto no tei kii nari*]. Such things should be feared and guarded against in the future, which is why I am writing this. The man was more than twenty years old and held the status of courtier.[53] A thing like this that has never been witnessed—how can it pass unnoticed? I later heard that the responsible party has been summoned.[54]

Munetada's account of the conflict and violence is steeped in a rhetoric of the strange. For him, the physical appearance of the *dengaku* performers is strange (*itei kii*), and the event writ large is also strange (*koto no tei kii*). He likens Ietoshi and his *dengaku* performers to a nocturnal procession of demons (*hyakki yagyō*), a heterotopic image that contrasts sharply with the cheerful intimacy of courtiers gathered at Moromichi's residence as they partake in song and flute playing.[55] The former embodies restless movement, the latter normative stillness. Munetada's account hence posits a binary relationship between two modes of cultural practice: open crowds and closed crowds. It is both a record of interpersonal conflict and an index of symbolic conflict between non-elite and elite, one reframed in different guises throughout the medieval period: by retired emperors in order to construct a new politics of culture, and by heads of performance troupes in order to articulate repertoires in line with the tastes of elite patrons.[56]

53. "Courtier" translates *unkaku*, a term that, beginning in the mid-Heian period, referred to aristocrats of fourth, fifth, or sixth rank who had permission to enter the Seiryōden, the emperor's private residence. It is synonymous with *tenjōbito* and *kumo no uebito*. See table I.1.

54. *Chūyūki*, DNK 2:66.

55. On the emergence of *hyakki yagyō* in Heian literature and its later articulation in painted scrolls, see Faure, *Gods of Medieval Japan*, 74–79. For a systematic overivew of the appearance of *hyakki yagyō* in classical and medieval literature, see Itō Masahiro, "'Hyakki yagyō dan' jō"; and Itō Masahiro, "'Hyakki yagyō dan' ge."

56. For an example of the latter, see Zeami's description of the *rikidōfū* (violent movement style) in his "Nikyoku santai ningyō zu" (Figure drawings of the two arts and the three modes; 1423). This style, and the highly restricted use that Zeami specifies for it, embodies the binaries of potency/abstention and danger/taboo that characterize

It might be argued that Munetada's invocation of a rhetoric of the strange simply works to imbue the account with a critical tone, but it also reflects an active process of identification at work. For Munetada, the strange, through its upwardly directed violence and transgression of various norms (vestimentary, kinetic, musical), demarcates the boundaries of his identity, but in its difference, it also invites the reactionary assertion of a superior authorial "self." By figuring the *dengaku* performers with this rhetoric, Munetada effectively "kills and ingests" their alterity, "preserving" it in his diary as a "remainder," a stylized but never wholly integrated object of discourse.[57] Significantly, this is only one of a range of acts of identification that marks Munetada's relationship with *dengaku*, acts that are recurrent yet inconsistent. As discussed in chapter 3, Munetada's record of his own participation in the Great Dengaku of 1096 reveals a moment in which he seemingly transgresses the boundary between self and other, as the narrating subject becomes a simultaneously narrated object, and identification and desire collapse in on each other.[58]

Munetada's status as a member of the upper nobility—and furthermore as an important figure in the burgeoning development of the *insei* system—is thus constituted by an ambiguous but motivated relationship with those events and phenomena that embody the violence and difference of the other. He writes with condemnation, but by othering the unruly *dengaku* performers, he also calls attention to the ambiguity of his own identity. He is endowed with the privilege of surveillance and judgment yet also perpetually on the verge of being displaced by disorder—a threat that, it should be added, is frequently tied to implementations of law and order. As will be seen in accounts

many of the performances I discuss in this book. Zeami, *Zenchiku*, NST 24:129. Reginald Jackson argues that Zeami's treatment of the style illustrates that "in order to choreograph tradition, the punctual is displaced for the durative." See Jackson, "*Midare* Performance," 158.

57. The quoted words are from Diana Fuss's discussion of the "totem meal" that Sigmund Freud develops in *Totem and Taboo*: "Identification is only ever partially secure and never complete. The whole unconscious process functions as a form of psychical memorialization in which the subject must repeatedly kill and ingest what it wishes to preserve a remainder of inside." Fuss, *Identification Papers*, 34.

58. Fuss, *Identification Papers*, 11–12.

of the Great Dengaku of 1096, strategies of appropriating and rendering legible such disorder played a significant role in the production and assertion of elite identities and authority.

Dengaku and Strangeness

The historical tale *Eiga monogatari* contains countless descriptions of cultural and religious activities sponsored by Fujiwara no Michinaga, the most powerful political figure in early eleventh-century Japan. Much has been made of the way Michinaga successfully parlayed these activities—many of which broke with established precedent in spectacular fashion—into political gains for himself and his family. For example, in an essay on the inscribed screens commissioned by Michinaga for display at his daughter Shōshi's (988–1074) extravagant court entrance ceremony in 999, Joseph T. Sorensen notes that "Michinaga used his authority and resources to commission works of art, and these aesthetic symbols, in turn, reinforced his political clout."[59] Later in life, after taking Buddhist vows, Michinaga would devote much time and energy to constructing Hōjōji, a massive temple complex.[60]

Michinaga's spectacular and sometimes shocking breaks with precedent inform our perception of him as a cunning politician, but there are other moments when his actions also indicate an identification with the other. In the "Onmogi" chapter of *Eiga monogatari*, we read of his enthusiasm in transforming the ordinarily mundane planting of a nearby rice field into a spectacle to be observed by his daughter Shōshi, his principal wife Rinshi (964–1053), and their ladies-in-waiting. It is the fifth month of 1023, and Shōshi has been staying with her father at his Tsuchimikado residence. Michinaga asks the officials in charge of the planting to have the planters dispense with their official clothing and instead do it "as is, no matter how unseemly or strange."[61]

59. Sorensen, "The Politics of Screen Poetry," 96.

60. On the formation and cultural influence of the Muryōjuin (Hall of Amitāyus), the focal point of the complex, see Yiengpruksawan, "The Eyes of Michinaga."

61. *Eiga monogatari*, SNKBZ 32:345–46.

Michinaga furthermore has an earthen wall that separates two properties torn down so that the festivities can be viewed by the women with ease.

The day of the planting arrives, and Shōshi gathers with her mother and their ladies-in-waiting. They look out and see:

> Some fifty or sixty young and unblemished girls formed into a line. They wore exceedingly white skirts and white, wide-brimmed hats. They had dyed their teeth black and made up their faces red. There was an old man known as the field master dressed in very strange [*ito ayashiki*] festival garb, holding a large, dilapidated parasol and wearing tall unfastened clogs. His wife [*ayashi no onna*] wore a black glossed-silk robe, and her face was dappled with white powder. She too carried a parasol and wore tall clogs. There was also a *dengaku* troupe, consisting of ten or so proud and beaming men who fastened crude-looking drums [*ayashiki yau naru tsuzumi*] to their waists, played flutes, struck things known as *sasara*, and performed various dances, while other lowly men [*ayashi no otoko*] sang songs. Among them was what is known as a "field drum," which unlike a regular drum produced a thunderous sound [*goho-goho*]. Shōshi's confidantes watched from the eastern veranda, and young aristocrats of the fourth and fifth rank leaned against the railing and looked on excitedly. Next some very large buckets and delicacy boxes were carried out, which must have contained their food. Watching this assortment of unusual spectacles, Shōshi felt exceedingly special and delighted.[62]

This passage has received particular attention from performance historians because it contains one of the earliest extant descriptions of *dengaku*.[63] Mediated by several quotatives ("what is known as a 'field drum,'" "things known as *sasara*") and appeals to "lowliness" or "strangeness" (*ayashi*, which, depending on the context, can signify both meanings), *dengaku* in this context is alien and unknown, something that necessitates bracketed explanation because of its difference

62. *Eiga monogatari*, SNKBZ 32:346–47.

63. Nose Asaji uses it as the point of departure for his study of *dengaku*, although he is mostly interested in clarifying the meaning of the word. He argues that despite linguistic ambiguities in the passage, *dengaku* does not refer to a type of drum but rather the performance as a whole. See Nose, *Nōgaku genryū kō*, 1444–49.

from more conventional cultural practices. The word *ayashi*, used several times throughout the passage, signifies the inassimilable otherness of the performers as well as their identifiably base appearance and sound.

This heteromorphic assemblage of musicians and planters is not distanced from sites of elite power and privilege; rather, it takes shape right next to Michinaga's mansion, engineered for the viewing pleasure of his daughter and her entourage. This kind of elite observation recalls the ninth-century descriptions of rice-planting rites discussed earlier in this chapter, which dramatize the centripetal function of the emperor's gaze. But in this case the act does not have the same symbolically fortuitous function that it does in earlier accounts. Instead, the ambiguous status of the performance as both the object of elite diversion and the agent of elite abjection reveals the increasingly untethered position of non-elites amid the shift away from *ritsuryō* social organization. Furthermore, in this case, it is not the emperor but rather Shōshi and her entourage who gaze out at the agricultural performers, an index of the Fujiwara family's ascendency and their domination of court politics during the regency period.

Of course, the word *ayashi* is not confined to this particular passage in *Eiga monogatari* and can be found throughout early medieval texts, often signifying "strange," "uncouth," "beyond the pale," or some combination thereof. It appears, for example, in the well-known opening of *Sarashina nikki* (Sarashina diary; ca. 1060), written by Sugawara no Takasue's daughter (b. 1008). She writes, "As one who grew up beyond the terminus of the Eastern Road [in Kazusa Province], how uncivilized [*ayashikari*] I must have been! I'm not sure how it started, but I would often think, 'How I wish I could have a look at those tales I hear about.'"[64] Here the narrator remembers the several years she spent living with her father when he served as governor of Kazusa. Given the physical and cultural distance between the capital and Kazusa (part of modern Chiba Prefecture), she recalls just how uncivilized she must have been in her youth. *Ayashi* hence signifies a spatial periphery, somewhere beyond the routes established to guide flows of goods from capital to countryside and vice versa. She hears of

64. *Sarashina nikki*, SNKBZ 26:279.

the marvelous tales that convey the splendor of the court, but her only way of accessing them is through the memories of those around her. She fetishizes tales to the point that she finally has a statue of Yakushi built just so she can pray for an imminent move to the capital.

In this way, *ayashi* often conjured notions of a spatial disjuncture. To return to the passage in *Eiga monogatari*, the field master's clothing (*ayashiki saiginu*), his wife (*ayashi no onna*, literally "strange woman"), the drums (*ayashiki yau naru tsuzumi*), and the "lowly" singers (*ayashi no otoko*) are all denoted by various invocations of the word *ayashi*—strange, low, and other. Furthermore, *goho-goho* (literally "thud-thud," which I translate as "a thunderous sound") appears near the word *ayashi*, making it a mimetic signal of the close tie between the strange and the low.

Although the text notes Michinaga had asked the officials in charge to have the planters appear as is, without affectation, as a ceremony the whole event is of course consummately staged. There is a theatricality about the field master and his wife, as though they are there to perform the salutary archetypes necessary for the ritual to function properly. Ueki Yukinobu has speculated that the two figures do not simply oversee the planting but also signify through imitation (*monomane*) the fecundity of a union between husband and wife.[65] The text describes them as "an old man known as the field master" (*tanushi to ifu okina*) and "a strange woman"; they both carry parasols and wear tall sandals (*takada*, often referred to as *takaashida*). Ueki proffers that such parasols were a sign of the sacred and therefore signify the couple's metonymic relationship to symbolic power.[66] On the other hand, Hashimoto Hiroyuki has noted how tall sandals enable a unique perspective for the wearer even as they turn the wearer into a kind of spectacle.[67] These two perspectives indicate the dual nature of the event as both ceremonial and functional. Perched on their tall sandals and shaded by the parasols, the field master and the woman oversee the work done by the planting girls, while simultaneously conducting a more ritualistic kind of work. The presence of these two

65. Ueki, *Chūsei geinō*, 30.

66. Ueki, *Chūsei geinō*, 30.

67. Hashimoto, *Engeki no seishinshi*, 202–3.

figures—husband and wife, man and woman—and the way they interface with the planting girls (as visualized in fig. I.1, the old man looks at the planting girls, and a planting girl looks at the old man) suggests a microcosmic vision of the agricultural fundamentalism espoused by the *ritsuryō* state. In this way, the strangeness of the old man and his wife, of the *dengaku* performers and their instruments, becomes part of a larger performance of productivity.

Far from being disturbed by the strangeness of the field master and the *dengaku* performers, Shōshi and her retinue are delighted by what they see and are in fact drawn into participating in the performance, contributing poems:

> Next she gathered with the others to watch [the girls] energetically planting rice, which she found quite delightful. It was also very delightful to watch the *dengaku* musicians who, though seemingly restrained while on their way to the planting fields, let loose with boisterous performances once there. Just at that moment a light rain started to fall, soaking the planting girls' robes. Apparently having heard about the event at some point, countless people [*yohito*] were arrayed [outside the fence], and even their watching faces were delightful to see.
>
> She listened to the poems being sung by the planting girls:
>
> > Our trains drenched in the fifth-month rains—
> > may these fields we plant nourish our lord for myriad years to come.
> >
> > *samidare ni mosuso nurashite uuru ta o*
> > *kimi ga chitose no omakusa ni sen*
>
> She also heard:
>
> > Countless, the years since we began planting—
> > let us gather and store the rice stalks, endless as the sky,
> > from our lord's fields.
> >
> > *uuru ni yori kazu mo shirarezu ohozora o*
> > *kura ni zo tsuman omakusa no ine*[68]

68. *Eiga monogatari*, SNKBZ 32:347–48.

In this section, the emphasis on "delightful" (*wokashi*) contrasts sharply with the rhetoric of the strange found in the previous passage. Shōshi delights in watching the planting girls, the *dengaku* musicians, and even the faces of those who have gathered to watch the festivities. Here the *Eiga* narrator supplants strangeness with delight, anticipating a rhetorical move seen in later accounts of non-elite performance.

It is noteworthy that the songs sung by the planting girls take the form of *waka* and not the sort of folk songs overheard by Sei Shōnagon when she encountered the planting women on her way to Kamo Shrine. It is not impossible that the planting girls would have been familiar with such poems and poetic forms, but the performance of *waka* during rice-planting rites was not customary.[69] It is as though the words of the elites have been placed in the mouths of the planting girls or, alternatively, as though the ladies-in-waiting are hearing their voices through the internalized filter of court culture. Naturalized in this way, the songs of the planting girls—songs that pledge support for the emperor and the agricultural well-being of the realm—are intelligible, in both form and content, to Shōshi and her entourage, prompting them to participate in one last poetic exchange:

> With such poems being created, the aristocrats were thrilled with the way the stable attendants had organized the event. It is not known who composed it, but when a *hototogisu* flew by singing, a lady-in-waiting recited:
>
> The *hototogisu* cries out just as the rice sprouts are planted:
> "field master of the underworld" is indeed an apt description.[70]
>
> *sanahe uuru ori ni shimo naku hototogisu*
> *shide no taosa to mube mo ihikeri*

69. One example of a non-elite composing *waka* is found in an episode in *Uji shūi monogatari* (A Collection of tales from Uji; ca. 1221), "How a Woodcutter Made a Poem" (3:8), in which a woodcutter composes a *waka* so clever that it prompts a mountain guardian to return his confiscated axe. *Uji shūi monogatari*, SNKBZ 50:118.

70. The call of the *hototogisu* was thought to sound like the words *shide no taosa* (field master of the underworld). As described in the Ten Kings Sutra, Mount Shide is a steep mountain that the newly deceased must pass on their way to the court of Enma.

> Looking on, someone else sang:
>
> Hearing the sound of the *hototogisu* from beyond the clouds,
> the planting girls' trains are thoroughly drenched.
>
> *hototogisu kumowi naru ne ni kikoyuredo*
> *shibori mo ahezu tago no tamoto wa*
>
> The rice-planting rite came to an end, and the stable attendants were summoned to receive rewards for being so thoroughly entertaining. In this way, nothing was overlooked in putting on a satisfying and entertaining event.[71]

The passage ends on an auspicious note, with the attendants responsible for the event rewarded and Shōshi and her entourage thoroughly entertained. As a whole, the passage can be read as an inversion of the power of the strange: though the field master and his wife, the *dengaku* musicians, and the planting girls first appear as strange and excessive, their actions and performances eventually meld into the space of court culture and elite diversion. The seamlessness of this transition—this is not an account of violence or disorder, unlike other narratives of *dengaku*—succeeds in masking the political violence required to stage such a performance of forced labor. Although Shōshi is first drawn in by the strangeness of the other, by the end of the passage, she delights in an encounter with the same.

Dengaku and Humor

In addition to triggering a fear of violence and an ambivalent desire for the strangeness of other, *dengaku* also provoked laughter. The performance's comic unsuitability in certain elite spaces is at the core of a story from *Konjaku monogatari shū* (Collection of tales of times now past; early twelfth century). Entitled "The District Official of Yabase in Ōmi Holds a *Dengaku* Performance to Consecrate His

71. *Eiga monogatari*, SNKBZ 32:348–49.

Temple" (28:7), the story transforms the anxieties occasioned by performances of *dengaku*—excess and transgression, low social status, rural epistemologies and practices—into an amusing punchline.[72]

In the story, a provincial official visits the monk Kyōen (979–1047), who became abbot of the powerful temple Enryakuji in 1038, and asks him to perform the dedication ceremony for his recently completed temple in Yabase, on the east coast of Lake Biwa. The monk accepts the invitation and requests that the official commission *bugaku* performers for the ceremony—no small feat given the official's relatively insignificant position. The man nevertheless assures the monk that it will be no trouble at all and goes on his way.

On the day of the ceremony, Kyōen travels down from Mount Hiei and east to Lake Biwa, crossing it in the direction of Yabase. When he reaches the shore, he is met by a group of ten men dressed in white and accompanied by a throng of unranked attendants (*genin*). Puzzled, Kyōen proceeds on his way but cannot help but take a closer look at the men, who have started to perform: "Some had pitch-black drums fastened to their waists, their thrust-out hands clutching plectrums; others played flutes, or struck rhythm boards or *sasara*, or waved hoes in the air.[73] They performed two acts and then three, striking their drums and blowing their flutes. There was no limit to their crazed movements [*kurufu koto kagiri nashi*]."[74] Kyōen has no idea who these performers are and wonders if he is witnessing the village's annual *goryōe*. Thinking he has stumbled into the middle of the festival, he becomes vexed and worries that he might be seen by an acquaintance.

The monk proceeds to the official's residence, making sure to keep his face covered to hide his identity. But he cannot shake the performers, who surround him and "beat and twirl their drums, strike their *sasara* on the edges of their hats, and raise up their hoes in a sign of

72. *Konjaku monogatari shū*, SNKBZ 38:177–82. For an English translation, see Dykstra, *Buddhist Tales of India, China, and Japan*, 894–98.

73. The text is corrupted toward the end of the sentence, but based on context and what we know of *dengaku* practice in general, "*sasara*" was likely the intended word. See *Konjaku monogatari shū*, SNKBZ 38:180n6.

74. *Konjaku monogatari shū*, SNKBZ 38:180.

FIGURE 2.1 *Dengaku* performers surround the monk Kyōen. Similar to fig. I.1, this illustration was created to be included in an early modern edition of the text. *Konjaku monogatari shū*, 1721, vol. 10, ed. Izawa Banryō. Courtesy of Waseda University Library.

welcoming, blocking his passage" (fig. 2.1).[75] When Kyōen at last arrives at the official's residence, he asks about what he has just encountered. The official responds, "When I visited you at Saitō Temple, you told me, 'True merit is brought about by music [*gaku*],' so I assembled musicians. Furthermore, since someone said, 'The monk in charge of the ceremony should be greeted with music [*gaku*],' I sent them to meet you."[76] Kyōen realizes that the official has confused *dengaku* with *bugaku*, thinking that the former would be an appropriate musical performance (*gaku*) for the solemn occasion. But in Kyōen's estimation, the only appropriate type of performance is *bugaku*. The monk proceeds to conduct the ceremony and returns to Enryakuji, where he tells a group of young monks about the unfortunate misunderstanding. The young monks laugh and ridicule the official, exclaiming, "Even

75. *Konjaku monogatari shū*, SNKBZ 38:181.
76. *Konjaku monogatari shū*, SNKBZ 38:182.

rural folk know at least that much. This district official is a real ignorant boor!"[77]

The story is infused with appeals to the strangeness and otherness of the *dengaku* performers and the unranked attendants who accompany them. Initially Kyōen does not even recognize them as performers, and as they start playing music, the narrative highlights their unusual assortment of instruments and their "crazed movements" (*kurufu koto*). Although the sound of their music is not described explicitly, the combination of musical instruments and strange playing styles evokes a soundscape dominated by noise: the striking of rhythm boards and *sasara*, the pounding of drums, the shouts and calls that animate the crowd. The performers' "crazed" dancing furthermore shows how performing bodies were often understood as excessive, beyond control, and unintelligible to orthodox religious and cultural practices. Lastly, the performers are not confined to a stage but instead range multidirectionally through the landscape: they appear at the port and follow Kyōen, periodically encircle their target, and pulse with a fugitive energy.

In his reading of this story, Komine Kazuaki notes how a broad composite parallel—between the capital, Mount Hiei, and *bugaku*; and the countryside, local administration, and *dengaku*—creates a sense of cultural difference that, through Kyōen's telling of the story to the young monks, becomes an occasion for derisive laughter.[78] Kyōen is initially shocked by his encounter with the *dengaku* performers, but once back in his temple, he views the experience with amusement. The play of oppositions and the overturning of expectations makes for a good story (Kyōen, we are told at the outset, is an accomplished storyteller), and sure enough, Kyōen provokes the desired response from his audience.

But the way *dengaku* is represented by the *Konjaku* narrator does not simply convey the center's sneering appropriation of a peripheral custom. As can be seen elsewhere in the archive, *dengaku* itself was a festive and oftentimes amusing performance that had many functions, one of which was to entertain through transgression. Oppositions like

77. *Konjaku monogatari shū*, SNKBZ 38:182.

78. Komine, *Inseiki bungaku ron*, 873.

capital/countryside and elite/non-elite may provide the basic structure that allows the story to succeed in its primary aim (eliciting laugher from the young monks and, presumably, the reader), but the story also shows how dialectically interrelated the terms of these oppositions could be. Kyōen does not live in a bubble: his ceremonial duties take him into the countryside, where he encounters various kinds of social, cultural, and performative difference. Once the festive energy of the *dengaku* performers emerges, it remains at the center of the narrative, clinging to Kyōen despite his attempts to shake it off. In this sense, the monk's fashioning of a humorous anecdote can be read as an attempt to transform a transgressive and threatening encounter into a playful misunderstanding—a border breached and then repaired. The interplay of breach and repair is central to the functioning of transgression, and as discussed in the next chapter, a particularly large breach requires an extraordinary effort of repair.

CHAPTER THREE

From the Ground Up

The Great Dengaku of 1096

The mass-performance event that would come to be known as the Great Dengaku of 1096 (Eichō dai dengaku) spanned several summer months and left traces across a range of texts, including diaries, retrospective accounts, historical digests, and tales. These records not only document and transmit the embodied practices that constituted the performances but also enable a sustained consideration of their ability to function as a medium of transgression and facilitate acts of identification. Simply put, the Great Dengaku was an extraordinary event that brought high and low together in spectacular performances of excess.

I begin with a summary of the events leading up to the Great Dengaku and continue with an exploration of its robust documentation. I treat the texts chronologically to show how the narrative of the event shifted over time, from one that described and interpreted the embodied excess of unruly open-crowd performances to one that foregrounded the subsequent death of a member of the imperial family and the pathos experienced by the elites who mourned her. As a transgressive event, the Great Dengaku provoked a range of bodily and textual chain reactions, resulting in a historical record as uneven as it is ambivalent.

The Great Dengaku: Social and Political Background

The late eleventh century was a time of widespread political and economic changes, as can been seen in the shift away from the Fujiwara regency and the reassertion of imperial power through the establishment of the *insei* system. In the 1070s, Emperor GoSanjō instituted a new policy of equal provincial levies (*ikkoku heikin no kayaku*) to raise funds for projects related to the maintenance of imperial power, including the reconstruction of the imperial palace and Ise Shrine. The court enacted a levy in 1094 (Kahō 1) in preparation for the vicennial reconstruction of Ise Shrine two years later.[1] It was met with resistance in the provinces, which eventually led to the capital police (*kebiishi*) being dispatched to reassert control.[2] Two courtiers involved in the enforcement of the levy left behind the most detailed extant documents about the Great Dengaku, which seems to have been precipitated in part by popular unrest in the provinces. Ōe no Masafusa, who authored *Rakuyō dengaku ki* (An account of the dengaku in the capital; ca. 1100), served as the "noble-in-charge" (*shōkei*) of the reconstruction of the shrine, and Fujiwara no Munetada, who wrote at length about the event in his diary *Chūyūki*, served as Masafusa's assistant.[3] It is thus likely that both had firsthand knowledge of the political conditions that led to the eruption of the Great Dengaku.

The events of summer 1096 can be traced more proximately to an incident at Sumiyoshi Shrine in the third month.[4] Tsumori no

1. For details on the levy and its implementation, see Toda, "Shōen taisei kakuritsu ki," 9. On the regular reconstruction of the two shrines at Ise, see Hardacre, *Shinto*, 84–87.

2. The capital police force was established in the early Heian period to preside over the policing, prosecution, and corporal punishment of lawbreakers. Its functionaries, however, did not always enforce the law in accordance with the wishes of nobles and sometimes participated in the very activities they were supposed to suppress. Moriya Takeshi notes that far from being an exception to the rule, accounts of *kebiishi* "neglect" abound throughout the archive. Moriya, *Chūsei geinō no genzō*, 61–62.

3. Fukazawa, *Chūsei shinwa no rentanjutsu*, 66.

4. The following summary is based on an entry in the fourteenth-century abridged history *Ranshōshō* (Selection of origins). *Ranshōshō*, 336. A full translation of the entry is included in appendix 1.

Kunimoto (1023–1102), at the time governor of Settsu Province and head of Sumiyoshi Shrine, had arranged for an officiating priest and musicians to conduct a ceremony for a recently completed dedication hall. Visitors arrived in droves, overrunning the grounds of the shrine and prompting a *kebiishi* named Miyaji no Norikata to dispatch a group of functionaries to remove them.[5] In protest of this forced removal, thirty-eight revelers flung themselves into the shrine's pond and drowned, their deaths leading to the symbolic pollution (*shokue*) of Norikata and one of the musicians.[6] Both Norikata and the musician then returned to the capital and entered the imperial palace; when it was discovered that the pollution had been transmitted there, the court immediately canceled several upcoming shrine festivals. This included the annual festival scheduled for Matsu-no-o Shrine, much to the dismay of those wishing to attend. As dissatisfaction increased during the following weeks, a prophetic song (*wazauta*) circulated—"The deity will not abide by this!"—and revelers engaged in raucous performances of *dengaku* in a preview of what was to overtake the capital a few months later.[7]

This series of events demonstrates, among other things, the power of transgression to trigger fears of contamination. The purity of the emperor and the wider imperial system could be maintained only through the vigilant ritual management of pollution, which was perpetually on the verge of exceeding the boundaries set in place to contain it. This was an imperfect and fragile system: the court took evasive maneuvers to protect its symbolic center from becoming contaminated but did not anticipate that by canceling festivals it would reap the whirlwind. Taboo led to transgression, high and low alike crossed borders, and the situation spiraled out of control as the court lost its grip on order.

5. According to Munetada, the number of visitors was "several thousands." See his entry dated 1096/3/16 (Eichō 1). *Chūyūki*, DNK 3:37.

6. Munetada reports that "several tens of people, old and young, man and woman" drowned themselves. *Chūyūki*, DNK 3:37. Toda reads these suicides as "the people's silent protest against the violent suppression of their beliefs." Toda, "Shōen taisei kakuritsu ki," 9.

7. *Ranshōshō*, 336.

Rewriting Transgression: Multiplicity in *Chūyūki*

The senior noble Fujiwara no Munetada left behind a diary brimming with observations about everyday life at the court, records of court ceremony and protocol, and noteworthy events in and around the capital. He developed close relationships with Retired Emperor Shirakawa and his son Emperor Horikawa, and he was an important figure in the early development of the *insei* system of government.[8] There are other extant courtier diaries from the same period, but only Munetada's covers the Great Dengaku in detail. His multiple diary entries convey conflicting opinions about the spectacle, ranging from harsh condemnation to awe. In general these revolve around the poles of phobic distancing of *dengaku* performed by non-elites and acclamation for *dengaku* performed by elites (including himself), which would seem to indicate that Munetada simply hews to class boundaries in his assessments. But since *dengaku* performances by attendants were the catalyst for those by elites like Munetada, it becomes difficult to categorically separate the two. They are, in a sense, united by a single transgressive trajectory toward excess.

The transit between attraction and repulsion is in part a reflection of the medium in which Munetada wrote. Each entry in a diary represents a specific temporal occasion of writing and contributes to an increasingly layered narrative—each entry succeeds the last—as the author continues to write. Unlike other forms of narrative, a diary is in principle something that develops along with the rhythms of everyday life.[9] This is not to say that diaries, in their progressive unfolding,

8. For a detailed description of Munetada's relationships with Shirakawa and Horikawa, including his decades-long admission into the privileged *hokumen* (northern side) of Shirakawa's palace, see Akiyama, *Chūsei kuge shakai*, 100–105. In 1095 Munetada was appointed a director in the Office of the Retired Emperor (In no bettō) under Shirakawa. Many of the courtiers who participated in *dengaku* performances during the summer of 1096 were affiliated with the burgeoning *insei* government, a fact emphasized by scholars who view the Great Dengaku as an attempt by pro-*insei* forces to consolidate their political legitimacy. See Inoue, "Eichō gannen no dengaku sōdō," 11–14.

9. In *Kujō ujōshō ikai* (Parting lessons of the Kujō minister of the right; ca. 950s), Fujiwara no Morosuke (908–960) touches on diary keeping in his delineation of proper court conduct. After waking up and performing a series of Daoist and Buddhist

are somehow less mediated than other forms of writing, but the basic stratification of entries makes a comparison of objects and topics across periods of time implicitly possible—and not only for an external reader. In composing his daily entries, Munetada writes the present (by depositing the goings-on of the day and registering his thoughts about them) even as he revises his own construction of the past (by referring to earlier entries or by revising or reintroducing a past event). In this way, the diary medium can work to produce multiple visions and revisions (or presentations and representations) of subjects and events, an aspect that in turn concretizes the possibility of layered identifications. With their multiple selves and others that emerge and recede, Munetada's diary entries parallel the heterogeneous movements of a transgressive crowd.

The first relevant entry is dated 1096/6/12 (Eichō 1), some three months after the incident at Sumiyoshi Shrine. Munetada writes of how the Gion *goryōe* has occasioned disruptive performances of *dengaku* by unranked attendants (*zōnin*, *shimobe*), including functionary guards (*aozamurai*). Munetada's attention is drawn to these rowdy performances: "Everyone performs *dengaku* and the streets are clogged. The sound of drums and flutes resounds, greatly inconveniencing those coming and going." Toward the end of the entry, he wonders, "Could this be the result of the strange rumors [*yōgen*] circulating these days?"[10] For Munetada, the Great Dengaku emerges as an event amid the Gion *goryōe*: the performers he describes in this entry are not peasants from the countryside but instead urban residents that constitute the lower ranks, the nameless "base" (*senmin*) tasked with menial labor and often involved in various types of performance that took place at shrines and temples and on the streets of the capital. The entry also mentions functionary guards, who have their own evening performances, perhaps an indication of the burgeoning power of armed attendants. But Munetada does not

devotions, as well as using a toothpick to clean one's teeth, the diligent courtier is supposed to "next record what happened yesterday (in the case that there are many things, you should record them throughout the day)." "Kujō ujōshō ikai," NST 8:296 (CJ: 116). For a partial English translation, see Sansom, *A History of Japan to 1334*, 181–83.

10. *Chūyūki*, DNK 3:65.

differentiate between the two groups when criticizing: both are part of a larger crowd (animated, he speculates, by the circulation of strange rumors) that produces disturbing sounds and movements. He describes a group of urban performers that seems to have reached a point of discharge—the point at which the group has effectively become an open crowd—a transgression that necessitates commentary.

Two days later, on 1096/6/14, this amorphous low-ranking crowd of *dengaku* performers is eclipsed by attendants of the imperial family who have organized into several *dengaku* groups. This time, Munetada bases his account on hearsay, since he was busy tending to the emperor for the duration of the day. He reports, "Some four hundred of the retired emperor's male attendants performed *dengaku*, along with more than seventy young attendants from his Chamberlains' Office and thirty from the emperor's Chamberlains' Office."[11] The entry ends with a comment about the unusually large number of spectators present for the Gion *goryōe* and a note about an imperial order to dispatch offerings to the major shrines in the area.[12] Here Munetada describes, in something close to real time, the point at which *dengaku* has spread to elites.

After this entry, Munetada falls silent about the *dengaku* for a full month. But on 1096/7/12, the event comes back into focus with a lengthy and detailed description of a group of aristocrats engaged in extravagant performances. In contrast to his previous entries, the main social actors here are not non-elite attendants but instead courtiers, senior nobles, and members of the imperial family—in other words, the upper echelon of court society. This development raises several questions about relations between the elites and non-elites, as well as the role of performance in mediating their relationships. Should this appropriated form of *dengaku* (what Yamaji Kōzō refers to as "extravagant *dengaku*," as discussed in the introduction) still be considered *dengaku*? Is Munetada's more positive attitude toward these performances simply due to the high class of the performers? What changes and what stays the same in this courtier "version" of *dengaku*?

11. *Chūyūki*, DNK 3:66.
12. *Chūyūki*, DNK 3:66.

At first glance, it seems to differ greatly from most of the performances that took place during the previous month. Instead of an intractable crowd of nameless performers, Munetada describes courtiers who dazzle one another (and the gathered imperial spectators) with lavish dress and spectacles of virtuosity:

> I retired [from the palace] early in the morning, but visited again at the Hour of the Monkey [4:00 p.m.]. During the evening, courtiers [*unkaku*] ordered that a *dengaku* performance take place, to be watched by the emperor. A council was held and it was decided that it should certainly include a performance of *The Head of the Field*, and that Chamberlain Junior Counselor [Minamoto no] Narimune was just the person to fill the role. This was reported to the emperor, who presently issued his sanction. A messenger dispatched by the retired emperor communicated that he should certainly like to watch the courtiers perform *dengaku*, and especially have a look at Narimune's performance of *The Head of the Field*. As a result, he ordered that they [also] visit his palace.
>
> [News of] the event spread far and wide. All attendants were present. First, everyone prepared their *dengaku* attire in the private rooms of the palace. (The instruments were on their way from the retired emperor's palace.) With the moon shining bright, people prepared their costumes and gathered before the emperor. (They wore crimson undergarments and gathered trousers with a pressed silver-foil pattern, and they placed broad hats on their heads (as one would place a lid on a box) and adorned them with the long tail feathers of pheasants. Young participants indulged in other types of finery, including flowers made of embroidered silk, lacquered shoes, and silk slippers.) The emperor first watched them perform in the Southern Courtyard in front of the Seiryōden, then they left the courtyard and circled west [around the inner palace]. The emperor watched them again at the Kita-no-Jin Gate [on the northern extremity of the greater palace compound]. They were guided by a strange power [*ma ni iri*] and performed pieces of exceptional beauty.
>
> Captain of the Right Palace Guards Masatoshi summoned attendants and accompanied the *dengaku* performers to the retired emperor's palace. (Carriages were used to get there.) The retired emperor watched them perform from inside the Kitanaka Gate. He was greatly impressed,

> especially with Narimune's mysterious and awe-inspiring [*fukashigi shinmyō*] performance of *The Head of the Field*. Lord [Minamoto no] Akimasa's pole hopping and Lord [Fujiwara no] Tsunetada's and [Fujiwara no] Munesuke's stilt walking proved to be the finest acts.
>
> Next Ikuhōmon'in appeared and watched them perform pieces of exceptional beauty [*myōkyoku*]. Afterward they crossed back to the Southern Courtyard, exited through the West Gate, and returned to the inner palace. Finally, they gathered around the Kita-no-Jin Gate and spent the rest of the night immersed in song and dance, retiring when the cocks began to crow. (Some ten Takiguchi guards and four or five functionaries from the Chamberlains' Office were ordered to pick up the stilts [that had been used].)[13]

In his account, Munetada documents the capacity of *dengaku* to command the attention not only of courtiers and senior nobles but also of the emperor, the retired emperor, and the retired emperor's daughter. The order to commence the performances comes from the assembled courtiers; the emperor approves this, and before long, the retired emperor has requested that the performers visit his compound as well. Thus begins an all-nighter featuring extravagant costumes and virtuosic performances that take place in various locations throughout the capital, from the courtyard of the Seiryōden, to sites within the greater palace compound, to the retired emperor's compound.

Bialock notes that "outbreaks of vestimentary excess" like this were an especially visible sign of the "breakdown in the symbolic codes that had been integral to the center's ritual management of space."[14] Just as the performances one month earlier had transgressed with their strange sounds and disorderly movements, so too did the courtiers' performances transgress with their displays of sumptuous excess. Munetada relates the event with an air of enchantment, noting how Emperor Horikawa watched as participants "guided by a strange

13. *Chūyūki*, DNK 3:74–76.

14. Bialock, *Eccentric Spaces, Hidden Histories*, 218. For an overview of the semiotics of dress as they relate to early medieval performance, see Moriya, *Chūsei geinō no genzō*, 41–76.

Table 3.1. Courtier participants in the 1096/7/12 (Eichō 1) *dengaku* performance

Governor of Harima Lord Fujiwara no Akisue	*kaketsuzumi*	Fourth-Rank Lieutenant Lord Minamoto no Akimasa	*kaketsuzumi*, pole hopping
Right Controller Lord Fujiwara no Munetada	*kaketsuzumi*	Minister of the Left Bureau of Horses Lord Minamoto no Morotaka	small *tsuzumi*
Latter Fourth-Rank Lieutenant Lord Minamoto no Yoshitoshi	small cymbals	Acting Captain Lord Fujiwara no Akizane	*kaketsuzumi*
Governor of Inaba Lord Fujiwara no Nagazane	small *tsuzumi*	Minister of the Right Bureau of Horses Lord Fujiwara no Kanezane	flute
Fourth-Rank Lieutenant Lord Fujiwara no Ariie	*kaketsuzumi*	Fourth-Rank Acting Lieutenant Lord Fujiwara no Toshitada	small *tsuzumi*
Governor of Suō Lord Fujiwara no Tsunetada	*sasara*, stilt walking	Former Vice-Director of the Palace Guards Lord Fujiwara no Nagatada	small cymbals
Fourth-Rank New Lieutenant Lord Minamoto no Akimichi	*sasara*	Acting Right Controller Lord Minamoto no Shigesuke (wearing a wide-brimmed cypress hat)	small *tsuzumi*

power [*ma ni iri*] [. . .] performed pieces of exceptional beauty [*myōkyoku o sōsu*]"; Retired Emperor Shirakawa delighted in the "mysterious and awe-inspiring" (*fukashigi shinmyō*) presence of troupe leader Narimune; and Shirakawa's daughter Ikuhōmon'in observed the "exceptional beauty" (*myōkyoku*) of the performances.

After narrating these events, Munetada proceeds to list the participating courtiers and the instruments played by each (see table 3.1).[15] This is how we know that Munetada himself participated in the

15. A total of twenty-nine courtier musicians are listed by name: nine played *kaketsuzumi*, seven played *kotsuzumi*, eight played *sasara*, three played *dobyōshi* (small

Chamberlain Junior Counselor Minamoto no Narimune	*The Head of the Field* (wearing tall rain clogs)	Chamberlain Right Junior Controller and Acting Captain of the Right Gate Guards Taira no Tokinori	small cymbals
Lieutenant Minamoto no Arikata	*kaketsuzumi*	Chamberlain Lieutenant Fujiwara no Munesuke	*sasara*, stilt walking
Governor of Misaka Fujiwara no Mototaka	small *tsuzumi*	Vice-Director of the Palace Guards Minamoto no Morotoki	small *tsuzumi*
Acting Senior Assistant Minister of Population Affairs Fujiwara no Motokane	*sasara*	Senior Assistant Minister of Population Affairs Minamoto no Yukinobu	small *tsuzumi*
Captain of the Palace Guards Fujiwara no Sanetaka	*kaketsuzumi*	Junior Assistant Minister of Civil Affairs Fujiwara no Kanesue	*kaketsuzumi*
Acting Minister of the Right Bureau of Horses Minamoto no Iesada	*sasara*	Senior Assistant Minister of Civil Affairs Fujiwara no Atsukane	*sasara*
Chamberlain Minamoto no Moroshige	*kaketsuzumi*	Chamberlain Aide to the Ministry of Ceremonial Fujiwara no Munenaka	flute
Chamberlain Assistant Minister of the Bureau of Cookery Moriie	*sasara*	Chamberlain Aide to the empress Minamoto no Masamoto	*sasara*

SOURCE: *Chūyūki*, DNK 3:75–76.

performances, having played the *kaketsuzumi*, a large drum fastened to the hip. Courtier diaries often report hearsay, but in this instance, the author of the entry could not have been closer to the action. Despite *dengaku*'s more plebian provenance, what unfolds in Munetada's

cymbals), and two played flute. The table should be read from left to right, top to bottom. *Chūyūki*, DNK 3:75–76.

account is a kind of carnival put on by elites for elites, a performance of disorder and excess tailored to fit the wider shape of court culture.[16] The cast of *dengaku* performers shifts from unnamed urban attendants to named and titled courtiers, and the protean open crowd is replaced by the closed crowd of a structured list. This shift enables and perhaps necessitates a mode of viewing—both in Munetada's narrative and presumably among the courtiers themselves—that highlights individual acts of virtuosity as exemplary moments within the larger event. For example, Munetada comments that Minamoto no Akimasa's (1074–1136) pole hopping (*issoku*) and the stilt walking (*nisoku*) of Fujiwara no Tsunetada (1075–1138) and Fujiwara no Munesuke (1077–1162) are especially splendid.[17] These courtiers elevate such feats of balance from lowbrow entertainment to highbrow diversion, transposing the kinetic energy of the open crowd into a mark of elite distinction.

What drew the most attention was Narimune's performance of *Tanushi* (The head of the field). The word *tanushi* usually refers to a person in charge of the management and cultivation of a rice field, though in this case it seems to indicate a dramatization of such a figure. In the passage from *Eiga monogatari* discussed in chapter 2, the head of the field and his wife preside over a rice-planting rite that Fujiwara no Michinaga has arranged especially for his daughter Shōshi. Here, Munetada records only that Narimune played the role of the head of the field, but considered in relation to the description found in *Eiga monogatari*, his performance can be read as an act of symbolic inversion in which an urban elite appropriated the customs and appearance of a rural farmer. By momentarily transforming himself into a social other, Narimune seems to have ensured the delight and won the praise of his audience.

It would be misleading to characterize Munetada's description of the courtiers' *dengaku* performances as wholly recapitulating existing

16. The courtier Fujiwara no Suenaka (1046–1119) recorded a nearly identical account of the 1096/7/12 *dengaku* in his diary, which has been preserved in Minamoto no Akikane's (1160–1215) collection of tales *Kojidan* (Stories of ancient matters; ca. 1215). See *Kojidan*, SNKBT 41:104–6. A full translation is included in appendix 1.

17. These practices likely derived from *sangaku*, discussed at length in chapter 5.

court diversions. There is, instead, a doubling—something so often associated with transgression and inversion—in which a discourse of awe displaces a discourse of strangeness. Whereas Munetada previously used words and images denoting the strange and supernatural to create a negative characterization of the *dengaku* performances in the sixth month, here he employs a parallel vocabulary to mark the courtiers' *dengaku* as otherworldly in a more positive sense. As his shift in linguistic register indicates, the strange (*ki*) has been eclipsed by the sublime (*myō*).

Munetada's entry for the following day, 1096/7/13, describes another round of extravagant *dengaku* performances and its attendance by several senior nobles and the empress, Tokushi Naishinnō (1060–1114):

> At the Hour of the Monkey [4:00 p.m.], I hurried to the palace. The retired emperor's courtiers had assembled to perform *dengaku*. People soon gathered at the palace to watch, but there were some courtiers who abstained. Among those who came, however, were [Fujiwara no] Nagazane and Tsunetada, and due to the presence of the retired emperor's officials and the line of *dengaku* performers, once nightfall came, more than thirty of the retired emperor's courtiers performed *dengaku* on the grounds of the palace. The emperor watched them as they moved along the hallways toward the Kita-no-Jin Gate. People said, "The governor of Bizen Fujiwara no Suetsuna is truly second to none at playing the *kaketsuzumi*. He has really mastered it." The chamberlains gathered torches and placed them under the eaves.
>
> For costumes, they wore formal upper robes and wide-legged divided skirts. They attached fans to their heads and wore broad hats adorned with the long tail feathers of pheasants. Words cannot describe the extravagant articles of clothing on display: they featured gold, silver, and embroidered silk and included skirts made from Chinese brocade.
>
> Four senior nobles accompanied [the performers]. (Director of the Left Palace Guards [Fujiwara no] Mototada, Minister of Civil Affairs [Fujiwara no] Michitoshi, Captain of the Right Palace Guards [Minamoto no] Masatoshi, and the New Consultant Captain [Fujiwara no] Munemichi.

> They were all attired in ordinary court clothing. Servers from Ise Shrine accompanied the two consultants and carried long poles crested with fans.)
>
> Next they visited the empress. They crossed the Southern Courtyard, left through the West Gate, and then returned. It was truly awe inspiring [*shinmyō*]. With the entertainment far from over, some twenty of the emperor's courtiers performed *dengaku* for him. They next visited the nearby Reizei Palace and performed pieces of exceptional beauty [*myō-kyoku*] before the Nakayama deity. They also visited the residence of the imperial consort [Fujiwara no Kanshi] (in the Imperial Kitchens), spending all night entertaining themselves before finally retiring at daybreak.[18]

Here Munetada devotes considerable space and praise to the courtiers' performance of *dengaku*, using the same lavish language found in the previous entry and a similar rhetoric of individual virtuosity. But at the end of the entry, Munetada makes an abrupt digression and launches into a more general criticism of the sounds and movements of the *dengaku* craze that had spread throughout the capital during the summer months. He concludes:

> Starting in the fifth month, the realm has witnessed daily *dengaku* performances put on by both the venerable and the base [*kisen*]. Some visit Iwashimizu and Kamo, and others visit Matsu-no-o and Gion. The streets are congested with the sounds of drums and flutes. Praising it as something favored by the deities, myriad people perform *dengaku*. Still others speak in a trance and rapidly form groups. They delight in the strange rumors [*yōgen*] of the day. This is truly a dangerous situation.[19] Is it ordained by heaven? Although matters have escalated greatly, no one knows.[20]

18. *Chūyūki*, DNK 3:76.

19. Literally, "Truly have water and fire entered." While this phrase can signify floods and conflagrations, here Munetada uses it metaphorically to suggest a dangerous situation.

20. *Chūyūki*, DNK 3:76–77.

Despite Munetada's positive valuation of the sounds and movements of the courtiers' *dengaku*, his description of the wider arc of the event remains critical. Although the performances of 1096/7/12 and 1096/7/13 have not occasioned physical violence, from the viewpoint of elite observers like Munetada, they are still ultimately tainted by their association with *dengaku*, especially acknowledging that by this point *dengaku* had come to signify not only a repertoire but also a range of transgressive behaviors linked to violence and otherness. The ongoing strength of these associations explains why *dengaku* retained its subversive valence even in the context of urban elite performance.

At the end of the 1096/7/13 entry, Munetada specifies both elites and non-elites as targets of his ire, which means this is not simply a critique of an outside group. Furthermore, whereas in his earlier accounts of the *dengaku* craze Munetada was careful to articulate the different social groups participating in the performances, in this moment of retrospective judgment, he unites the diversity of social actors under a simple two-character compound: *kisen*, the "venerable and base," two of the three categories of *ritsuryō* social typology, but also a conventional way of signifying everyone, high and low. In casting a narrative glance back over recent events, Munetada melds the heterogeneous group of social actors into a single legible figure of disorder. The final verdict given, the past is recreated—but the diary format preserves points of difference, foregrounding contradictions that a more polished narrative might have elided. These contradictions remain unresolved, a fitting end for an event that brought self and other together in transgression, with the fugitive energies of *dengaku* mediating the performance of temporary identifications and ever-shifting social boundaries.

Displacing Transgression: *Dengaku*'s Supernatural Animation

If Munetada's diary entries chart the drift of his ambivalent reactions to the Great Dengaku across a swath of time and shifting circumstances, Ōe no Masafusa's account, entitled *Rakuyō dengaku ki*, presents a more polished and politically savvy narrative. A quasi-historical account (*ki*), over time it became the most frequently reproduced and referenced summary of the event.[21] The account, written in literary Sinitic prose, presents a streamlined description of the Great Dengaku contextualized by an appeal to the performative ability of language to control the uncontrollable and reinstate order in the aftermath of transgression.

Rakuyō dengaku ki is one of several accounts composed by Masafusa, a prolific Confucian scholar who left behind an oeuvre that spans compilations of court ceremony and protocol, collections of tales and biographies, several quasi-historical accounts, and hundreds of ceremonial dedications.[22] Several of his accounts center on populations that were, from the viewpoint of the court, socially peripheral but perhaps more symbolically central than openly recognized: troupes of puppeteers, itinerant courtesans, and of course *dengaku* performers. As crowd-like entities that both repel and attract, these "others" seem to prompt a dual identification from Masafusa. On the one hand, he asserts himself through his writing as learned (prodigiously literate) and politically valuable, in contrast to their ignorance (illiteracy) and political marginalization. But on the other hand, considering his unprecedented and extraordinary political success, it seems possible that he had misgivings about his own status, which may have prompted a sort of positive identification with his objects of representation. For example, although historical records indicate that puppeteers (*kugutsu*) were subject to aggressive policies of integration, Masafusa's evocation of them in *Kairaishi no ki* (An account of puppeteers; ca. late eleventh century) is strikingly quixotic:[23]

21. Miyoshi Tameyasu (1049–1139) includes the account in the belles lettres (*bunpitsu*) section of his *Chōya gunsai* (Compendium of texts for court and provinces; initially compiled in 1116), a voluminous collection of model court documents. See *Chōya gunsai*, SZKT 29:68–69. The encyclopedia *Koji ruien* (Encyclopedia of ancient matters; ca. 1896–1914) furthermore describes *dengaku* using language particular to Masafusa's account. *Koji ruien*, 687. A translation of the entry is included in appendix 1.

22. For an excellent study of Masafusa and his writings, see Shibayama, "Ōe no Masafusa and the Convergence of the 'Ways.'"

23. For more on *kugutsu*, see Yamaji, *Chūsei geinō no teiryū*, 161–69. For a view of *kugutsu* as female entertainers and their relationship to *asobi*, see Kawashima, *Writing Margins*, 27–30. In chapter 7, I discuss a story about a provincial official with a history as a *kugutsu* performer who, upon hearing a group of *kugutsu* playing drums in the distance, reawakens to his former performance practices.

> They do not plow even one *se* of rice fields, nor do they pick even one branch of mulberry. In this manner, they do not subject themselves to local officials, none of them is a regular dweller, and they are naturally equivalent to "drifters." They do not recognize even the royalty at the top, nor do they fear the provincial governors among them. They take not having any taxes and levies as their lifetime enjoyment. At night they worship the *hyakugami*, clamorously beating drums and dancing, praying for aid in bringing good fortune.[24]

Masafusa imagines these bands of puppeteers as embodying a culture that is fundamentally distanced from the influence of the court and its bureaucracy. He constructs the figure of the puppeteer as a symbol of political and cultural freedom, conjuring it as beyond the reach of imperial authority and its systematized agricultural foundation.[25] As Jane Marie Law writes, the *kugutsu* depicted here "tell us more about what a noble court scholar (such as Ōe) was *not* (and perhaps what he secretly at times wished he could be) than what a puppeteer was."[26] Law goes on to argue that Masafusa's "fantasy" marks "the beginnings of the invention of the Other—in this case, itinerant performers—in Japanese history."[27] Though this may hold true for the history of puppetry and other *kadozuke* (attached to the gate) performance genres,

24. "Kairaishi no ki," NST 8:308 (CJ: 158). I have used Kawashima's English translation, with slight modifications. See Kawashima, *Writing Margins*, 297–98. *Hyakugami* literally means "one hundred deities." There is debate about whether this word should be interpreted as "myriad deities" or as a reference to *hyakudayū*, which Kawashima describes as "deities of crossroads and sexual unions, also known as *dōsōjin*" (31). Since Masafusa uses *hyakudayū* in another text, Jane Marie Law argues for the "myriad deities" interpretation but also states that we should understand *hyakudayū* to be included in this collection of deities. Law, "Of Plagues and Puppets," 114–15.

25. The narrator of the Kakuichibon version of *Heike monogatari* uses similar language to describe the inhabitants of faraway Kikai-ga-shima: "The men wear no *eboshi* hat; the women do not let their hair hang loose. / Going unclothed as they do, they little resemble people. / Having no food, they think only of slaughtering living beings. / The peasants till no hillside paddies, / and so it is that they have no rice; / since they lack mulberry trees and leaves, / they have nothing resembling silk." *The Tale of the Heike*, 106.

26. Law, *Puppets of Nostalgia*, 101.

27. Law, *Puppets of Nostalgia*, 103.

Masafusa's description of the *dengaku* performances in the summer of 1096, which he wrote around the same time, involves a more nuanced perspective on non-elite performance.[28]

If *Kairaishi no ki* presents a wistful vision of a drifting lifestyle, *Rakuyō dengaku ki* highlights the more ambivalent fusion of fear and fascination that non-elite performance routinely triggered among elites. In the account, Masafusa narrates the relentless spread of *dengaku* throughout the capital's social topography, developing a sustained examination of the connection between crowds and non-elite performance. A complete translation follows:

> During the summer of the first year of Eichō [1096], there were many *dengaku* performances in the capital, but no one knows where they began. They started with people from the countryside and spread to the senior nobles. There was stilt walking and pole hopping; the playing of [large] hip drums and small drums, small cymbals and *binzasara*; and rice-planting rites conducted by young women and their attendants.[29] Performances continued day and night without end; the noise was extreme, and people were truly amazed by what they heard. Various district officials, government bureaucrats, and guards each formed their own groups, some making pilgrimages to temples and others filling the streets. It was as though everyone in the capital had gone mad—perhaps it was the deed of a spirit fox. Their costumes exhibited the utmost beauty and refinement, appearing as though engraved and polished, and their clothes were made from embroidered silk adorned with gold and

28. *Kadozuke* refers to a variety of practices (including *senzu manzai* and *matsubayashi*) involving outsider performers visiting the thresholds of residences to conduct ritual performances, typically around the new year. For an overview, see Law, *Puppets of Nostalgia*, 77–86.

29. *Koshitsuzumi* (hip drum) and *furitsuzumi* (small drum) are different names for the instruments Munetada refers to in his diary respectively as *kaketsuzumi* and *kotsuzumi*. "Rice-planting rites conducted by young women and their attendants" translates *ueme, tsukime*. *Ueme*, glossed by Yamaji Kōzō as *saotome*, refers to a role in rice-planting rites. In these rites, young women (*saotome*) planted seedlings designated as divine manifestations (*yorishiro*) while singing; meanwhile, men (*saotoko*) stood on the footpaths and played music. *Tsukime* (literally "hulling women") refers to attendants who brought food and drink to the ritual performers. Yamaji, "Nōfu, denpu no gaku," 271, 281.

silver. The wealthy made use of their ample resources; the poor were stretched thin as they tried to imitate.

Ikuhōmon'in, daughter of Retired Emperor Shirakawa, became especially interested in *dengaku*, and performances thrived on the grounds of her father's palace. In several dwellings and places, people formed groups and performed. Not only the young but also the old—both monk and layman—formed groups. Buddhist sculptors and reciters of sutras each led groups of their own, wearing caps and long embroidered overcoats.[30] They performed [*bugaku*] dances such as Ryōō and Batō. Afterward, officials in the Documents Bureau planned their own performances of the dances. Lord Koremune no Takakoto performed the Man'en Show with his wizened body.[31] Lords Fujiwara no Aritoshi, Fujiwara no Arinobu, Fujiwara no Suetsuna, Fujiwara no Atsumoto, and Sugawara no Ariyoshi [were also in attendance]. All were equally successful bureaucrats who held the Diploma of Letters. Some were attired in formal robes, others wore armor, and still others had their robes hiked up.

Warriors gathered in a group, and as nightfall approached, they entered the retired emperor's palace, drumming, dancing, and leaping around. They wore extravagant robes and skirts that had been outlawed. The capital police also took part in the *dengaku* performances. All wore extravagant clothing and moved around the streets in broad daylight.

30. *Ryōra*; these overcoats were part of official court dress.

31. "Man'en Show" translates *man'en no gi*. In Zhang Pingzi's *Xijingfu*, the *man'en* (Ch. *manyan*) appears as a fearsome beast: "There was a giant beast one hundred *xun* long; / This was the *manyan*. / A sacred mountain, tall and rugged, / Suddenly appeared from its back. / Bears and tigers climbed on, grappling one another; / Gibbons and monkeys leaped up and clung to a high perch. / Strange beasts wildly capered about, / And the great bird proudly strutted in. / A white elephant marched along nursing its calf, / Its trunk drooping and undulating. / A great sea-fish transformed itself into a dragon, / Its form writhing and wriggling, twisting and twining." David Knechtges, whose translation appears here, explains that "the *manyan* show must have included a large number of performers: the dancers inside the *manyan* costume (if it were as long as the prototype, there would have been several hundred!) and the performers dressed as tigers, bears, gibbons, and monkeys, who were carried on the sacred mountain." See *Wen xuan*, 230–33. Additionally, in *Kairaishi no ki*, Masafusa mentions that the nomadic puppeteers' skill in animating their dolls resembles the *man'en* performance. See "Kairaishi no ki," NST 8:308 (CJ: 158).

> Guests of the retired emperor also formed a group and went to his palace.
>
> Attendants gathered at the emperor's palace. The acting middle counselor Fujiwara no Mototada thrust a nine-*shaku* fan into the air, Fujiwara no Michitoshi wore rush sandals decorated with strips of paper, and advisor Fujiwara no Munemichi wore half sandals made of straw. One can only guess how their attendants were dressed. Some were completely naked save for a red robe wrapped around the waist; others sported unruly hair under [wide-brimmed] field hats. They traveled back and forth between several locations on Rokujō and Nijō, kicking up dust in the streets and blocking traffic.[32] Why have strange [*kikai*] events like these increased as of late?
>
> Ikuhōmon'in later became sick and, before long, died. Her *dengaku*-viewing attendants now accompanied her funeral carriage. This is the result of a strange omen [*yōi*] that exceeds human control. Who among even the wise and the powerful can escape such things?[33]

Just like in Munetada's diary entries, Masafusa highlights the heterogeneous mix of performances and the transgressive space they produced. He also emphasizes the extravagant clothing on display, noting the shocking appearance of courtiers and their attendants. The vision of courtiers bedecked in prohibited finery, described at length by Munetada, is here complemented by the naked bodies and unfurled hair of attendants cavorting along the avenues of the capital.

Masafusa emphasizes *dengaku*'s ability to move between different social spaces, with rich and poor, old and young, monk and layman all getting involved in the performances. He wonders why "strange events" such as this one have occurred recently, and proposes a potential answer in the figure of the "spirit fox" (*reiko*). Foxes were transgressive figures thought to straddle the human world and the spirit

32. Retired Emperor Shirakawa's palace was located to the south on Rokujō (Sixth Avenue); Emperor Horikawa's palace was on Nijō (Second Avenue), not far from the greater palace compound.

33. "Rakuyō dengaku ki," NST 23:219 (CJ: 218–19). Two English translations have been published: Raz, "Popular Entertainment and Politics," 297–98; and Addiss et al., *Traditional Japanese Arts and Culture*, 113–14.

world: they might use their powers to help a courtier succeed, or they might possess and prey on humans.[34] As noted at the beginning of the chapter, Masafusa was appointed noble-in-charge for the 1096 rebuilding of Ise Shrine and tasked with managing the implementation of the levy, a burden that played no small role in exacerbating unease and resentment in the provinces. In terms of the origins of the *dengaku* disturbance, there is no conclusive explanation as to why Masafusa favors supernatural rhetoric over political backstory. Some scholars have interpreted this to mean that he did not understand the cause of the event and simply defaulted to that which explains the unknowable.[35] But a more interesting reading might take Masafusa at his word, or lack thereof. Fukazawa Tōru has argued that by deliberately eliding the central role played by the Gion *goryōe* in the *dengaku* craze, Masafusa attempted to transpose the festival's symbolic efficacy into his own account.[36] In other words, his invocation of the supernatural rendered a transgressive event manageable through existing symbolic forms. In this interpretation, the account becomes a placatory text that obscures visible political conditions, and the transgressive possibilities they signified, with a veil of supernatural rhetoric.

Komine Kazuaki agrees that the Gion *goryōe* (and *goryō* belief in general) exercised a prime influence on the account. He reads Masafusa's account more broadly, as an attempt to articulate the shadowy "underside" (*uramen*) represented by the Great Dengaku, in contrast to the "official" (*omotemuki*) duties he was obliged to carry out before and after.[37] The absence of the Gion *goryōe* in the account relieves

34. Faure, *Gods of Medieval Japan*, 89–93.

35. For a discussion of this interpretation, see Fukazawa, *Chūsei shinwa no rentanjutsu*, 69.

36. Fukazawa, *Chūsei shinwa no rentanjutsu*, 71. A more extreme example of this elision can be seen in the reaction of the regent Fujiwara no Moromichi, who, as discussed in chapter 2, was assaulted by *dengaku* performers in 1094. Whereas Masafusa obscures certain details of the event, Moromichi ignores it entirely, writing in his diary *GoNijō Moromichi ki* on 1096/6/19 only that he commissioned sutra readings from monks on Mount Hiei "due to society's instability." *GoNijō Moromichi ki*, 202. Fukushima Masaki has also pointed out that the shake-up caused by the Great Dengaku augured the dissolution of the political partnership that Moromichi had cultivated with Emperor Horikawa. See Fukushima, *Nihon chūsei no rekishi*, 44–45.

37. Komine, *Inseiki bungaku ron*, 880.

Masafusa of the burden of political diagnosis, since the lack of a social explanation enables him to assert the efficacy of his own acts. His appropriation of the ritualistic utility of the festival suggests the power of narrative to refocus the eye of history. By reframing the event in terms of the supernatural, Masafusa displaces the placatory thrust of the festival onto his own act of writing, a work of inversion that seeks to absorb the socially peripheral and reassert the reach of order.

After Transgression: Narrating Elite Trauma

In addition to his appeals to strange phenomena, spirit foxes, and crazed behavior, Masafusa introduces a more directionally specific vector of contagion in support of his interpretation. The *dengaku*, he writes at the beginning of his account, "started with people from the countryside [*ryōri*] and spread to the senior nobles [*kuge*]." This claim is mirrored by the account's underlying structure: it begins with speculation about an unknowable rural origin and concludes with the shocking sickness and death of Ikuhōmon'in, daughter of Retired Emperor Shirakawa, a description of which makes up the entirety of the account's fifth and final section.

In contrast to Munetada's ranging ambivalence, here Masafusa recasts the Great Dengaku as a traumatic moment in which transgressive excess triggered a crisis for elites. He uses parallelism and symmetry to emphasize the connections between Ikuhōmon'in's interest in *dengaku* and her untimely death. This is especially evident in the original text:

自田楽御覧之戸	Her *dengaku*-viewing attendants
蓋見御葬送之車	now accompanied her funeral carriage.[38]

In Masafusa's literary Sinitic, "*dengaku*" and "her" parallel each other, as do "viewing attendants" and "funeral carriage." This creates an impression of the inevitability of Ikuhōmon'in's passage from life into death, a sudden transition wrought by the malevolent force of

38. "Rakuyō dengaku ki," NST 23:219 (CJ: 219).

dengaku.[39] At the same time, this transformation of performing into mourning suggests the resumption of court ceremony over and against non-elite performance, reorganizing the narrative of the Great Dengaku around a theme of elite loss. In the space of a single seven-character couplet, Masafusa has those who ardently participated in the performances morph into the attendants at Ikuhōmon'in's funeral, signaling a return to the order of reality after a detour through the fictitious supernatural terrain of *dengaku*.

Entries in Munetada's diary in the wake of the *dengaku* craze record actions undertaken to allay Ikuhōmon'in's illness, including sutra readings, the imposition of a general amnesty, and a series of elaborate mourning rituals performed after her death—a court spectacle that lasts the better part of a month.[40] The swift substitution proposed by Masafusa, on the other hand, yokes these post-performance developments into the present moment of the narrative, suggesting a more general shift in the relationship between event and context. Ikuhōmon'in's illness and death become the foreground in a story of tragic loss, pushing the *dengaku* performances into the background.

Later narratives of the Great Dengaku show how this refocusing spread beyond Masafusa's account. In the chronicle *Hyakurenshō* (One hundred tempered selections; thirteenth century), a series of brief entries renders the *dengaku* performances secondary to the fate of Ikuhōmon'in and the grief experienced by her father.[41] Likewise, in *Imakagami* (Mirror of the present; late twelfth century), a vernacular history spanning the eleventh and twelfth centuries, Ikuhōmon'in's death becomes a provocative symbol of the wider disorder that rocked the capital.[42] In effect, this shift suggests how court elites used narrative

39. "Her" translates *kengyo*, which, as Moriya Takeshi notes, refers to one who has the affection of the emperor and here indicates Ikuhōmon'in. "Rakuyō dengaku ki," NST 23:219, header note.

40. Munetada's description of these rituals—leading up to, surrounding, and postdating Ikuhōmon'in's death—can be found in several entries in his diary between 1096/7/19 and 1096/8/7. *Chūyūki*, DNK 3:77–83.

41. See the entries dated 1096/7/12, 1096/8/7, and 1096/8/9 in *Hyakurenshō*, SZKT 11:43. A full translation of these entries is included in appendix 1.

42. On *Imakagami*'s approach to narrating the past, see Brightwell, *Reflecting the Past*, 34–83.

to maintain their hold on a particular vision of history and culture amid the destabilization of social order.[43]

The relevant passage in *Imakagami* begins with an explicit reframing of the Great Dengaku in terms of elite mourning:

> [Ikuhōmon'in] passed away on 8/7 of Eichō 1 [1096]. That year, something called the Great Dengaku brought traffic to a standstill even in the streets of the capital and continued unabated at the various shrines. People said, "Given the state of affairs, it's no wonder such a thing has come to pass." It goes without saying that Retired Emperor Shirakawa lamented her death. As a result, he shaved his head [and became a monk]. Words like "surprising" hardly begin to convey what happened.[44]

As in Masafusa's account, a cause-and-effect relationship between the *dengaku* disturbance and Ikuhōmon'in's death is established. The general difference between these later accounts and Munetada's day-to-day reportage highlights the implicit political orientation of the writing of history. With "people" spreading rumors about the destabilizing capacity of *dengaku*, Ikuhōmon'in's interest in such performances must be downplayed in favor of recasting her as a tragic victim. One strategy for accomplishing this transformation is by reorienting the narrative to reflect the pathos and trauma that her loss signifies, as opposed to the unruly performances that were thought to have caused it. In this way, the later narratives—and, by extension, the retrospective imaginative function of court-centered histories—neutralize the threat of non-elite performance by staging elite loss.

Another passage in the *Imakagami* account enacts this displacement through an evocation of the pitiful mourning activities of a young man named Fujiwara no Tomonobu, the son of Ikuhōmon'in's wet nurse. Consumed with sadness, he retreats from the world and resettles in a remote area outside the capital. In an exchange of *waka* poems that takes place one year after Ikuhōmon'in's death, the lingering

43. This is not to say that the archive does not preserve points of difference. For example, the record of the Great Dengaku found in *Kojidan* does not even mention Ikuhōmon'in. *Kojidan*, SNKBT 41:104–6.

44. *Imakagami zenchūshaku*, 507.

bereavement experienced by Tomonobu and his poetic interlocutor Haku no haha finds expression in a sympathetic response from the natural soundscape. He writes:

> I thought my sadness would have ended last autumn—
> but this year, too, I cannot help but weep along with the crying insects!
>
> *kanashisa ni aki wa tsukinu to omohishi o*
> *kotoshi mo mushi no ne koso nakarure*

And she responds:

> This autumn the insects cry out all the more,
> and it feels like your departure was long ago.
>
> *mushi no ne wa kono aki shimo zo naki masaru*
> *wakare no tohoku naru kokochi shite*[45]

The sound of insects (*mushi no ne*) crying conventionally signifies autumnal valediction, and the speakers of both poems use this figure to express their grief over Ikuhōmon'in's untimely death. Tomonobu's encounter with this chorus causes him to confront his sadness and realize that he is not beyond mourning, and Haku no haha describes how the sound's unusual intensification makes her feel even more distanced from the moment of parting.

Amplified in this way, the sound of crying insects becomes a central signal within the narrative's soundscape, just like the clamorous *dengaku* performances described in earlier texts. In their accounts, Munetada and Masafusa describe the prodigious noise of the *dengaku* performances, allowing readers to hear something of what reverberated throughout the capital. In this scene of poetic exchange, that very noise is silenced by the invocation of a more conventional poetic sound. What we hear is not the rasping of the *binzasara* or the thrumming of drumbeats but instead a mournful cry bearing witness to Ikuhōmon'in's absence. By invoking a soundscape built on the conventions of *waka*

45. *Imakagami zenchūshaku*, 509.

poetics, the narrator mutes the transgressive noise of the Great Dengaku with a powerful aural expression of court culture.

During the summer of 1096, *dengaku* staged by a heterogeneous mix of performers—high and low, rich and poor, urban and rural, old and young, monk and layman—engulfed the capital. How, in the end, should we understand this event? Political, social, and religious factors are surely relevant, but as I have argued, the more fundamental efficacy of *dengaku* lay in its transgressive appeal for a variety of performers. There was a widespread desire to cross boundaries, and *dengaku* enabled this as the medium of the moment. Although accounts of the Great Dengaku often sought to distinguish between performances by elites and those by non-elites, both groups confronted authority with spectacles of transgression that could not be rendered fully legible in writing. In Munetada's diary entries, it is Munetada himself who mediates between these groups: he is the eyes and ears that report on the raucous festivities as well as the performing body that gets autoreported. In Masafusa's account, *dengaku* becomes a supernatural force that pummels its way through the capital's various social boundaries, overturning the court's symbolic defenses, traumatizing the emperor and the court, and necessitating an attempt at repair through retrospective narration.

As time went on, *dengaku* was absorbed into rural festivals throughout the provinces and became increasingly professionalized as troupes formed and affiliated with temples and shrines.[46] But elites—courtiers and warriors alike—remained troubled by *dengaku*'s accrued associations with violence, otherness, and transgression. Pondering why *dengaku* never became an institutionalized court performance, Okimoto Yukiko speculates that Ikuhōmon'in's death intensified its status as taboo.[47] Indeed, the relationship between taboo and transgression encapsulates the fraught way in which *dengaku* lingered in elite social and symbolic spaces. *Dengaku*'s transgressive force both attracted and repelled, a potent combination that ensured its abiding association with disorder throughout the medieval period.[48] In 1129,

46. Yamaji, "Nōfu, denpu no gaku," 282.
47. Okimoto, *Ranmai no chūsei*, 16.
48. Matsuo, *Girei kara geinō e*, 118.

the poet and courtier Minamoto no Morotoki (1077–1136), who appears in Munetada's diary as one of the courtier performers of *dengaku*, wrote in his diary about a rice-planting event featuring *dengaku* and *sarugaku* performers. Bifukumon'in (1117–1160), future consort of Retired Emperor Toba (r. 1103–1123), departed early from the event because the clamorous sound of drums and flutes was deemed to be inauspicious for a pregnant woman to hear.[49] In an entry dated 1247, the history *Azuma kagami* (The mirror of the east; 1180–1266) mentions reports from local inhabitants that describe the nightly gathering of *dengaku* troupes in the mountains as a "strange phenomenon" (*kaii*).[50] In 1311, Tōin Kinkata (1291–1360) warned in his diary *Entairyaku* (Diary of the Nakazono grand minister; 1311–1360) of an epidemic "known popularly as '*dengaku* disease,'" registering the metaphoric slippage between *dengaku* and illness.[51] And the warrior tale *Taiheiki* (Chronicle of the great peace; late fourteenth century) includes two narratives that dramatize *dengaku*'s strangeness and excess: one that interprets Hōjō Takatoki's (1303–1333) private *dengaku* parties as evidence of the impending downfall of the realm and one that details a *dengaku* performance in 1349 that elicited such raucous responses from the audience that several viewing stands collapsed, bringing death and discord to the assembled crowd.[52] As a lingering medium of transgression, *dengaku* continued to signify violence, excess, strangeness, and political instability, registering a basic incompatibility between spontaneous eruptions of open-crowd performance and administrative apparatuses that sought stasis and longevity. If the cultural politics of early Japan can be characterized by a centripetal orientation, the Great Dengaku highlights the centrifugal excesses that would come to characterize the medieval period.

49. *Chōshūki*, ZST 16:268.

50. *Azuma kagami*, SZKT 33:395.

51. *Entairyaku*, 94. See chapter 7 for a discussion of this and other accounts of "*dengaku* disease."

52. *Taiheiki*, SNKBZ 54:254–57 and 56:322–28. Bialock reads these passages as heteromorphic topoi in which "everything has been turned inside out." See Bialock, *Eccentric Spaces*, 238–39.

CHAPTER FOUR

Audience as Crowd

Shin sarugaku ki, Social Typology, and Urban Life

Predating *Rakuyō dengaku ki* by some four decades, Fujiwara no Akihira's *Shin sarugaku ki* is the longest extant Heian-period text devoted to non-elite performers and audiences. Though both texts describe a range of performance practices within the broader space of festivity, *Shin sarugaku ki* does not document a specific historical event nor is it even predominantly concerned with *sarugaku*. It begins by listing performers and performances typically present at the annual Inari Festival, proceeds to describe the excessive behavior of several members of the audience, and then shifts to a description of the attributes and professions of a large family that has come to watch. Akihira's inclusion of *sarugaku* and other non-elite performances makes it a valuable text for understanding their status and form in the mid-eleventh century. But the text mostly consists of a description of the audience: the diverse populations that lived, worked, and played in the capital.

Compared to the documents written about the Great Dengaku, which collectively embody an upper-aristocratic view of non-elite performers, *Shin sarugaku ki* describes the gathered audience members in order to evoke a broader view of mid-ranking nobility and low-ranking officials and functionaries. Akihira's text effectively flips the narrative perspective from viewing performance to performing viewing, resulting in an emic ethnography of spectatorship. To read *Shin sarugaku ki* is not only to learn about the repertoire of non-elite performances (*sarugaku* and all the others listed at the beginning of the text) but also, more substantially, to view the broader social topography of the capital transposed into the form of a diverse and memorable audience. By shifting the focus from performers as crowd to audience as crowd, this chapter furnishes a more expansive understanding of crowds in the Heian period, returning to the questions first posed in the analysis of *Nenjū gyōji emaki* in chapter 1.

A focus on language, embodiment, and their intermingling permeates *Shin sarugaku ki.* Akihira vividly describes virtuosic bodies engaged in activities associated with their professions or dominant attributes, typically to an excessive degree. Just like the festival that provides the setting, the family members described in succession are neither wholly fabricated nor mimetically "real" in any historically specific sense. They are instead impressions, often archetypal and caricatured, of the range of people who populated the capital and who are now gathered to take in the performances. By organizing these impressions, Akihira crafts a typological view of society even as he playfully subverts the viability of representation. To read the text thoughtfully—that is, to consider how it stages an intersection of classical form and vernacular content—is to inhabit this ambiguity.

Like Masafusa's quasi-historical accounts, *Shin sarugaku ki* was written in the style known by modern scholars as *hentai kanbun*: literary Sinitic studded with vernacular Japanese words and syntax. To consider how to read and interpret such a text, a quick look at roughly contemporaneous attitudes about textual hierarchies will be helpful. In *Genji ippon kyō* (A dedicatory proclamation for *The Tale of Genji*; 1176), the monk Chōken (1126–1203) considers the purpose and significance of different kinds of texts and enumerates them in order of prestige. Buddhist sutras and treatises are at the top, followed by Confucian classics, Chinese histories, Chinese poetry, vernacular poetry (*waka*) and, lastly, vernacular prose.[1] This schema elevates *kanbun* above *wabun* (vernacular Japanese writing), but it is a distant view that cannot account for the particularities of how specific texts make hybrid use of forms and figures from the larger textual system.

1. "A Dedicatory Proclamation," 189–90.

Consider, for example, *waka* composed on Buddhist topics (*shakkyōka*). The religious merit embodied by such poems might, according to Chōken's schema, make them superior to poetry composed on the topic of unrequited love. Conversely, Chōken lauds *kanbun* verse that describes "the pleasures of spring scenery and the views of the autumn hills," but what about more "marginal" *hentai kanbun* prose works that cover local topics such as folk tales and practices, acrobatics, female entertainers, and puppetry?[2]

The scholar-officials who wrote texts of this sort, which can be understood as classical in form and vernacular in content, were by and large affiliated with the State Academy (Daigakuryō), an important institution within the court bureaucracy.[3] Instead of being a precise replica of its continental models, it abounded with local adaptations. One particularly striking difference was the structure of the academy and the social status of those who pursued knowledge within it. Although the examination system in China was a practical means to advance one's social and political status, at the Heian court (especially by the tenth century), political power flowed largely according to lineage and kinship, not merit. For the low-ranking Heian scholar-official, producing *kanbun* texts was not a dependable way to advance one's career, given that it was, according to Brian Steininger, "increasingly excluded from court ceremony" and "came to be understood as a technical skill of limited value."[4] Furthermore, as Satō Michio notes, by the eleventh century, "the official duties of Confucian scholars were reduced, and the actual contents of a scholar's everyday service were evolving into the mere act of drafting lavish compositions that had nothing to do with the ideal of 'building the state and ruling society' [*keikoku chisei*]."[5]

The decline of classical Chinese learning's functional utility precipitated a new kind of *kanbun* writing in the eleventh and twelfth centuries. I argue that, as scholar-officials in the academy became

2. "A Dedicatory Proclamation," 190.

3. For an overview of the structure of the State Academy, see Steininger, *Chinese Literary Forms*, 129–38.

4. Steininger, *Chinese Literary Forms*, 15.

5. Satō, *Heian kōki Nihon kanbungaku no kenkyū*, 9.

increasingly distanced from political authority and were no longer assuming an active role in governance, their writing turned toward the here and now: increasingly they wrote about the world around them, including local performance practices and popular festivals. These hybrid texts recalibrated the relationships within *kanbun* writing between form and content, classical and vernacular, "there" (China) and "here" (Japan), and—most importantly for this book—elite self and non-elite other.

Fujiwara no Akihira, Scholar of the Social Fringe

What happens when a classical prestige style converges with a dynamic vernacular world? The works of the scholar-official Fujiwara no Akihira provide an excellent point of departure for answering this question. Prior to the eleventh century, the State Academy was dominated by two clans of Confucian scholars, the Sugawara and the Ōe. Akihira was born into the Fujiwara clan, the northern branch of which catapulted into political power and cultural standing under the shrewd leadership of Michinaga around the turn of the eleventh century. The wealth amassed by Michinaga included precious books from the continent, holdings that created the conditions for the Fujiwara to challenge the Sugawara and Ōe monopoly on literary Sinitic learning.[6] It was in this context that Akihira, a member of an "upstart house" (*kike*), as regarded from the perspective of the entrenched scholarly clans, began his decades-long journey through the academic bureaucracy. Despite his obvious talent, it took him nearly thirty years to pass the civil service examination (*taisaku*) after enrolling in the academy, an extraordinarily long period of time.[7] He was nonetheless able to achieve several accolades late in life: for example, in 1062 he

6. Satō, *Heian kōki Nihon kanbungaku no kenkyū*, 5–6.

7. The examination was modeled on continental precedents, but its function was more narrowly tied to one's status within the academy and not the court or society at large. See Saitō, *Kanbunmyaku*, 14. For a recent discussion of Akihira's rise through the ranks, see Shigeta, *Kakyū kizokutachi*, 122–27. For a compact but informative biography of Akihira in English, see Rabinovitch and Bradstock, *No Moonlight in My Cup*, 402.

became the academy's sole professor of Chinese history and belles lettres (*monjō hakase*), obtained the respectable rank of junior fourth lower, and was appointed tutor to the crown prince.[8]

Akihira's writings were anthologized in notable collections of the day, and he left behind three longer works. He is well-known as the compiler of *Honchō monzui* (Literary essence of this court; ca. 1060), a monumental collection in fourteen volumes of model *kanbun* texts that were based on *Wenxuan*.[9] He also wrote *Meigō ōrai*, which consists of 213 model letters written in *kanbun* about a variety of everyday topics and situations. As discussed in chapter 1, this latter work contains passages describing the sights and sounds of urban festivals, including the Inari Festival, and can therefore be read in tandem with *Shin sarugaku ki* as an engagement with local vernacular practices through the idiom of literary Sinitic.

Not unlike Masafusa and GoShirakawa, Akihira displays in his oeuvre a diversity of subject matter, which ranges from practical primers for navigating social interactions to the tumult of urban festivals. This diversity is remarkable, and yet there have been no sustained attempts to evaluate its significance. Most scholars seem to believe it is a function of Akihira's outsider status: Ōsone Shōsuke notes his "eccentric" spirit, and Satō Michio attributes his pronounced interest in "street" topics to his "personal disposition."[10] There may indeed be biographical reasons why Akihira wrote on these topics, but to fully explore the significance of his writings, it is more productive to ask the question of *how*. How did Akihira treat non-elite performers and the audiences that showed up to watch them? How does the interplay between form and content in Akihira's texts index the status of *kanbun* writing as a medium for knowledge about the world? Answering these questions will enable a contextualization within broader literary and historical currents, beyond the intentional fallacy that lingers behind appeals to "the personal."

8. Akihira's new rank placed him in the middle of the middle nobility (see table I.1); for a further discussion, see Shigeta, *Kakyū kizokutachi*, 13–15.

9. For more on Akihira's role in compiling this text, see Steininger, *Chinese Literary Forms*, 61–63.

10. Ōsone, "Fujiwara no Akihira"; and Satō, *Heian kōki Nihon kanbungaku no kenkyū*, 8.

Form and Seriality in *Shin sarugaku ki*

In *Shin sarugaku ki*, Akihira not only represents the diverse residents of the capital but also schematizes its overall social shape. He accomplishes this by beginning with a pretext for people to gather: a performance of *sarugaku*. There are many records of *sangaku* and *sarugaku* performances in the archive, as will be discussed in chapter 5, but Akihira's account is unique for both its high level of detail and how it uses *sarugaku* to register the rapid socioeconomic changes taking place in the capital.

The text begins with the narrator placing himself in the audience and observing the performers who have gathered to participate in what scholars believe to be the Inari Festival:[11]

> Over the past twenty years,
> I have observed the east and west sides of the capital,
> but never has there been [a *sarugaku* performance] as spectacular as the one tonight.[12]
>
> It included *jushi* exorcists, dwarf dancers, *dengaku* performers, puppeteers, illusionists, knife-and-bell jugglers, diabolo throwers, ball jugglers, mimes who acted out wrestling matches and games of *sugoroku*, boneless dancers, and muscular dancers.
>
> I saw District Head Endō's strutting
> and the shrimp-catching attendant's careful tracking;
> the bunched-up trousers of a low-ranking Hikami monk
> and an embarrassed woman from Yamashiro who hid her face behind a fan.
>
> There were tales recited by blind lute priests

11. Kawaguchi Hisao speculates that the performances would have taken place as part of the parade that followed the *mikoshi* back to Mount Inari, in a vacant area just south of the Eastern Market at Shichijō and Ōmiya. *Shin sarugaku ki*, ed. Kawaguchi, 32. See fig. 1.4 for a visualization of audiences gathered to watch the parade.

12. Two characters are illegible due to worm damage in the oldest extant manuscript, but scholars agree that the two missing characters are those that comprise the word *sarugaku*.

and the *sake*-blessing *senzu manzai* musicians;
people drumming their round bellies and chest bones
and dancers imitating a praying mantis.

The monk Fukukō groped around for his surplice
and the nun Myōkō begged for diapers;
a first-class court lady revealed her beautiful face
and a quick-witted chamberlain whistled.

There was the amusing dance of an old musician
and the powdered face of a female shaman;
and some unruly street urchins
who teased an easterner newly arrived in the capital.

There was even the appearance of boisterous musicians
and the sight of their troupe leader.

With all the *sarugaku* skills and foolish lines,
you couldn't help but split your belly and dislocate your jaw
with laughter.[13]

In addition to establishing a point from which to view the festival (that of the gathered audience), this opening passage introduces the form of listing that structures the account. Though I have interpolated subjects and verbs ("there was," "I saw") into my translation, the original text contains no such language, with the notable exception of the narrator's initial "I have observed" (*rekikan*). Because of this, the text in its *kanbun* form is even more list-like, consisting of a catalogue of twenty-eight performers or acts arrayed one after the other, devoid of conjunctions and commentary. This enumeration of performers can be divided into two categories: the first twelve (starting with exorcists and ending with muscular dancers) perform practices incorporated by or related to *sangaku* and *zōgei*, and the remaining perform a variety

13. "Shin sarugaku ki," NST 8:301 (CJ: 134). For Joan Piggott's partial English translation of *Shin sarugaku ki*, including this opening passage, see "An Account of the New Monkey Music," 491–97. My translation uses lineation to replicate something of the structure of the original, which often creates parallel correspondences between groups of characters.

of entertainments, including mimetic drama, dance, percussion, and narrative music. There is such a range of performance types that the passage can be read as an introduction to the emerging culture of medieval performance and some of its main characters: blind lute priests (*biwa hōshi*), *dengaku* performers, and actors putting on dramas akin to those of the medieval comic theater (*kyōgen*). The opening passage, in short, depicts the emergence of a new cultural phenomenon on the streets of the capital. As Matsuoka Shinpei has argued, the world of urban performance that had appeared by the late eleventh century was no peripheral development but rather the very essence of medieval culture in embryonic form.[14]

The serial introduction of performers sets the tone for the entire work, but Akihira does not linger for long on the performances themselves, instead shifting the narrative gaze toward the audience and eventually settling on one large family from "the west side of the capital" (*saikyō*) that has gathered among the onlookers to watch.[15] The family consists of a nameless lieutenant of the Right Gate Guards and his three wives, sixteen daughters, eleven sons-in-law, and nine sons. The two Gate Guard bureaus (*emonfu*) were charged with securing the boundary around the greater palace compound, work that involved more contact with those outside the palace than that of the other guard bureaus. Lieutenants were low-ranking functionaries: their position was the third of the four levels within the bureau, and their rank was typically senior sixth (though fifth-rank lieutenants also existed).[16] From the very beginning, then, the family is marked as not only socially but also geographically marginal: many functionaries lived to the west of the greater palace enclosure, and the western half of the capital in general was underdeveloped compared to the east.

The remainder of the text consists of a description of the lieutenant's family members, though many are skipped—including, interestingly, the lieutenant himself (see table 4.1). These descriptions consist mostly of lists of technical terms that evoke each character's

14. Matsuoka, *Utage no shintai*, 7.

15. "Shin sarugaku ki," NST 8:301 (CJ: 135).

16. *Shin sarugaku ki*, ed. Kawaguchi, 31–32. For more on office and rank in *Shin sarugaku ki*, see Shigeta, *Kakyū kizokutachi no ōchō jidai*, 9–15.

Table 4.1. List of the lieutenant's family members in *Shin sarugaku ki* and their professions or affinities

#	Relationship to lieutenant	Profession and/or description	Relationship to family member	Profession and/ description
1	First wife	Old, ugly		
2	Second wife	Seamstress, ordinary		
3	Third wife	Young, beautiful		
4	First daughter*		Husband	Gambler
5	Second daughter*		Husband	Warrior
6	Third daughter*		Husband	Agriculturalist
7	Fourth daughter	*Miko*	Husband	Smith
8	Fifth daughter*		Husband	Scholar
9	Sixth daughter*		Husband	Wrestler
10	Seventh daughter	Glutton	Husband	Horse-and-cart lender
11	Eighth daughter*		Husband	Carpenter
12	Ninth daughter*		Husband	Physician
13	Tenth daughter*		Husband	Divination mast
14	Eleventh daughter*		Lover	Musician and p
15	Twelfth daughter	Beauty	Suitors*	Several courtiers
16	Thirteenth daughter	Hag	Suitor	Rustic old man
17	Fourteenth daughter	Short, flat forehead, big mouth	Husband	Braggart
18	Fifteenth daughter	Virtuous widow		
19	Sixteenth daughter	Courtesan		
20	First son	Calligrapher		
21	Second son	Shingon priest		
22	Third son	Craftsman		
23	Fourth son	Attendant of a provincial official		
24	Fifth son	Tendai scholar-monk		
25	Sixth son	Painter		
26	Seventh son	Buddhist sculptor		
27	Eighth son	Merchant		
28	Ninth son	Court musician in training		

NOTE: Asterisks denote figures who are mentioned by the narrator but not described.

profession, position, or attributes, in effect creating a lexical tableau of the capital's diverse social and professional terrain.[17] Most strikingly, each description inhabits its own bounded narrative space. The characters do not interact: it is as though each figure occupies a sealed room in a large house. The narrator—and by extension, the reader—has an unobstructed view of minutiae related to them, just as picture scrolls often use the compositional device of the "blown-off roof" (*fukinuki yatai*) to enable viewers to see interior spaces. But unlike in picture scrolls, here the characters have no ability to see or hear anything beyond the narrative walls that separate them.

The encyclopedic nature of Akihira's lists suggests a didactic function. The text may have indeed been written for a young aristocrat or future emperor, a theory supported by Akihira's appointment as tutor to the crown prince toward the end of his life. In this sense, *Shin sarugaku ki* bears a similarity to other didactic manuals written at the court, such as Minamoto no Tamenori's (d. 1011) *Kuchizusami* (Verbal amusements; 970) and the anonymous *Nichūreki* (Two portable encyclopedias; ca. 1210). But whereas these texts present catalogues of terms meant to acquaint the reader with an encyclopedic range of knowledge, Akihira arranges his lists into a unified matrix, the cells of which furnish information about the capital's social terrain.[18] Such a master list depends on models and archetypes, resulting in a broad yet compressed capitalscape built on an exhaustive cataloguing of skills, objects, and features. By transposing the particularities of embodied practices into a grid of *hentai kanbun* text, *Shin sarugaku ki* enables readers versed

17. Lists appear in other literary works of the Heian period, most famously *Makura no sōshi* but also *Ryōjin hishō*. For a study of the former, see Morris, "Sei Shōnagon's Poetic Catalogues."

18. Particularly relevant for the present discussion is the thirteenth volume of *Nichūreki* ("Geinō"), a section of which lists several artistic pursuits, performance practices, and occupations (all signified by the broad meaning of *geinō*), each one followed by the names of exemplars. The section includes names of string and wind musicians, warriors, power brokers, paragons, able officials, Confucian scholars, law scholars, scholars of math, divination masters, doctors, astrologers, horoscope astrologers, stick diviners, physiognomists, dream interpreters, painters, craftsmen, Buddhist sculptors, carpenters, wrestlers, Inner Palace Guard attendants, *gagaku* musicians, dancers, kickballers, *go* players, *sugoroku* players, zealots, thieves, *jushi* exorcists, *sangaku* performers, *yūjo*, puppeteers, *miko*, and the excessively self-interested. *Nichūreki*, 234–40.

in literary Sinitic to slip into a virtual space that simulates the city's vibrant social life. The text, in other words, processes heterogeneous content into a homogenous form, with the lists serving as contact zones in which elite learning mediates a range of vernacular experiences.

Making *Shin sarugaku ki*: Formal and Social Contexts

As a text that represents the practices of non-elites, *Shin sarugaku ki* calls to mind a sequence of literary Sinitic poems (*kanshi*, "Han [Chinese] poetry") about the dispossessed written by the scholar-official Sugawara no Michizane and titled *Kansō jūshu* (Ten poems on the early arrival of the cold; 900). Each of the ten poems begins with the question, "To whom does the cold come early?" and supplies a different answer, highlighting the plight of non-elites: a vagrant, a peasant fleeing taxation, an old widower, an orphan, an herb farmer, a relay station attendant, a ferryman, a fisherman, a salt peddler, and a woodcutter.[19] Because the sequence cycles through several different professions, modern scholars have typically situated it within a group of texts known as *shokunin zukushi* or "exhaustive lists of workers." *Shin sarugaku ki* is often approached in similar fashion, but the tone cultivated by Akihira is markedly different. Michizane's sequence depicts the conditions of impoverished workers in the provinces (a gesture likely influenced by Bai Juyi's (772–846) socially aware *xinyuefu* or "new music bureau ballads"), inciting sympathy in the reader and serving as a potential call to action. Akihira's account, on the other hand, appeals to a broader range of emotions: although there are indeed moments of sadness, there is also plenty to evoke laughter, awe, disgust, and excitement. If *Kansō jūshu* performs a frigid lament, *Shin sarugaku ki* operates more generally as a theater—a "seeing place," as per the ancient Greek word *theatron*—in which characters enter and leave the stage in succession.[20]

19. "Kansō jūshu," NKBT 72:259–65. For a partial English translation, see Watson, *Japanese Literature in Chinese*, 93–94.

20. On the fifth-century BCE *theatron*, see Nellhaus, *Theatre Histories*, 57–60.

Shin sarugaku ki may differ in tone from Michizane's poems, but its form and structure echo those of several tenth- and eleventh-century *kanbun* quasi-historical accounts. Akihira was undoubtedly familiar with Yoshishige no Yasutane's (d. 1002) *Chiteiki* (An account of a pond pavilion; 982), which documents the rapidly changing conditions of the capital and prescribes worldly detachment as an antidote for the vagaries of life as a low-ranking scholar-official.[21] Not only did Akihira include the text in the anthology *Honchō monzui*, but he also repurposed its opening line for *Shin sarugaku ki.*

To set the tone for his narrative of decline and deliverance, Yasutane begins with the following couplet: "Over the past twenty years, I have observed the east and west sides of the capital. / The west side has gradually become devoid of people and dwellings and is mostly reduced to ruins."[22] Akihira chose slightly different characters for his opening couplet, but the meaning is virtually the same: just like Yasutane's, his text begins with the narrator performing an act of visual mastery over the capital. Yasutane's narrator casts a melancholic gaze across the capital, a gesture that activates a poetics of decay that remains palpable throughout the text. (As Yasutane writes, and as noted in the previous section, large portions of the western half of the capital were indeed devoid of dwellings, while the northeastern part of the capital was becoming more dense.)[23] Akihira's narrator, on the other hand, uses the introductory statement to emphasize the exceptional nature of the day's *sarugaku* performances. Where Yasutane sees loss, nearly a century later, Akihira sees vibrant presence, albeit one that indexes a shift away from the central role of scholar-officials in justifying the importance of bureaucratic structures in ruling the realm. If Yasutane's opening lines register discontinuity, loss, and a desire for detachment, Akihira's riff on them pushes in the opposite direction, with the narrator placed within and not separate from the

21. For a full English translation, see "Chiteiki."

22. *Honchō monzui*, SNKBT 27:35 (CJ: 86).

23. Stavros, *Kyoto*, 30–31. Stavros notes that whereas Yasutane (and others after him, including modern scholars) posit the decline of the western half of the capital, recent archeological evidence indicates that large sections of it may have never been developed in the first place.

crowd, observing first the performances and then his fellow audience members.

Given *Shin sarugaku ki*'s investment in representing the external world of the wider capital, as opposed to the internal world of the court, the immediate social context is also important for interpreting its meaning. Akihira's decision to cast a lieutenant of the Right Gate Guards as the text's anchoring figure is worth highlighting here. I have already discussed how the Gate Guard bureaus were tasked with maintaining the greater palace compound's physical order, making their functionaries liminal figures who bridged high and low, purity and impurity, and order and violence. Akihira himself once served in the Right Gate Guards, so the lieutenant may be thought of as a kind of surrogate for (or parody of) the author. Conversely, the lieutenant's liminal status suggests something of Akihira's own circumstances as a low-ranking courtier and scholar who remained on the "social fringe" for much of his career.[24]

Shin sarugaku ki's social and authorial context converge most directly in the description of the fifth daughter's husband, a scholar who has mastered the four fields of knowledge taught at the academy:

> The fifth daughter's husband is a regular student at the academy who studies Chinese history and belles lettres, law, the Confucian classics, and math. His surname is Sugawara, his given name is Masafumi, and he goes by Kanryōsan in his writings. He has thoroughly studied *Selections of Literature*, *Collected Works of Bai Juyi*, *Records of the Grand Historian*, *History of the Han*, *The Analects*, *The Classic of Filial Piety*, *The Classic of Poetry*, and *The Commentary of Zuo*, in addition to the administrative codes, penal laws, supplementary regulations, and procedures. He is hence skilled in writing Chinese poems and rhapsodies, poem prefaces and addresses to the throne, imperial edicts, oral edicts, certificates of rank, memorials to the throne, dedicatory vows, prayers, orders, memoranda, reports, decrees, factual records, petitions, letters, primers, and documents of consent.[25] His writing is exceedingly clear and does

24. Smits, "The Way of the Literati," 117–18.

25. "Reports" translates *keusho* and follows the semantic meaning of the graphs, but the specific nature of these documents is unknown.

> not diverge from established forms; his rhetoric is polished, and his poems and rhapsodies break neither rhyme nor topic. So how could he possibly be inferior to Mochitoki, Masashira, Fumitoki, or Naomoto?[26] Of course, he has not a single weakness when it comes to multiplying and dividing large figures, multiplying single-digit numbers by themselves, estimating quantities, square roots, cube roots, measuring the total area of a field, arithmetic, and [reading] math treatises. If you consider those recently at the academy—scholarship students, graduate students, letters students, graduate students of letters, graduates, and scholars—who could possibly stand shoulder to shoulder with him?[27]

In this entry, Akihira conjures up an impossibly accomplished scholar through lists of books, documents, and techniques, which work to emphasize the encompassing nature of the scholar's knowledge. His surname, Sugawara, recalls the famous scholar clan (from which Michizane hailed), and his given name, Masafumi, combines two graphs that appear in the given names of several well-known scholars, including two mentioned in the entry. The fictionality of this "Sugawara no Masafumi" is hence not to be found in his name but instead in his outlandish accomplishments: we are told that he excels in all four tracks of the academy's curriculum, an unimaginable feat given how each track involved decades of study. Akihira himself is an extreme demonstration of this: as noted earlier in this chapter, despite moving steadily through various prestigious positions within the academic hierarchy, he did not pass the civil service examination until he was thirty-nine years old, and it was not until late in life that he left behind his long-held status as a low-ranking aristocrat.

Masafumi's virtuosic interdisciplinary knowledge captures a wider dynamic that characterizes *Shin sarugaku ki*. It would be wrong to say that Masafumi is entirely made up since, of course, there were scholars (including Akihira himself) who studied the exact books, documents, and techniques mentioned in the passage. It is as if Akihira

26. Ōe no Mochitoki (955–1010), Ōe no Masahira (952–1012), Sugawara no Fumitoki (899–891), and Koremune no Naomoto (active late ninth century) were four successful and well-known scholars.

27. "Shin sarugaku ki," NST 8:303 (CJ: 139–40).

has taken a variety of life experiences, detached them from their contexts, and patched them together into a composite that is simultaneously of and yet beyond reality. Masafumi can thus be interpreted as a kind of wish fulfilment of the scholarly unconscious: at a time when scholars no longer enjoyed a central advisory role in governance, the dream of a prodigiously overqualified scholar appeared. By fashioning an impossibly skilled scholar, Akihira ironically suggests the crisis for him and his contemporaries: if they are no longer needed to help "build the state and rule society," what is their value?

Performers and Audiences in *Shin sarugaku ki*

The particulars of Akihira's fabrication of the scholar Masafumi provide some direction for how to read the text's overall evocation of the capital's social terrain. A rhetoric of heightening the exceptional (and, along similar lines, lowering the excessive) can be found earlier in the account, after the initial evocation of festive feats and acts, when specific performers—the good, the bad, and the ugly—are evaluated. "High and low are not the same in *sarugaku*," begins the narrator, "and so the two must be distinguished":

> Hakuta exalts thoughts of awe;
> he is unrivaled in both past times and the present.[28]
>
> Jinnan, whenever he performs and without fail,
> earns the admiration of the crowd.
>
> Jōen is the god of humorous antics;
> one's belly splits upon a single glance at him.
>
> Keinō is a *sarugaku* immortal;
> he dislocates everyone's jaw without saying a word.

28. The description of Hakuta precisely replicates the praise for Kakinomoto no Hitomaro (d. ca. 710) in the *mana* preface of *Kokin wakashū*. See *Kokin wakashū*, SNKBZ 11:424 (CJ: 425). For an English translation, see *Kokinshū*, 382. See the supplementary note for "Hakuta" in "Shin sarugaku ki," NST 8:395.

The master of Agataido has good comical form,
but his speech is exceedingly rough and he sometimes forgets his lines.

The Sesonji transmitter has a natural talent,
but he uses too many words and makes people yawn.[29]

Sakanoue no Kikumasa is boring at first
but becomes more interesting by the end.

Modorihashi no Tokutaka is lively at first
but has no good puns by the end.

Ōhara no Kikutake has already disappeared from this path;
he favored his own success over people's affection.

Ono no Fukumaru is a nonperson [*hinin*] in the extreme;
a beggar should certainly not be counted among the others.[30]

Of the ten *sarugaku* performers introduced, the first four are lauded, the next four are deemed middling, and the last two are criticized. Hakuta and Jinnan, the first two, surface elsewhere in the archive. *Sarugaku* performers named Hakutō and Hakutōta appear in *Nichūreki* and Akihira's *Meigō ōrai*, respectively; and performers named Jinnan and Jinnan (written with different sinographs) appear in *Nichūreki* and *Honchō seiki*, respectively.[31] These traces do not reveal anything substantive about Hakutō/Hakutōta, although here Hakuta's prowess is suggested by an implicit comparison to Kakinomoto no Hitomaro. Jinnan, on the other hand, is elsewhere noted as the "real name" of Mukotsu, the performer who caused a scandal and earned Michinaga's ire in 999 (see chapter 5). But because this

29. A transmitter (*dōtatsu*) was an attendant monk who, during an esoteric rite, conveyed the sponsor's petition to the monk, who then read it out loud. Groner, "Annen, Tankei, Henjō," 150. Ōsone Shōsuke interprets this "Sesonji transmitter" as a *sarugaku* performer who was particularly well-known for imitating this specific role. See the supplementary note for "Sesonji no dōtatsu" in "Shin sarugaku ki," NST 8:395.

30. "Shin sarugaku ki," NST 8:301 (CJ: 134–35).

31. *Nichūreki*, 239; "Unshū shōsoku," 192; and *Honchō seiki*, SZKT 9:213.

occurred some five decades before *Shin sarugaku ki* was likely written, it is unclear if the two Jinnans are the same figure.

Three of the four lauded performers are described according to their ability to impact audiences, either by earning their admiration or making them laugh so hard their bodies fall apart.[32] It is the same with the middling performers: whether they succeed or fail depends on their ability to connect with the audience. Good comical form, natural talent, being interesting, and being lively enable performers to entertain, but rough speech, forgetting lines, inducing yawns, being boring, and not having any puns cause audiences to turn away. As for the last two performers, one is criticized for putting himself above his audience, and the other is dismissed because of his low social position. The qualities that signify a bad performance therefore range from baseness to lack of skill to excess: rough speech, forgetting one's lines, talking too much, and failing to rouse the audience. The narrator seems to have a particular distaste for roughness and low social status, which is most apparent in his evaluation of the master of Agataido and Ono no Fukumaru. These comments show that although *sarugaku* performers were mostly unranked urban commoners, expectations about permitted behavior and desired performance styles still drew on a logic of social differentiation. In this way, the text imposes an evaluative hierarchy that encodes rough speech and poverty as negative and excludes performances associated with them. The narrator concludes the section by stating that, as of late, there are only four or five exceptional performers, a tidy demonstration of the tension between inclusivity and distinction displayed throughout the *Shin sarugaku ki*.

Before describing the lieutenant's family, the narrator details the audience's raucous reaction to this handful of accomplished performers:

> At this point clerics and laymen, men and women, venerable and base, and high and low all flung their clothes at the performers in acclamation.

32. In literary Sinitic, "split bellies and dislocated jaws" (*danchō kaii*) was a conventional signifier of mirth. The same figure of speech is used at the end of *Shin sarugaku ki*'s opening passage (see earlier in this chapter) and questioned by Emperor Murakami (r. 946–967) in *Ben sangaku* (see chapter 5).

> It came down like rain and collected like clouds. A few returned home naked and others departed [on all fours] like dogs. By the next morning, it was cloudy and raining, so people tied straw together to make raingear and split sedge mats to make wide-brimmed hats. Some bunched up their trousers and showed their monkey heels; others pulled up their undergarments and displayed their crane legs. Some wrapped themselves in tatami and rolled around in the mud; others put on straw mats and tumbled into the Hori River. It was impossible to count the number of people who looked on with scornful laughter.[33]

The narrator writes that all present—high and low, venerable and base—offered thanks to performers by assailing them with their clothing. Known as *kazukemono*, this was a conventional way for an audience member to convey appreciation to a performer.[34] But the text also specifies the antics of a particular group of spectators, those driven mad by the spirit of performance. They are figured as animals: naked, dirty, rolling around in the muck, and left to fashion makeshift clothing from whatever materials they have on hand. Some of their behavior suggests feats associated with *sarugaku*: the appeal to monkeys is the most obvious, but the exposing of bare feet and legs also recalls Yukitsuna's bawdy performance for Emperor Horikawa described in a story from *Uji shūi monogatari* (A collection of tales from Uji; ca. 1221), as discussed in chapter 5. Once again, a hierarchy emerges. Some members of the audience transgress social norms in their excessive enthusiasm, while others sneeringly look on (fully clothed, presumably).

Bodies and Knowledge in *Shin sarugaku ki*

To return to the question of form, *Shin sarugaku ki* is a markedly liminal text. It inhabits the space between fiction and nonfiction, classical and vernacular, performer and audience, author and character,

33. "Shin sarugaku ki," NST 8:301 (CJ: 135).

34. On *kazukemono*, see Raz, *Audience and Actors*, 48–49; and Moriya, *Chūsei geinō no genzō*, 44–45.

and person and thing. Akihira wrote it at a time when the Heian capital was shifting from a command economy toward a market economy, a new socioeconomic environment in which centralized planning gave way to multifarious patronage relationships between powerful aristocrats and workers.[35] This meant an increasing diversity of social actors (unranked attendants and low-ranking court functionaries), a profusion of things (goods from all over the archipelago and beyond), and a general tilt toward social instability.

These shifts can be gleaned from the historical record, but it is *Shin sarugaku ki* that presents a unified view of this new world. Akihira's lists effectively "stitch together the lively movement of bodies and the dynamic state of the world" and, in doing so, model a mode of representing the world in its multidirectional unfolding.[36] Central to this mode is the morpheme-heavy *kanbun* style that presents readers with a deluge of objects, aspects, and techniques. By zooming in on the crowds of performers and audiences present for the festival, Akihira evokes the wider composite of vernacular bodies that populated the Heian capital—bodies that dance, sing, build, forge, plant, calculate, transport, seduce, repulse, trick, eat, drink, fight, and write.

Earlier in this chapter, I interpreted the artificiality of the scholar (the fifth daughter's husband) as a commentary on the scholar-official's diminished social importance in Akihira's day. Here, I develop the idea of artificiality further through *Shin sarugaku ki*'s persistent focus on how bodies fuse with the world (textual and phenomenal) around them. The text teems with bodies in action or being acted upon: the three wives are described mostly in terms of their physical appearance, the twelfth and thirteenth daughters evoke male heterosexual ideas of desire and disgust, and many of the daughters' husbands are defined by their relationship to physical labor (the smith, the wrestler, the carpenter).[37] Any one of these entries can be read for what they say about

35. Piggott, "Mō hitotsu no Heiankyō," 223.

36. Sakura, "Chūsei no retsujo," 121. The latter portion of Sakura's article argues for *Shin sarugaku ki*'s formal influence on a variety of medieval texts. See especially pp. 123–30.

37. Intriguingly, the sons' professions—calligrapher, Shingon priest, artisan, attendant of a provincial governor, Tendai scholar-monk, painter, sculptor, merchant, musician—depend less on physical labor than those of their brothers-in-law.

bodies and bodily labor, but the way language mediates the fusion of corporeality and objecthood is most memorably demonstrated by the description of the eighth daughter's husband, the carpenter. As with the description of the scholar, the passage consists almost entirely of technical terms:

> The husband of the eighth daughter is from Hida Province. He is a fifth-rank carpenter named Hinokuma no Sugimitsu.[38] He transmits the plans for building the Hasshōin and the Burakuin, and understands the principles of constructing palaces and shrines. In terms of temple architecture, he can build the lecture hall, the main hall, the sutra repository, the belfry, the pagoda, the monks' dormitory, the main gate, the inner gate, the second story of a building, a simple cottage, base rafters, [structures using] unrefined timber, square-shaped buildings, and bedrooms. In terms of private residences, he is skilled in building the western and eastern houses, the main house, the covered passageway, the bridgeway, the attendants' quarters, the kitchen, the carriage stall, the stables, the log storehouse, and the *kafukura*.[39]

Just like the scholar, the carpenter's prodigious skill enables him to do the work of several specialized workers. Akihira takes this "stitching" further in the final passage of the entry, in which he represents the carpenter's body as a prosthetic composite of the tools he uses:

> The carpenter has inkpots for eyes: he can see when a line is not straight;
> he has saw bits for teeth: he can slice the corners off a block of wood.

38. Based on how Sugimitsu's rank is introduced, Shigeta Shin'ichi infers the following biography: he came to the capital as a commoner, became a court functionary, and worked his way into a mid-ranking position. Shigeta, *Kakyū kizokutachi*, 174–75.

39. "Shin sarugaku ki," NST 8:303 (CJ: 141–42). "Private residences" translates *jinka*, which, based on the components included, seems to refer to residences built in the *shinden* style. Stavros describes this style as "a key part of the formalized paraphernalia of classical authority." Stavros, *Kyoto*, 24. The exact meaning of the final term, *kafukura*, is difficult to determine but it refers to some kind of log storehouse.

He has an adze for a neck: he is a master carpenter;
he has a mallet for a head: he is the leader of this Way.

His fingers are bamboo brushes;
his arms are squares.

His back is the flat part a chisel;
his feet are hammers.

Starting with his body, he is in every way a preternaturally skilled carpenter.[40]

If tools are objects that enable a body to act on the material world in prescribed ways, then embodiment is here defined solely in terms of the instruments of labor. Inkpots stand in for eyes because of their shape and because both are necessary for measuring. A saw resembles a row of teeth; both function to separate one thing from another. The adze and mallet are associated with the neck and head, respectively, perhaps due to a general correspondence of shape. Bamboo brushes evoke fingers because of their visual similarity but also because of the metonymic relationship between the two: fingers are required to use brushes, so brushes become fingers. Lastly, the square mimics the shape of a bent arm, and the chisel and hammer resemble a back and a foot, respectively. In this moment, the carpenter himself becomes an instrument of measurement, separation, inscription, and production, and the distance between his body and the objectified material environment vanishes.

The convergence of subject and object in the figure of the carpenter is achieved through the ordered parallelism of *kanbun* writing, which my translation suggests through lineation. There are eight embodiments described, and they proceed mostly along a vertical axis from top to bottom: eyes, teeth, neck, head, fingers, elbows, back, and feet. The first four are situated on or around the head and perform "higher-order" acts (measuring by sight, leading other workers); the latter four take place in lower or peripheral areas of the body, suggesting acts

40. "Shin sarugaku ki," NST 8:303 (CJ: 142).

that are more directly physical (inscribing, hammering). Formally, the passage is arranged into four couplets (with character counts of 8–8, 10–10, 4–4, 4–4) and punctuated by a final comment. In terms of both form and content, then, this entry-ending passage epitomizes how *Shin sarugaku ki* works as an artificial composite that reorders social bodies and their relationships with the world.

Artificial bodies can be found elsewhere in *Shin sarugaku ki*, most notably in the description of the twelfth and thirteenth daughters: the hag and the beauty. But whereas the carpenter's body is recast as a machine that transcends the duality of subject and object, here the two daughters' bodies are figured through a lens of male desire grounded in literary Sinitic allusions and tropes. The twelfth daughter's physical appearance is described as follows:

> Her hair is smooth like the wings of a kingfisher;
> her elegant countenance is relaxed and composed.
>
> Closing her lotus-blossom eyelids and smiling, she exudes limitless coquetry;
> arching her blue eyebrows and tilting her head, she attracts endless affection.
>
> Though she does not apply powder, her face is still white;
> though she does not apply rouge, her cheeks are still red.
>
> Her moist lips are like the red *bimba* fruit;
> her lustrous skin is white as snow.
>
> Her arms contend with the radiance of jewels;
> her teeth embody the whiteness of seashells.[41]

As with the carpenter, the twelfth daughter's physical features are sometimes situated in the same ontological space as the objects used to describe them, suggesting the hybridity of classical locution and vernacular body. This can be seen in phrases like "lotus-blossom eyelids" and "her teeth embody the whiteness of shells." Consisting of

41. "Shin sarugaku ki," NST 8:304 (CJ: 144).

comparisons to resplendent objects and allusions to historic beauties such as Yang Guifei (719–756), the description of the twelfth daughter straddles the boundary between classical and vernacular, "China" and "Japan."

The entry on the thirteenth daughter displays a similar relationality, but the content is the opposite of that found in the entry describing her older sister:

> Her hair is a tangle of mugwort and her forehead is narrow;
> her mouth hangs open and her chin protrudes.
>
> Her ears droop and her jawbone is large;
> her cheeks are enlarged on top and sunken at the bottom.
>
> There are gaps between her teeth and she speaks with a lisp;
> her nose is low, flat, and stuffed up.
>
> She is a hunchback and her chest protrudes like that of a pigeon;
> her stomach is bloated and she has the belly of a frog.
>
> She is bowlegged and moves from side to side when she walks;
> her skin is covered with scabies and rashes.
>
> She has a short neck, causing her collar to bunch up;
> her robes are too short for her tall stature.
>
> Her body exudes a foul stench;
> her clothes are infested with lice.
>
> Her hands are like iron rakes;
> her feet are like hoe blades.
>
> When she applies powder to her face, it resembles that of a fox;
> when she applies rouge, it looks like a monkey's ass.[42]

Using a series of brisk couplets, Akihira strings together a list of images—tangled hair, protruding chin, drooping ears, bloated

42. "Shin sarugaku ki," NST 8:304 (CJ: 144–45).

stomach—to form an excessive and grotesque body that parodies the previous entry. In addition to being unattractive, physically deformed, and afflicted with disease, the thirteenth daughter's "hands are like iron rakes; her feet are like hoe blades"—imagery that associates her with rustic agricultural labor and recalls the merging of body and tools in the passage devoted to the carpenter.

Even though this entry describes a body in meticulous and colorful detail, it still has the effect of contributing to the archetypal (and artificial) ordering found throughout *Shin sarugaku ki.* This is because the thirteenth daughter, like all other members of the lieutenant's family, cannot do anything in a narrative sense once she is introduced: as readers, we take in the minute details of this portrait and move on to the next. The formulaic structure of the text, coupled with the profusion of lists, serves to minimize narrative movement and cross-entry interaction, leaving room for only a rudimentary plot that supplies little more than the occasion for the audience to gather. The text's narrative consists of an extended act of viewing, enabling readers to gaze at figures who have been put on the textual stage and take them in like a diorama of life in the Heian capital. *Shin sarugaku ki* is not a case of language documenting experience, but rather a transposition of embodied action into an archetypal knowledge that is figured in terms of exhaustive serialization. It distils the excess of the popular carnival into a classical textual form, making the messy bodies of the multitude artificially legible.

In conclusion, *Shin sarugaku ki* evokes the Heian capital as it underwent rapid socioeconomic changes during the mid-eleventh century. Akihira produces a monument frozen in time and bearing the imprint of his own tools. This is an overwhelming and crowded artifice: the lists of technical jargon, the parade of one family member after another, the multitude of practices and techniques. In its textual excess, *Shin sarugaku ki* becomes something grounded in yet apart from the vernacular world that informs the text. It is in this way that the festive energies of performers and audiences find their way into the text, contributing to a classical-vernacular fusion crafted by a scholar-official whose own professional techniques sought new applications.

PART II

BODIES

CHAPTER FIVE

Transgressive Bodies

Sangaku, *Sarugaku*, and *Zōgei*

In part 1, I argued that tracing the cultural practices of crowds, especially open crowds, enables a relational view of social interaction and structure, one that is not reducible to the bifurcation of high and low. In part 2, I shift attention to the virtuosic bodily acts of *sangaku*, *sarugaku*, *zōgei*, *imayō*, and *kugutsu* performance, replacing crowds with bodies as the basic unit of analysis. This is ultimately an arbitrary distinction, since crowds are made up of bodies and bodies often work in concert as crowds. It follows that I view the two parts of this book as not only complementary but also integrated in their focus on understanding the dynamics of transgression. The performers of the practices explored in the next three chapters use their bodies, often in spectacular fashion, to transgress conventional social boundaries and trigger various acts of identification. The result is a repertoire of practices that were both heavily suppressed and joyfully celebrated.

But first, what are bodies? "The body" is a contested term in contemporary scholarship. In her illuminating study of bodies and embodiment in Heian literary texts, Rajyashree Pandey surveys the contemporary debate between materialist and social constructivist positions about how to define the body, arguing that neither is particularly useful for understanding how bodies work in premodern East Asian contexts. "The choice," she writes, "between the natural versus the social/cultural body that is on offer in these debates is part of a very particular history that belongs to the West, and hence necessarily inadequate to thinking about other traditions of embodiment."[1] In particular, bodies in a Heian-period text or illustration should not be apprehended as objective Cartesian representations of the physical but rather as zones in which the physical and the psychic converge in diverse ways: thinking and feeling have as much to do with the body as bodily acts have to do with thinking and feeling. This approach not only aligns with the operative "epistemic framework" of the times, one informed by Daoist and Buddhist understandings of the body and its fluid relation to surrounding environments, but also reflects the ambivalence that often surrounds bodies and bodily acts.[2] The body in the Heian period—far from being dismissed as inferior to the mind, as the Cartesian view would have it—signified a wide range of fears, desires, virtues, and vices.

The body's ambiguity and attendant ambivalence have been emphasized in several recent studies by scholars of Japanese literature, history, and performance. In her history of leprosy in Japan, Susan Burns notes that in premodern times, "the body of the *rai* sufferer was simultaneously the object of both reverence and fear, a corporal embodiment of pollution, the power of karma, and the possibility of salvation."[3] Michelle Osterfeld Li, in her study of medieval *setsuwa* (explanatory tales), examines the recurrence of a grotesque body type that "is marked by a blending of boundaries: men can eat women and vice versa; birds can be murderers; foxes can be wives."[4] And Matsuoka Shinpei, in his pathbreaking study of embodiment, reframes the history of medieval Japanese performance culture as the tensile relationship between two types of bodies: the virtuosic, acrobatic body and the restrained, unmoving body.[5] These analyses share an interest in how physical bodies—especially those that, in their illness, excess, or liminality, mark difference—activate psychic ambivalence. Similarly, the

1. Pandey, *Perfumed Sleeves*, 17.

2. Pandey, *Perfumed Sleeves*, 12–13.

3. Burns, *Kingdom of the Sick*, 31.

4. Li, *Ambiguous Bodies*, 43.

5. Matsuoka, *Utage no shintai*, 1–4. For a recent translation of the entire work, see Matsuoka, *Embodied Performance*.

regularity with which bodies become more, multiple, and other is a central feature of embodiment in Heian Japan.

Corporeal ambiguity and the ambivalence it provoked are notable features of the *sangaku* ("minor performances," later *sarugaku*) and *zōgei* (miscellaneous performances) repertoires in the Heian period. These repertoires astounded audiences with a range of acrobatic feats, from sword swallowing to transfiguration to balancing acts.[6] At the same time, the perilous ontologies embodied by these feats troubled established sociopolitical and religious orders, resulting in the potential for performers to be incarcerated or otherwise restricted. Spectacles of limit breaking captured the elite imagination even as they threatened to undermine the rituals and etiquette that constituted social order.

As discussed in the introduction, *sangaku* was an "imported" repertoire; the long history of similar practices in China is attested by representations in literary works like *Wenxuan*. The history of *sangaku* in Japan traces both the influence of Sinitic literary and performance culture among scholars familiar with classical Chinese texts, and that of the living repertoires practiced by performers active in the court and at shrines and temples. At the time of writing, then, the practices were simultaneously present in the archive and the repertoire, and accounts of performances often drift between describing contemporary forms and encoding practices within a literary Sinitic intertextual framework.

Unlike *dengaku*, *sangaku* had an institutional home within the *ritsuryō* bureaucracy, resulting in a closer and earlier integration into court culture. By the end of the eighth century, this integration had given way to separation, at which point elites started to treat *sangaku* with more ambivalence. In this chapter, I explore the variety of identifications triggered by the spectacular bodily feats of *sangaku* and *zōgei*, focusing especially on how they were subjected to scholarly epistemologies and administrative imperatives. This exploration affords an opportunity to understand the moves and countermoves that

6. Scholars sometimes use the term *yokyō* (attraction, sideshow) to refer collectively to practices like these, the idea being that they typically supplemented "main draws" like *bugaku* and *kagura*. See, e.g., Ishii, *"Monomane" no rekishi*, 45.

constitute transgressive processes. If astounding bodily feats signify a violation of conventional economies of movement, the texts that render them as legible can be read as attempts to repair the breach. My core concern here is the dynamic nature of this social process—how disparities of class and medium give birth to contestation and realignment.

Minor Performances: *Sangaku*/*Sarugaku*/China/Japan

As described in the introduction, *sanyue* emerged in medieval China as a diverse repertoire of acrobatic feats, mimetic drama, and illusion. It is unknown exactly when or in what form *sanyue* first arrived in Japan, but by the early Nara period, the Sangaku Division had been established within the Gagaku Bureau. The earliest appearance of a *sangaku* technique in the archive is found in *Shoku Nihongi* (Chronicles of Japan, continued; 797), in an entry dated 735/5/5 (Tenpyō 7), which briefly touches on Emperor Shōmu's (r. 724–749) observation of performances of Chinese and Korean music and spear twirling put on by performers from the Tang (618–907) court.[7] The division was abolished nearly fifty years later, according to an entry in *Shoku Nihongi* dated 782/7/11 (Enryaku 1).[8] The exact reasons remain unknown, but by then *sangaku* had been incorporated into a number of other performance practices and contexts, perhaps making it less necessary for it to have its own division.[9]

For example, there are ninth-century records of *sangaku* being performed as part of the annual wrestling ceremony (*sumahi no sechi*)

7. "The emperor went to the Hokushōrin [Northern Pine Grove] and watched mounted archery. Emissaries to the Tang court as well as people from Tang performed music from Tang and Silla, and then twirled spears." *Shoku Nihongi*, SNKBT 13:288.

8. *Shoku Nihongi*, SZKT 2:486.

9. Tsunoda, "Sangaku no geinō," 292. Ishii Kōsei surmises that some *sangaku* performers became court musicians and many others were taken in by large temples throughout the archipelago as "slaves" or "bound servants" (*nuhi*). Ishii, "*Monomane*" *no rekishi*, 45. Takemoto Mikio points out that there were other offices in the *ritsuryō* bureaucracy that were downsized or abolished around the same time. Takemoto, "Geinō ichiba," 23n1.

by officials from the Bureau of Palace Guards (Konoefu), low-ranking functionaries tasked with protecting the emperor from physical and ritual threats.[10] In the 860s, imperial interest in *sangaku* was revived by Emperor Seiwa, who also viewed farmers performing rice-planting rites, as discussed in chapter 2. *Nihon sandai jitsuroku* reports that on 861/6/28 (Jōgan 3), the emperor observed a boys' wrestling competition. After nine matches, "both right and left performed music, along with varieties of miscellaneous skills [*zōgi*] and *sangaku*, including pole climbing [*tōshō*], somersaulting [*juteki*], and juggling [*rōgyoku*]. They performed [competed] in the manner of the wrestling ceremony."[11] This entry indicates that acrobatic feats—pole climbing, somersaulting, and juggling—were central components of the kind of *sangaku* performed in this ceremonial context.[12] Four years later, on 865/7/23 (Jōgan 7), *Nihon sandai jitsuroku* again records Emperor Seiwa's viewing of *sangaku* as part of a wrestling ceremony, although in this case the term *hyakugi* or "one hundred acts" is used.[13] Taken together, these entries show that in the mid-ninth century the court was still able to furnish those who could perform some of the skills and techniques included in the early *sangaku* repertoire.

By the early tenth century, the word *sarugaku* started to replace *sangaku* in the records of wrestling ceremonies, a shift that has prompted much debate among performance historians about how to understand the relationship between the two.[14] As discussed by

10. On the emergence of this "aristocratic *sarugaku*" (*kizokuteki na sarugaku*) in the context of the wrestling festivals, *kagura* performances, and banquets, see Nose, *Nōgaku genryū kō*, 1–48. Hayashiya Tatsusaburō questions whether these performances by low-ranking guards should be considered "aristocratic." Hayashiya, *Chūsei geinōshi no kenkyū*, 290.

11. *Nihon sandai jitsuroku*, SZKT 4:78.

12. Tsunoda Ichirō notes that although the meaning of *juteki* (somersaulting) is unclear, it is probably similar to, if not the same as, *kaheriutsu*, one of the miscellaneous entertainments listed in *Wamyō ruijū shō*, as discussed below. Tsunoda, "Sangaku no geinō," 293.

13. *Nihon sandai jitsuroku*, SZKT 4:161.

14. The stakes of this debate are heightened by the fact that *sarugaku* was the term used to refer to noh between the fifteenth and nineteenth centuries, so the question of how earlier forms like those discussed in this book influenced noh often lingers in the background. See Pinnington, *A New History of Medieval Japanese Theatre*, 25–28.

Hayashiya Tatsusaburō, the early performance historians Konakamura Kiyonori and Nose Asaji both highlighted the close linguistic relationship between the two words, using this as evidence that they were two names for the same sets of practices.[15] But Hayashiya instead points to several records of wrestling ceremonies that list performances of both *sangaku* and *sarugaku* (as part of a wider program of *bugaku* dances) to support his argument that *sarugaku* had, by the tenth century, emerged as a discrete song-and-dance act within the wider repertoire of *sangaku*.[16] The *sangaku* and *sarugaku* listed in records of tenth- and eleventh-century wrestling ceremonies do not include mention of specific acrobatic feats, as in the case of earlier records; instead, they appear amid a string of *bugaku* pieces and seem to refer to mimetic dances, perhaps similar to those briefly described at the beginning of *Shin sarugaku ki*.[17]

It is clear, then, that both the form and function of *sangaku* had changed since the eighth century, when it was formalized as a division within the court's Gagaku Bureau. Given this history, *sangaku*'s association with low-ranking aristocrats (and, one can assume, non-elites) posed a problem for the court. How should the diverse practices that made up *sangaku* be used within the ritual matrix of court ceremony? A text anthologized in *Honchō monzui* and dated 963 (Ōwa 3) explores this and related questions. Typically referred to as *Ben sangaku* (An inquiry into sangaku) in contemporary scholarship, it discusses the history and contemporary practice of *sangaku* through the medium of parallel-prose essay prompts (*sakumon*) and responses (*taisaku*) found on the civil service examination.[18] (See appendix 1 for a full translation.)

The text naturally has two parts: question and answer. The question ("Inquiry into sangaku") is written by Emperor Murakami, and the answer is provided by a certain "Lord Hada no Ujiyasu, graduate

15. Hayashiya, *Chūsei geinōshi no kenkyū*, 288.

16. Hayashiya, *Chūsei geinōshi no kenkyū*, 296–98.

17. For example, see entries in *Shōyūki* dated 988/8/19 (Ei'en 2), 1005/7/29 (Kankō 2), 1013/8/1 (Chōwa 2), 1019/7/28 (Kannin 3), and 1023/7/28 (Jian 3). The relevant sections of these entries are reproduced in Hayashiya, *Chūsei geinōshi no kenkyū*, 297.

18. In earlier scholarship, the text was often referred to as *Sangaku sakumon*. See, e.g., Tsunoda, "Sangaku sakumon kō" and Hayashiya, *Chūsei geinōshi no kenkyū*, 300.

student of *sangaku*, functionary of the Ancillary Guard, senior sixth upper rank."[19] The State Academy of course had no curriculum in *sangaku*, and there is furthermore a note following the title of the answer that reads, "It is said that chamberlain and graduate student of letters Fujiwara no Masaki wrote this."[20] It seems the actual author was Masaki, a scholar and confidante of the emperor.[21] But the reference to Hada no Ujiyasu is significant due to the figure's central position in the legendary history of *sarugaku*, as related by the actor and playwright Zeami in his treatise *Fūshi kaden* (Transmitting the flower through effects and attitudes; 1400–18).[22] There, Zeami tells of a baby discovered during the reign of Emperor Kinmei (r. ca. mid-sixth century) in a vessel floating down the flooded Hatsuse River. This person was later given the name Hada no Kōkatsu and called upon by Prince Shōtoku (574–622) to "perform sixty-six acts of dramatic imitation" (*rokujū roku ban no monomane*), which brought order and peace to the realm.[23] Zeami later references how none other than Emperor Murakami read Prince Shōtoku's *Sarugaku ennen no ki* (The records of sarugaku and ennen; likely an apocryphal source, according to Tom Hare): "When the dances of *sarugaku* were performed, the nation was at peace, the people tranquil, and lives long; since this was revealed truth in Prince Shōtoku's very hand, Emperor Murakami determined that *sarugaku* be used as prayer throughout the realm [*tenga no gokitō taru beki to te*]."[24] Ujiyasu is then brought into the narrative, seemingly during Murakami's reign: "The descendant to whom this Kōkatsu had transmitted the arts of

19. *Honchō monzui*, SNKBT 27:175 (CJ: 30). The clan name Hada can also be read Hata.

20. *Honchō monzui*, SNKBT 27:175 (CJ: 30).

21. Shigeta, "*Honchō monzui* shoshū 'Ben sangaku' no kisoteki kenkyū," 6–7.

22. Arthur H. Thornhill III describes Ujiyasu as "an actor who performed at the court of Emperor Murakami" and notes that "scholars acknowledge his existence and concede that he might have performed the art known as *sangaku*." Thornhill, *Six Circles*, 13. But Ujiyasu's association with *sangaku* appears to derive wholly from *Ben sangaku* and Zeami's treatise.

23. Hare, *Zeami: Performance Notes*, 48. For the original, see *Zeami, Zenchiku*, NST 24:39.

24. Hare, *Zeami: Performance Notes*, 50. For the original, see *Zeami, Zenchiku*, NST 24:40. On *Sarugaku ennen no ki*, see Hare, *Zeami: Performance Notes*, 50n49.

sarugaku was Hada no Ujiyasu. [. . .] Counting from Hada no Ujiyasu, the line extends twenty-nine generations to its distant descendants"—that is, to the generations that directly precede Zeami's.[25] The appearance of Murakami in this evocation of a mythical lineage is intriguing. Regardless of who wrote the answer essay contained in *Ben sangaku*, the scholar Masaki or the shadowy Ujiyasu, it is clear that Murakami had an interest in understanding *sangaku*'s history and local articulation.

Ben sangaku abounds with literary Sinitic references, and although the meaning of specific phrases is not always clear, the overall narrative—the questions and the answers—can be read as an effort to legitimize the local performance of *sangaku* with reference to the longer history of continental practices. Murakami, in the role of questioner, highlights *sangaku*'s connection to humor and unusual acts, writing that the *sangaku* performed at court ceremonies is considerably different from the *sanyue* described in ancient texts like the *Zhou li* (The rites of Zhou; ca. third or second century BCE). He then asks about some eccentric feats—cracking a whip while riding a half-lattice carriage, approaching a pillar while holding a quiver—before inquiring about wrestling performances and puppetry techniques.

In his response, Masaki endeavors to strip *sangaku* of the potentially transgressive aspects raised by Emperor Murakami, such as excessively humorous or eccentric performances, by situating it within a conventional Confucian understanding of the social and political function of music.[26] He begins by describing the ideal relationship between music and rulership:

> When one's nature shifts between happiness, anger, pathos, and enjoyment, it is called emotion. When sounds [*koe*] respond to differences between instability, peace, order, and disorder, it is called music [*gaku*].

25. Hare, *Zeami: Performance Notes*, 50. For the original, see *Zeami, Zenchiku*, NST 24:40.

26. For an overview of Confucian theories of sound and music as elaborated in early and medieval Japan, see Bialock, "From *Heike* to *Nomori no kagami*," 173–80.

> Accordingly, when there is a wise ruler [*meiwau*], those endowed with virtue involuntarily dance with their hands and stomp with their feet.[27] When the realm is devoid of problems, those filled with benevolence express in words what they feel in their minds.[28]

Approaching *sangaku* as music in the orthodox Confucian sense enables Masaki to highlight its political utility, which in turn allows him to dismiss the outlandish practices brought up by Murakami as "rumors of the loquacious."[29]

Masaki uses the rest of his essay to argue that *sangaku* has a benevolent, formative influence on all within the realm, but he introduces a note of contrast toward the end. He writes, "Though the diminutive men who make their bodies lightweight during the *kagura* held on snowy nights might seem strange, we secretly detest the nobles who remain silent during the *tōka* dances held under spring skies."[30] Performances of *kagura* often took place in the cold, snowy twelfth month and featured acrobatics and other feats, and *tōka* were ceremonial group dances performed by aristocrats in the Shishinden courtyard on the fourteenth and the sixteenth day of the first month.[31] This is the only part of the text where Masaki allows for the potential transgressive interplay between orthodox and heterodox, between sticking

27. This is a reference to a phrase from the beginning of the famous "Great Preface" of *The Classic of Poetry* (Ch. *Shijing*). See Owen, *Readings in Chinese Literary Thought*, 41.

28. *Honchō monzui*, SNKBT 27:175 (CJ: 30–31).

29. *Honchō monzui*, SNKBT 27:175 (CJ: 32).

30. *Honchō monzui*, SNKBT 27:75 (CJ: 32). The meaning of the phrase I translate as "remain silent" (glossed as *shita o nomu*, literally "swallow one's tongue") is contested. The editors of the SNKBT version of the text, whose interpretation I follow, understand it to mean "to be silent." *Honchō monzui*, SNKBT 27:32. Tsunoda Ichirō, on the other hand, reads it as "to curl one's tongue in admiration." Tsunoda, *Ningyōgeki no seiritsu*, 280.

31. The dances were initially held during the night of the sixteenth day, with both men and women participating, but a prohibition was issued in 766 (Tenpyō-jingo 2) due to disorderliness. By the mid-Heian period, the ceremony had been reconstituted, with men performing on the fourteenth and women performing on the sixteenth. See Gamō, "Tōka." For more on the history of *tōka* and men's *tōka* see, respectively, Hirama, *Kodai Nihon no girei*, 37–65, 217–40.

to the script and breaching etiquette. He effectively inverts the expectations he has created earlier in his response. The spectacular feats performed by acrobats during the *kagura* "seem strange," but, it is implied, they are not; meanwhile, the nobles watching the annual *tōka* songs and dances in silence are "secretly detest[ed]" for suppressing their emotions. Masaki may have taken issue with Murakami's implication that *sangaku* actually made people dislocate their jaws in laughter, but at the end of his essay, he appeals to performance's ability—especially that of the virtuosic body and the crowd—to affect audiences.

Sangaku, *Sarugaku*, and Transgressive Humor

Sangaku's association with humor, which *Ben sangaku* seems to condone only reluctantly, strengthened throughout the eleventh century, as imitation skewed toward humor and *sangaku* became increasingly less connected to court ceremony. This is demonstrated by Fujiwara no Akihira's evocation of a "new *sarugaku*" in *Shin sarugaku ki* (see chapter 4) and the *sangaku* performance he describes as part of the Inari Festival in *Meigō ōrai* (see chapter 1), both of which involve humorous dramatic sketches performed by a pair of actors.

The intersection of humor, imitation, and an actor duo appears most memorably in a bawdy story anthologized in *Uji shūi monogatari*. The story, "How the Musicians Ietsuna and Yukitsuna Plotted against Each Other" (5:5), is set around the turn of the twelfth century and traces the antics of two brothers who serve as musicians attached to the Naishidokoro.[32] Even though the story concerns their participation in a performance of *kagura*, they are introduced by the narrator as "unparalleled *sarugaku* performers" (*yo ni naki hodo no sarugaku*). If the content of the story is any indication, to be the best

32. The following summary is based on the edition of the story found in *Uji shūi monogatari*, SNKBZ 50:177–79. For an English translation, see Mills, *A Collection of Tales from Uji*, 242–43. The Naishidokoro, also referred to as the Unmeiden and located within the palace compound, housed the sacred mirror associated with Amaterasu and thought to be one of the three regalia handed down from mythical times.

sarugaku performers in the realm meant to engage in trickery and entertain audiences with transgressive bodily acts.

The story begins on the night of an annual *kagura* performance that took place during the twelfth month in the courtyard of the Naishidokoro. Emperor Horikawa—the same emperor who attended performances during the Great Dengaku of 1096—makes an announcement ordering the performance of something unusual (*mezurashikaran koto tsukaumatsure*), at which point a chamberlain summons a musician named Ietsuna and tasks him with fulfilling the request.[33] Ietsuna accepts and calls over his younger brother Yukitsuna to discuss what they should do.[34] Ietsuna explains his idea: "When the bonfire is burning white, I'll pull my *hakama* way up, thrust out my boney shins and say, 'Late, late, it's getting late! Cold, cold, so very cold! I'll take these balls and warm 'em up!' Then I'll run around the bonfire three times. What do you think?" Yukitsuna responds that this might not be the best performance for an imperial audience; Ietsuna agrees and thanks his younger brother for his insight. When it comes time to perform, Ietsuna is summoned first, but unable to think of any additional ideas, he dallies before the assembled courtiers. Yukitsuna is summoned next, and he performs the exact routine described to him by his older brother, further embellishing it by running around the fire ten times instead of three. Everyone from the emperor on down bursts into laughter (*kami yori shimozama ni itaru made ohokata doyomitarikeri*). Ietsuna

33. Fujiwara no Ietsuna, the older brother in the story, appears several times in courtier diaries as a *kagura* performer, along with a companion—not his younger brother Yukitsuna but someone named Fujiwara no Tomosada. See Okimoto, *Ranmai no chūsei*, 13.

34. Little is known about Yukitsuna, but he appears in a story recounted in *Imakagami*. The passage describes a *marikai* (kickball competition) held at the imperial palace, featuring Yukitsuna (then the governor of Shinano Province, and apparently known as a skilled kickball player), his teacher Fujiwara no Morozane (1042–1101, regent at the time), and other courtiers. Morozane praises the skill of one of the other courtiers, and Yukitsuna becomes envious. Afterward, while washing his teacher's feet, Yukitsuna vents his anger by pinching Morozane's feet several times. Morozane is shocked, but instead of reprimanding his student, he addresses the root cause and praises his skill. Assuaged, Yukitsuna starts rubbing Morozane's feet. *Imakagami zenchūshaku*, 266–67.

realizes he has been duped, but rather than berating his brother, he decides to play nice and bide his time.

The story then jumps nearly a year into the future, to the *kagura* performed as part of the Special Kamo Festival.[35] The two brothers are there to perform, and this time Yukitsuna takes the lead, telling his older brother, "When I get up on the bamboo dais, I want you to say the line, 'What in the world is that?' Then I'll say, 'I'm a bamboo leopard, I'm a bamboo leopard!' and imitate a leopard." Ietsuna agrees to play the role as described. Yukitsuna is summoned to the dais and starts crawling around, waiting for his brother to say his line. But Ietsuna instead says, "What kind of leopard is that?" thereby ruining the joke by saying the punchline outright. With nothing left to do, Yukitsuna beats a hasty retreat. The story ends with the narrator noting that the emperor heard about what Ietsuna did and found it to be an extremely interesting performance (*nakanaka yuyushiki kyō nite arikeru to kaya*) and that people considered it revenge for how Yukitsuna had previously tricked him.

With its bodily exposures and tit-for-tat trickery, the story evokes *sarugaku* as a comical performance that centers on boundary play and sudden reveals and reversals. Yukitsuna's bodily antics seem designed to shock, but they are also authorized in advance by the emperor requesting "something unusual" without specifying what it should be.[36]

35. In a diary entry dated 1093/11/23 (Kanji 7), Fujiwara no Munetada notes that the *kagura* included in the return procession from the Special Kamo Festival featured *sangaku* performed by Ietsuna and Fujiwara no Tomosada, an act that "surprised people's eyes." *Chūyūki*, DNK 1:255. There is some disagreement about this line. The editors transcribe the character for "to sleep" (眠) but suggest that it is a scribal error for "eyes" (眼). Okimoto Yukiko reads the character as the former, coming up with a rather elaborate gloss ("people were surprised such that they woke from sleeping"). Okimoto, *Ranmai no chūsei*, 13. The idea that the *sangaku* "surprised people's eyes" is grammatically closer to the original, though both interpretations convey the sense that the performance seized the audience's attention.

36. It is not easy to determine how something like bare ankles or exposed testicles would have registered at the time. Yukitsuna's initial response to Ietsuna's idea indicates that it was unusual enough to at least raise a few eyebrows. In his account of the Great Dengaku, Masafusa describes mostly naked bodies and unfurled hair as contributing to the pandemonium (see chapter 3), while in *Shin sarugaku ki*, Akihira describes a few frenzied members of the audience running around naked (see chapter 4). The roughly contemporaneous *Tōhokuin shokunin utaawase emaki* (Illustrated scroll of

This sanctions the transgression since whatever happens will be contained within the parameters of the emperor's order. Yukitsuna transgresses vestimentary and musical norms by exposing himself and dancing around the fire ten times (excessive compared to the three times originally planned by Ietsuna), but he also violates the implicit agreement made with his older brother and makes him the butt of the joke within their own fraternal *sarugaku*. Yukitsuna hence transgresses two boundaries: the first, between actor and audience, is met with resounding laughter; and the second, between the two actors, triggers a further response since Ietsuna has been made a fool and must redeem himself.

The story demonstrates the multiple valences of transgression that operate within and through *sarugaku*. The excess of *sarugaku* performance provokes laughter, and the trickery on which it turns destabilizes relationships rapidly and dramatically. Even the manner of Yukitsuna's departure after being tricked evokes the virtuosic corporeality of *sarugaku* performance. He has not "slunk from the scene in shame," as one recent analysis of the story claims, but has instead "suddenly beat a hasty retreat" (*futo nigete hashiri irinikeri*).[37] The point is that he moves quickly and rapidly, in a manner that recalls a story from the collection *Kojidan* (Stories of ancient matters; ca. 1215) about courtier and *kemari*-enthusiast Fujiwara no Narimichi's (1097–1162) sensational ability to be "gone in a flash" (*chikuten*, literally "to chase after lightning").[38] Yukitsuna may or may not feel shame—the text says only that there was "nothing left for him to say" (*ifu beki koto nakute*)—but he certainly affirms his status as one of the top *sarugaku* actors in the realm by performing a disappearing act once his brother takes his revenge.

---

the Tōhokuin poetry contest between workers; 1214) depicts a gambler who has just lost a game of *sugoroku*: he sits crouched over the game board, completely naked (ankles, testicles, and all), except for an *ebōshi* cap, which remains fixed on his head. Kokuritsu Bunkazai Kikō, *Tōhokuin shokunin utaawase emaki*. Moriya Takeshi notes that in the medieval period, men rarely left their heads uncovered, even when sleeping, due to the belief that topknots possessed divine associations. Moriya, *Chūsei geinō no genzō*, 69.

37. Pinnington, *A New History of Medieval Japanese Theatre*, 31.

38. *Kojidan*, SNKBT 41:98.

Sangaku and *sarugaku* continued to broaden and incorporate new practices throughout the eleventh century, but virtuosic feats involving speed, acrobatics, mimicry, and trickery remained central to these forms' ability to command an audience. This is demonstrated by an entry in Ōe no Masafusa's *Gōke shidai* (Ōe family procedures; ca. 1111), in which he includes *sangaku* as one of several entertainments performed at the annual wrestling ceremony: "The *sangaku* consisted of one-footing and high-footing, a *jushi* exorcist who tossed the diabolo, and dwarf dances."[39] Balancing on a pole, a diabolo's midair suspension, and the dances of little people all registered as acts that pushed the boundaries of what bodies could do.

Sangaku, *Sarugaku*, and Ritual

One last development to note about the history of *sangaku* is its integration into temple rituals and shrine festivals by the early twelfth century—not the festive parades along the avenues of the capital discussed in chapter 1 but those centered around a handful of powerful religious institutions and designed to augment those institutions' authority. For example, there are several records of *sangaku* being performed as part of Shushōe, a penitential new year's rite enacted at the large temples in Nara and outside of Kyoto (see the last section of this chapter for a performer's mishap at one of these rites). Though the records do not describe the content of these performances, they typically appear alongside the ritual activities of *jushi* exorcists, which included "demarking sacred space, purifying it, chanting over offerings, and carrying out the sacred flame (*goma*) ritual."[40] *Sangaku* hence contributed to a ritual that revolved around revering the buddhas and purifying sins that had accumulated during the previous year.

This contribution continued well into the medieval period, with performances of *sarugaku* undertaken at the *ushirodo* or "backdoor" entrance to a temple building becoming an essential component of the

39. *Gōke shidai*, 257. "Dwarf dances" are sometimes referred to in the early chronicles, though there are no extant descriptions.

40. Pinnington, *A New History of Medieval Japanese Theatre*, 35.

Shushōe sub-rite *tsuina*.[41] These performances were dramas depicting the worship of Matarajin, a deity closely associated with performance, and the banishment of the demon Vināyaka.[42] Zeami describes just such a scene of demonic appeasement towards the beginning of the "Divine Matters" section of *Fūshi kaden*. He does not record a specific instance of *tsuina* but instead transforms the *tsuina* scenario into a mythic account of the origins of *sarugaku*, with the historical Buddha Śākyamuni's followers performing *sarugaku* as a way of pacifying the demonic adherents of the "outside teachings" (*gedō*):

> In the land where the Buddha lived, on the occasion of the consecration of the Jetavāna Monastery built by the rich man Sudatta, the Buddha Śākyamuni was preaching a sermon. Devadatta, in the company of ten thousand heathens [*mannin no gedō*], made such a great commotion dancing with festooned branches and sheaves of bamboo grass that it became difficult to continue the consecration. Buddha cast his gaze toward Śāriputra who, thus fortified by the Buddha's strength, prepared a performance with drums and songs at the back entrance to the temple, and there, through the ingenuity of Ānanda, the wisdom of Śāriputra, and the eloquence of Pūrṇa, they performed sixty-six acts of dramatic imitation so that the heathens, hearing the sound of the drums and flute, gathered at the back door [*ushirodo*] and settled down to watch. Given this respite, the Buddha continued with the consecration. Our vocation found its Indian origins in this.[43]

In this passage, Zeami demonstrates the importance of *sarugaku* by emphasizing its utility among Buddhist clergy looking to quell the raucous energies of the demonic horde, described as adherents of the outside teachings (*gedō*), or "heathens" in Hare's translation.

41. This may not have been a development confined to Buddhist rituals. As Takemoto Mikio points out, in the late Heian period, *sarugaku* was also performed in posterior (and therefore less ceremonially central) spaces within the inner palace in the capital, especially the back side of the Shishinden. Takemoto, "Geinō ichiba," 18.

42. Belief in Matarajin was transmitted to Japan from Tang China by Tendai monks. He is typically depicted as playing a drum and flanked by dancing children.

43. The translation is from Hare, *Zeami: Performance Notes*, 47–48; for the original, see *Zeami, Zenchiku*, NST 24:38.

Sarugaku is thus legitimized as a tool that helps propagate the dharma, but by occupying the space that separates believers from nonbelievers, it obtains a liminal character. And the back entrance is the spatial limen in which the pacification takes place, a site where the restless energies of heretical devotions are calmed.[44] Matsuoka Shinpei has observed that low-ranking *sarugaku* performers often played the role of Vināyaka, and higher-ranking *hōzushi* (exorcists) played the roles of Ryūten and Bishamonten, the deities who triumph over the demon.[45] This shows that the rite depended on a correspondence between social status and ritual position, as socially peripheral actors embodied demons who were ritually banished from sacred space. Nonetheless, the *sarugaku* performer plays an integral role: without someone to play the demon, there can be no rite. *Tsuina*, therefore, is yet another context in which the socially peripheral doubles as the symbolically central.

Sarugaku developed an especially close relationship to Buddhist institutions, but it was also frequently performed at Shinto festivals. For example, on 1136/9/17 (Hōen 2), Kasuga Wakamiya Shrine in Nara held its first annual festival (still performed today and known as Onmatsuri), which included *sangaku*, *dengaku*, and a variety of other performances aimed at entertaining the god who had been transported from the main shrine.[46] This festival, held consistently throughout the following decades and centuries, remained relatively stable in form and left behind a plethora of festival records (*saireiki*) and visual

44. At the end of the "Divine Matters" section, Zeami notes that the three *sarugaku* troupes (Shinza, Honza, and Hōjōji) perform at Hosshōji during the Shushōe rite. Hare, *Zeami: Performance Notes*, 52; for the original, see *Zeami, Zenchiku*, NST 24:41. Niunoya Tetsuichi interprets this as a reference to the *ushirodo* topos and furthermore makes a connection between the performers and the *kebiishi* functionaries who managed this ritual space. Niunoya, "Chūseiteki geinō no kankyō," 42–43.

45. Matsuoka, "Vinayaka kō," 229. As Matsuoka mentions elsewhere, Nose Asaji once hypothesized that the *tsuina* demons were played by outcastes (*sanjomin*), but low-status "professional" musicians seem to be more likely candidates. See Suzuki et al., "Sairei to engeki," 34.

46. For an overview of the establishment of the festival, see Hatakayama and Yasuda, *Sairei de yomitoku*, 3–23. On *dengaku*'s central role in the festival, see Yasuda, *Jisha to geinō no chūsei*, 18–26.

digests (*saireizu*) that are helpful in tracking how these performances have changed between the twelfth century and modern times.[47]

In conclusion, a *longue durée* overview of *sangaku* and *sarugaku* reveals a diverse repertoire of bodily feats that emerged as integral to court ceremony (Nara and early Heian periods), shifted toward a more transgressive function (mid- to late Heian period), and eventually became a mainstay of Buddhist rites and Shinto festivals (Heian period and beyond). Given the protean nature of *sangaku* and its attendant "one hundred skills," it should come as no surprise that its valences are multiple, unstable, and ambiguous. This breadth also meant that *sangaku* shared practices with other forms, including *dengaku* and *zōgei*.

Zōgei: Organizing Embodied Practices

In this section, I examine synchronic connections between *sangaku* and other practices. I have already touched on the relationship between *sangaku* and *dengaku*, but *sangaku* also shares genealogical and generic similarities with *zōgei*, or "miscellaneous performances." The term *zōgei* first appeared in classical Chinese texts and was imported along with the arts and performances it denotes, although, as might be expected for a term signifying the miscellaneous, the range of practices it covers is large and varies widely. In Japan, the earliest catalogue of *zōgei* is found in the scholar Minamoto no Shitagō's (911–983) encyclopedia *Wamyō ruijū shō* (Categorical miscellany of Yamato names; ca. 930s), commissioned for Emperor Daigo's daughter Princess Kinshi (904–938).[48]

The encyclopedia organizes knowledge according to a three-level structure: (1) sections, (2) subsections, and (3) entries. For example, the entry for "Wind" (*fū*) is found in the subsection "Wind and Rain" (*fūu rui*), which in turn is part of the "Heaven and Earth" section (*tenchi bu*). *Zōgei* constitutes its own subsection (*zōgei rui*), one of

47. Sorgenfrei, "Reversibility," 167. For transcriptions and reproductions of a variety of these records, see *Kasuga*, Shintō Taikei Jinja-hen 13.

48. For a discussion of *Wamyō ruijū shō*, see Steininger, *Chinese Literary Forms*, 196–210.

two in the "Arts and Skills" section (*gigei bu*), the other being "Shooting Arts" (*shagei rui*). Each entry in the "Zōgei" subsection contains "reverse cutting" (Ch. *fanqie*) pronunciations, brief attestations, and, in some cases, descriptions of the arts drawn from the classical Chinese corpus. As is the case elsewhere in the encyclopedia, this subsection is immediately followed by a parallel one in which related objects (*gu*) are described; by reading them together, one learns the pronunciation of the terms, what they signified, and what sorts of objects were involved. The twenty-three entries that make up the "Zōgei" subsection are shown in table 5.1.

The category of "Zōgei" encompasses a wide variety of activities, from simple diversions and tricks (tossing an arrow in a jar) to more demanding pursuits (horse racing, wrestling). The complementary subsection furthermore specifies not only objects like *go* stones and the *mari* ball used for *kemari* but also performance tools like puppets (*kairaishi*) and the diabolo (*ryūgo*).[49] Many of these diversions and pursuits appear in Heian court literature, where *go*, *sugoroku*, and *kemari* often function as opportunities for courtiers to vie with one another and demonstrate their skills.

The *zōgei* and *sangaku* repertoires both include acrobatics, games, and diversions. What makes *zōgei* distinct is how it encompasses practices that range broadly across class, location, and category. For example, the courtly diversion of kickball appears in the same list as virtuosic bodily feats and games played by gamblers on the streets of the capital.[50] As codified in the encyclopedia, "miscellaneous performance" signifies an expansive terrain that incorporates a variety of spaces, modalities, and ranks and classes.

Wamyō ruijū shō's systematic ordering of these practices adheres to a general encyclopedic structure through which the text organizes knowledge. But viewed from the perspective of performance history, the

49. *Shohon shūsei Wamyō ruijū shō*, 128–31.

50. The later sacralization of *kemari* is often tied to Fujiwara no Narimichi, whose prodigious speed I mentioned when discussing the story of Ietsuna and Yukitsuna's *kagura*. Tales about Narimichi's talent in *kemari* abound, and his *Narimichi-kyō kuden nikki* (Lord Narimichi's diary of oral instruction; twelfth century) details both his spectacular feats and his veneration for the trees and ball spirits that animate the game. See *Narimichi-kyō kuden nikki*, 386–87.

Table 5.1. *Zōgei* in *Wamyō ruijū shō*

tōko	throwing arrows into a jar
zōkō	find the hook
dakyū	polo
kemari	court kickball
keito	boat racing
kurabeuma	horse racing
shūsen	swinging
igo	*go*
dangi	battle *go*
chobo	flip-card gambling
yasugari	line *go*
sugoroku	backgammon
isen	coin throwing
hokotori	"spear" twirling
rōgan	juggling
sumai	wrestling
kobushiuchi	boxing
tagaheshi	arm wrestling
michikurabe	racing games such as *sugoroku* and *musashi*
kaheriutsu	somersaulting
toriawase	cockfighting
kusaawase	plant-comparing competition
ofusu	swimming

NOTE: Tsunoda Ichirō notes that in the Nara period, *hoko* signified a wooden shaft with both ends sharpened into points and usually used as a weapon. Today the character is read as *yari* (spear), but this usage did not develop until the end of the Kamakura period. See Tsunoda, "Sangaku no geinō," 289. Like *sugoroku* and *go*, *musashi* was played on a board, and the object of the game was to make lines with one's stones.

SOURCE: *Shohon shūsei Wamyō ruijū shō*, 122–28.

"Zōgei" subsection doubles as an early example of an archival fixing of a repertoire that otherwise remained fluid. The most well-known example of this kind of archiving in the Heian period is undoubtedly Akihira's *Shin sarugaku ki*, discussed in the previous chapter, which, like *Wamyō ruijū shō*, draws together a series of diverse bodily practices into a composite whole. Like Shitagō's encyclopedia, Akihira's account also attempts to forge a unity through ordering, although the centripetal pull of *sarugaku* is used as a point of departure for cataloguing the audience, which consists of various types of people who live in the urban capital. In this way, both texts are invested in organizing a range of heterogeneous and uneven elements into a seemingly coherent whole.

To further flesh out the context and content of *zōgei* and *sangaku*, and the way they facilitated bodily transgression, the following sections explore in greater depth two specific feats: illusion and acrobatics. Perhaps more so than other practices, illusion and acrobatics—tricking the eye and overwhelming the mind's conventional expectations—signified an unstable virtuosic excess and stoked fears of ontological instability.

Illusion, Disfigurement, and Heretical Teachings

The term "illusion" translates a wide variety of performance practices found in Heian-period texts. Premodern terms for these practices include *genjutsu* (the art of illusion), *kijutsu* (the strange art), *tejina* (legerdemain), *mekuramashi* (optical illusion), *gejutsu* (the outside art), and the term that appears at the outset of *Shin sarugaku ki: tōjutsu* (the Tang (Chinese) art). In Tang China, illusion was thought to constitute an important feature of the multifarious *sanyue*, as demonstrated by Du You's (735–812) comment that, "in general, *sanyue* [consists of] miscellaneous skills and many [types of] illusion."[51] Descriptions of illusion can therefore be found in the earliest Chinese sources that depict *sanyue*. For example, in the passage from *Xijingfu*

51. *Tongdian*, 764.

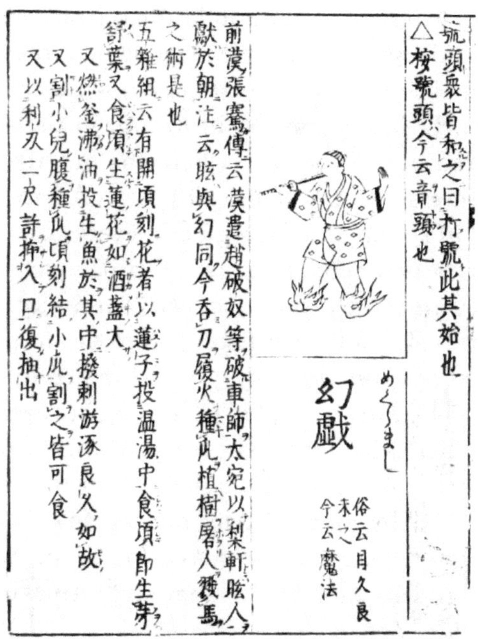
毬頭衆皆和之曰打毬此其始也
△按毬頭今云音頭也

幻戯 めくらまし
俗云目久良末之
今云魔法

前漢張騫傳云漢遣趙破奴等破車師太宛以犂靬眩人獻於朝注云眩與幻同今呑刀履火種瓜植樹屠人截馬之術是也
五雜組云有開頂刻花者以蓮子投温湯中食頃即生芽舒葉又食頃生蓮花如酒盞大
又燃釜沸油投生魚於其中撥剌游泳良久如故
又割小兒腹種瓜頃刻結小瓜割之皆可食
又以利刄二尺許揷入口復抽出

FIGURE 5.1. An illusionist (*mekuramashi*) swallows a sword and sets his feet ablaze. The image is part of an entry on illusion in Terajima Ryōan's encyclopedia *Wakan sansai zue* (1713). Courtesy of Waseda University Library.

discussed in the introduction, there are illusionists who change their appearance, swallow knives or swords, breath fire, and manipulate meteorological phenomena.[52] (Figure 5.1 depicts an illusionist swallowing a sword and lighting his feet on fire, two common feats of illusion.) Such entertainments came to Japan along with other *sanyue* techniques in the eighth century, but the dearth of descriptive records makes it impossible to know the precise nature of what was performed at the Nara court. There are, however, records from later time periods

52. *Monzen*, 153–56.

and literary works that offer some additional details about the characteristics of illusion and how people responded to them.

One of the most well-known examples of trickery based on optical illusion in early Japan appears in *Kojiki*, in the story of Amaterasu being lured out of the cave where she hid after her brother Susano-o's transgressions. Devising a ploy to get Amaterasu to return, the heavenly *kami* set up an offering of an evergreen tree decorated with curved *magatama* pendants, prayer strips, and a large mirror. Next, Ame no Uzume, the prototypical *kagura* performer, steps forward and "overturning a bucket [*uke*] before the entrance to Heaven's Boulder Cavern [*ame no iwaya*], she stamped loudly on it and became possessed [*kamugakari shite*], showing her breasts and pushing the girdle of her skirt down past her privates. / And so the high plains of heaven shook with the laughter of all the many spirits in their multitudes."[53] The sound of Ame no Uzume's performance and the gathered *kami*'s laughter intrigues Amaterasu, who peers out through a crack and asks for an explanation.[54] Ame no Uzume baits her by responding:

> "We laugh and dance because there is a spirit here who is even more magnificent than you, o mighty one."
>
> While she was saying this, the mighty ones Little Roof of Heaven and Solemn Soul took out the mirror and placed it before the great and mighty spirit Heaven Shining [Amaterasu].
>
> Thereupon the great and mighty spirit Heaven Shining grew more puzzled than before and started to creep out slowly toward it.
>
> Thereupon the spirit Strong-Armed Man of Heaven, who had been in hiding, grabbed her by her mighty hand and pulled her all the way out.

53. *The Kojiki: An Account of Ancient Matters*, 24. In his translation, Gustav Heldt translates the names of *kami* (and other proper nouns) literally, such that Amaterasu becomes "Heaven Shining." For the original, see *Kojiki*, SNKBZ 1:64 (CJ: 65).

54. On the overturned bucket's dual function as both a stage and "a magico-musical instrument," see Raz, *Audience and Actors*, 13.

> Straightaway the mighty one Solemn Soul drew forth a sacred boundary rope whose straw ends hung down, stretched it out behind her mighty back, and spoke, saying:
>
> "You shall not turn back past here!"
>
> So the great and mighty spirit Heaven Shining stepped forth, whereupon the high plains of heaven and the central realm of reed plains were lit up with her radiance.[55]

Ame no Uzume's performance, described by Benito Ortolani as "a treasure of information because of its projection of contemporary religious rites and dances into the legendary account of the myth," plays a crucial role in wider illusion's success.[56] Without her bawdy performance, there would have been no laughter, and without laughter, Amaterasu would not have peeked out from the cave and caught sight of her own reflection in the mirror. Furthermore, with its nudity, loud stomping, possession, and communal orientation, the performance includes many of the elements found in later records of performance, particularly *kagura* and *sarugaku*.[57] The combination of the performance's transgressive elements and its status as the lynchpin in the overall trickery make it a touchstone in the early history of illusion in Japan.

In Heian-period texts, depictions of illusion typically signify a social or ontological otherness. For example, in *Kairaishi no ki*, Ōe no Masafusa writes that puppeteers "toss twin swords and juggle seven balls, or manipulate wooden puppets and stage fights between dolls made of peach wood. They excel in the skill of making puppets act like humans, which generally resembles a performance of the fish-dragon *man'en*. By transforming sand and stones into golden coins,

55. *The Kojiki: An Account of Ancient Matters*, 24. For the original, see *Kojiki*, SNKBZ 1:66 (CJ: 67).

56. Ortolani, *The Japanese Theatre*, 4.

57. An early instance of this association is found in the first scroll of GoShirakawa's *Ryōjin hishō kudenshū*, of which only a small fragment remains. It includes the following line: "*Kagura* has been around since the Goddess Amaterasu was drawn by song to push aside her heavenly stone door and peer out." *Ryōjin hishō*, SNKBZ 42:341.

and changing grasses and trees into birds and beasts, they excel in [tricking] people's eyes."[58] Elsewhere in his account, Masafusa describes puppeteers as beyond the purview of the central state: they do not till fields, nor do they pay taxes or participate in corvée labor. Their productive capacities, he maintains, are instead directed toward creating entertaining illusions and other spectacular entertainments. The nature of this labor is somewhat ambiguous. It is not a stretch to imagine that audiences would be captivated by seeing birds transformed into beasts, but such manipulations of reality were not always viewed as innocent fun. Masafusa's account, which does not amount to a realistic depiction of puppeteers as they lived and worked at the time, rather draws on tropes and associations that work to create an aura of otherness.

Accounts that dwell on the more threatening valences of illusion can be found in several stories in *Konjaku monogatari shū*. In these stories, illusion is typically denoted by the word *gejutsu* (outside art), a pejorative term that signifies non-Buddhist magical beliefs and practices.[59] As Haruko Wakabayashi explains, *gejutsu* and its companion term *gehō* (outside teachings) "originally referred to non-Buddhist beliefs—particularly those of India—as opposed to *naidō* (inner way) and *naihō* (inner dharma), which were Buddhist teachings."[60] The first twelve tales of *Konjaku*'s twentieth volume—the last of the section focused on Buddhism in Japan—spotlight *tengu*, malign beings that are often associated with *gejutsu*.[61] Three of these tales mention or describe *gejutsu*; a fourth, dealing with similar subject matter but presented with a different tone, appears later in the collection.

58. "Kairaishi no ki," NST 8:308 (CJ: 158).

59. Buddhist and non-Buddhist practices, however, are not always diametrically opposed. Fujiwara no Sanesuke, in an entry of his diary *Shōyūki* dated 993/i10/14 (Shōryaku 4), reports a rumor that the spirit of Fujiwara no Morosuke was attempting to disrupt rites undertaken on behalf of the pregnant Fujiwara no Seishi (972–1025). Sanesuke writes, "When he was alive, Morosuke fervently sought to ensure the success of his descendants, be it by Buddhist rites or *gejutsu*." *Shōyūki*, ZST 46:95.

60. Wakabayashi, *The Seven Tengu Scrolls*, 27.

61. On *tengu*, see Wakabayashi, *The Seven Tengu Scrolls*, 3–12; and Faure, *Gods of Medieval Japan*, 79–84.

In the first story, entitled "A *Tengu* Transforms into a Buddha and Sits atop a Tree" (20:3), the sudden appearance of a buddha in a persimmon tree prompts people high and low to gather and pay their respects.[62] But the wise noble Minamoto no Hikaru (845–913) reasons that it would not make sense for a buddha to suddenly appear in this fashion, and he concludes that it must be the result of a *tengu* practicing *gedō*, another word for "heretical" non-Buddhist teachings.[63] He visits the manifestation and glares at it for hours until it suddenly changes into a kite (*tobi*) and falls to the ground, its wings broken. All those gathered are taken aback by this strange occurrence; a small boy soon approaches the kite and strikes it to death. Hikaru is subsequently praised for his intelligence.

Although this story deals with an illusion staged by a *tengu* and does not therefore describe the feats of human illusionists, it demonstrates the importance of vision in representations of illusion. The ease with which the crowd is duped is perhaps a foil for Hikaru's critical intelligence and skepticism, but also note that Hikaru exposes the demon by staring it down in a virtuosic act of looking. It is not just his knowledge of the demon's trickery but also his own performance of glaring, of not allowing his eyes to be tricked, that ensures his victory. The story thus stages an opposition between "true" Buddhist vision and the "false" illusions employed by beings like *tengu* who practice the "outside art."

The second relevant story is entitled "A Monk Who Worships *Tengu* Seeks to Teach the Skills to a Boy" (20:9).[64] It revolves around a boy who wants to learn the *gejutsu* techniques practiced by a "lowly" (*gesu*) monk who lives next door. The monk tells him that he must first observe austerities for seven days. The boy obeys, and after seven days

62. *Konjaku monogatari shū*, SNKBZ 37:37–38. For an English translation of the story, see Dykstra, *Buddhist Tales of India, China, and Japan*, 502–3.

63. In the version of the story that appears in *Uji shūi monogatari* (2:14), the term *gedō* is not used. Hikaru knows that something is not right because he does not expect to encounter a buddha in the "degenerate age" of *mappō*. *Uji shūi monogatari*, SNKBZ 50:102.

64. *Konjaku monogatari shū*, SNKBZ 37:52–56. For an English translation of the story, see Dykstra, *Buddhist Tales of India, China, and Japan*, 510–11.

the monk takes him to the mountains to meet his teacher. Though the monk has cautioned the boy not to bring along any weapons, the boy disregards these instructions and comes armed with a dagger. When they arrive, the teacher immediately senses the presence of the dagger, at which point everything suddenly vanishes, and the monk and the boy are forced to go home. The monk dies a few days later, and the narrator explains this was because his teacher was, in fact, a *tengu*. The story then ends with a warning about the evils of *gejutsu*.

The tale is noteworthy because it describes *gejutsu* techniques at some length. According to the narrative, the "low-ranking monk, who enjoys something called *gejutsu* and treats it as a profession," can perform a variety of illusions: "He can rapidly transform his clogs and straw sandals into puppies and make them crawl around, summon a fox from his breast pocket and make it cry, and enter the rear of a standing horse or cow and exit from its mouth."[65] The portrayal of the monk as a summoner of foxes, beings long perceived to be tricksters and shape-shifters, associates him with other heterotopic beings, including *tengu*, and his ability to transform objects and transfigure himself recalls the feats of puppeteers and *sangaku* performers.

The mention of "entering the rear of a standing horse or cow and exiting from its mouth" is a reference to a transformation technique that seems to have involved perspectival play. There is an illustration of the feat in the picture scroll *Shinzei kogaku zu* (fig. 5.2).[66] The image shows a diminutive illusionist mid-act, legs dangling out of the horse's rump, while his smiling face and flowing robes simultaneously extend from the animal's open mouth. An attendant holds the reins in one hand and uses the other to gesture in front of the horse, as though indicating

65. *Konjaku monogatari shū*, SNKBZ 37:52.

66. Details about the provenance of this work are few and far between, but it is certain that it was not all created by Shinzei, the dharma name of Fujiwara no Michinori. About four-fifths of the way through the scroll, we encounter two vertical lines of text that read: "A separate section based on the book of the Minor Counselor Monk (Shinzei) has been appended." Furthermore, although it has become conventional to refer to the scroll using Shinzei's name, the scroll itself specifies two titles: *Maizu* (Dance images) and *Tōmai-e* (Illustrations of Tang dance). For more on the history of the scroll, see *Shinzei kogaku zu*, 1–6.

FIGURE 5.2. The "Entering a Horse's Stomach Dance" (*nyūba fuku mai*). *Shinzei kogaku zu*. Courtesy of Tokyo Geijutsu Daigaku.

the space the illusionist will soon, incredibly, occupy. An impression of flow is created, a crucial element in any successful representation of illusion, since first and foremost illusion depends on the appearance of physical change or movement. Hashimoto Hiroyuki has noted that there is nothing unusual about actors associating closely with animals in the context of performance, and *Shinzei kogaku zu* contains several depictions of performers doing just that, as does the excerpt from *Xijingfu* discussed in the introduction.[67] But a representation of an illusionist at the precise moment he travels through a horse suggests a more transgressive corporeal transmutation.

Unsurprisingly, the narrator of the *Konjaku* story has few positive words to say about such feats. Insofar as the transformation of footwear into puppies, the summoning of foxes, and the transfiguration of

67. Hashimoto, *Engi no seishinshi*, 211. For additional images of *sangaku* performers dressing up as animals, see *Shinzei kogaku zu*, 72–75.

one's own body were associated with *tengu*, they are shunned as threats to the Buddhist teachings. The narrator concludes, "It seems that those who practice such techniques have committed an extremely and deeply sinful act [*kihamarite tsumi fukaki koto*]. And so, anyone who wishes to devote themselves the slightest bit to the Three Treasures must not, under any circumstances, consider learning [*gejutsu*]. Those who do are called *ningu* [human dogs] and they are not human."[68] In the same way that *Shinzei kogaku zu* portrays the momentary transgressive integration of illusionist and horse, man and beast, here those who practice *gejutsu* are described as *ningu*, a melding of *nin* (human) and the *gu* (dog) of *tengu*. By stitching together two different entities and orders, the narrator registers discomfort with the way illusionists made use of their bodies to both trick and captivate spectators.

The third tale brings *gejutsu* into the realm of sexual politics. In "How a Takiguchi Guard Was Sent to Collect Gold during the Reign of Emperor Yōzei" (20:10), a Takiguchi guard named Michinori has been sent to the north to retrieve gold from Mutsu Province.[69] While lodging at the residence of a district official in Shinano Province, he sleeps with the man's wife and then notices that his penis has disappeared. The same thing happens to eight of Michinori's attendants after they visit the wife in succession. The group flees the next morning, but before long they are stopped by one of the official's servants,

68. *Konjaku monogatari shū*, SNKBZ 37:56.

69. *Konjaku monogatari shū*, SNKBZ 37:56–64. For a translation and discussion of this story, see Li, *Ambiguous Bodies*, 71–80. For a more recent translation, see Dykstra, *Buddhist Tales of India, China, and Japan*, 512–15. A slightly different version of the story appears in *Uji shūi monogatari* (9:1), SNKBZ 50:272–77. For a translation, see Mills, *A Collection of Tales from Uji*, 300–303. The Takiguchi guards was a group of ten (later twenty) imperial bodyguards posted to the northeast of the Seiryōden in the inner palace and organizationally attached to the Chamberlains' Office. Emperor Uda (r. 887–897), a cousin of Yōzei, established the unit. (The anachronistic setting of this story is interesting, especially given later rumors of Yōzei's violence and instability.) In addition to providing security, these guards were tasked with conducting the nightly roll call (a vocal performance known as *nadaimen* or *monjaku*) and through this became linked to other kinds of performance including *dengaku* and *shirabyōshi*. See Okimoto, *Ranmai no chūsei*, 79–81.

who is carrying a box containing "the nine men's penises, gathered and wrapped like *matsutake* mushrooms."[70] It turns out the official had used a special technique to make the penises disappear. Amazed, Michinori returns to the district official's residence after completing his trip to the north. The official explains that he, too, had the same experience in his youth and that the man who had caused his penis to disappear taught him the technique. To learn the technique, Michinori is told to perform austerities (abstinence, bathing, reclusion) and renounce the Three Treasures; the speech act marks the practices as related to *gejutsu*. The official then has him confront fantastical beasts—a huge serpent and a large wild boar—with the instructions that he should grapple with them. Michinori flees from the serpent but manages to grab the boar. The official decides that although he cannot teach Michinori the more advanced technique of causing penises to disappear, he can at least teach him how to transform a simple object into something else. When Michinori returns to the capital, he demonstrates his newly acquired skills for the other Takiguchi guards: "He bet them that he could transform their shoes into puppies; he did, and made them crawl around. He also changed their old straw sandals into a three-foot-long carp and made it dance around on top of a serving table."[71] Emperor Yōzei hears of Michinori's abilities and summons him so that he, too, may learn the art of illusion. The emperor uses his new skills to project the Kamo Festival parade along the "top railing of a curtained screen."[72] The tale ends with the narrator speculating that Yōzei's dabbling in such practices, which shun the Three Treasures and venerate the *tengu*, resulted in his insanity.[73]

Li argues that the tale is "ultimately about the vulnerability of men to other men rather than to women."[74] It may begin with temporary castration brought about by intercourse with a woman, but the focus

70. *Konjaku monogatari shū*, SNKBZ 37:60.

71. *Konjaku monogatari shū*, SNKBZ 37:63.

72. This is Yoshiko Dykstra's translation. Dykstra, *Buddhist Tales of India, China, and Japan*, 515. For the Japanese, see *Konjaku monogatari shū*, SNKBZ 37:63.

73. As Dykstra notes, Yōzei's insanity is documented in several contemporary sources. Dykstra, *Buddhist Tales of India, China, and Japan*, 515n831.

74. Li, *Ambiguous Bodies*, 75.

is squarely on the homosocial experience of loss (and retrieval) and the masculine competition that recurs throughout the story. In this and the previous tale, the teacher of the techniques is a man of low-to-middle status (a lowly monk, a district official in the provinces), and those they teach are men or boys (a young boy, the Takiguchi guard, and Emperor Yōzei). In terms of class, the *gejutsu* skills are perhaps too freighted with the danger of ontological otherness to permit aristocratic interest; Yōzei might be read as an exception, but by the time the *Konjaku* story was written, he had long been coded as other due to his forced abdication "after killing the son of his wet nurse."[75] The first story discussed, despite being different from the second and third in that it concerns a *tengu* using *gejutsu* to transform into a buddha, nonetheless features the male noble Minamoto no Hikaru (son of Emperor Ninmyō) as the one who triumphs over the duplicitous creature. Altogether, the space of *gejutsu*'s performance and transmission is non-elite, homosocial, and filled with danger and foreboding. *Gejutsu* thereby obtains an ambivalence similar to that of *sangaku* and the other non-elite performances discussed in this book: it is at once powerful and virtuosic (the district official uses it not once but nine times—and on representatives of the emperor no less), even as it is overshadowed by the narrator's concluding appeal to the superior power of Buddhism.

The fourth and final *Konjaku* story that depicts *gejutsu* techniques appears in volume 28 of the collection, which also contains the story about the monk Kyōen and his unsettling encounter with *dengaku* performers (see chapter 3), in addition to the stories about the nuns and woodcutters dancing together and about the former puppeteer (see chapter 7). Marian Ury describes this volume as consisting of "humorous stories," and for the most part the stories are indeed lighter than those in volume 20, which treat *gejutsu* as threatening and tie it to violence and decline.[76] In "How *Gejutsu* Was Used to Steal and Eat Melons," (28:40) several "lowly men" (*gesudomo*) using packhorses to transport melons to the capital encounter "a wizened old man" (*toshi imijiku oitaru okina*), who asks them for a

75. Li, *Ambiguous Bodies*, 78.
76. Ury, *Tales of Times Now Past*, 4.

melon.[77] The men explain that they cannot share them since they belong to their master. Upset at their mistreatment of the elderly, the old man digs a hole and scatters some melon seeds into it; before long, seeds sprout, grow into vines, and bear large ripe melons. The men watch in amazement as the old man (who they now think might be a deity) feasts on the melons and hands them out to passersby, before heading off to parts unknown. When the men go to prepare their horses to continue toward the capital, they discover that all the melons are gone. Astonished, they realize that the old man has "tricked our eyes [*me o kuramashite*] without us noticing," and with no more melons to deliver, they head home.[78] Some passersby find the situation strange, others simply laugh. In conclusion, the narrator proposes a few explanations for the old man's behavior and identity before stating that, in the end, no one had a clue who he was.

Compared to the anxieties that inform the other three stories—the ability of *tengu* to covertly spread *gejutsu*, castration and emasculation, insanity—the stakes of this story are low. The others revolve around skills used to make objects disappear or turn one thing into something else, but here the old man's technique is explicitly described by the stingy melon transporters as an optical illusion (*mekuramashi*), just the kind that might feature in a performance of *sarugaku* at a marketplace or a crossroads. Indeed, in addition to the "stagecraft" of the illusion, the story contains elements that evoke a performance, such as the streamlined dramatic tension between the melon transporters and the old man, the structured narrative reveal, and the passersby, who at times take on the function of an audience reacting to the spectacle. This is a story about a performance of a particular kind of illusion, but it is also a story about performance writ large: how it works, what it involves, and what people make of it.

In its capacity to both entertain and threaten, illusion was viewed with ambivalence by elites. It might involve a captivating feat performed as part of a larger program of *sarugaku*, a playful trick played on others to get what one wants, or a malicious threat to the authority

77. *Konjaku monogatari shū*, SNKBZ 38:269–71. For an English translation, see Dykstra, *Buddhist Tales of India, China, and Japan*, 946–47.

78. *Konjaku monogatari shū*, SNKBZ 38:271.

of the court or Buddhist institutions. And it continued to fascinate well into the early modern period, as attested by the many stories about the (likely fictitious) illusionist named Kashin Koji, who used his techniques to playfully subvert warlord authority.[79] The lingering interest in those who could invert social hierarchies and manipulate ontological states makes illusion, like the broader repertoire of *sangaku*, a socially peripheral practice with a symbolically central importance.

Juggling and Midair Suspension

Just like illusion, juggling involves using one's body to manipulate objects in a way that astounds audiences. As a feat within the *zōgei* and *sangaku* repertoires, juggling relied on timing, coordination, and in some cases the threat of bodily harm for its dramatic effect. Performers juggled a wide variety of objects, including balls, bowls, scythes, candles, and knives. Nakazawa Shin'ichi has drawn attention to the sacred connotations of midair suspension, an experience of which was transmitted by practices like juggling, acrobatics, and *kemari*. He writes, "By fixing their bodies acrobatically mid-air and by the feat of throwing various things up into the air without dropping them, the mythological thinking prevalent in Neolithic cultures sought to experience that 'intermediary space' unrelated to the physical world. This is the space in which spirits reside."[80] In this sense, juggling is not only a crowd-pleasing entertainment but also feeds the desire to experience something beyond everyday reality.

An early visual representation of several *sangaku* feats, including juggling, can be found in the form of black-ink paintings brushed on the surface of a wooden catalpa bow preserved in the Shōsōin storehouse at Tōdaiji. Known as *sumie no dankyū*, this slender bow

79. For example, see Nakayama Sanryū's (1614–1684) *Daigo zuihitsu* (The Daigo miscellany; 1670), which includes an anecdote about Kashin Koji battling the fierce warrior Matsunaga Hisahide (1510–1577) by conjuring his dead wife so realistically that Hisahide cries out in agony. *Daigo zuihitsu*, 57–58.

80. Nakazawa, *Seirei no ō*, 10.

FIGURE 5.3. A juggler depicted on the *sumie no dankyū*. The Shōsōin Treasures. Courtesy of the Imperial Household Agency.

measures 162 centimeters in length and was most likely made in China, though it remains unclear exactly when and where.[81] The paintings depict a gathering of *sanyue* performers who play instruments, dance, and execute virtuosic feats including balancing on poles attached to the heads of large men. Figure 5.3 shows a performer juggling six balls, his hands open in anticipation of catching them and his head tilted toward the sky.

81. Tsunoda, "Sangaku no geinō," 291.

The earliest textual record that explicitly mentions juggling, and perhaps describes something similar to what the image depicts, is found in *Shoku Nihon kōki* (Later chronicle of Japan, continued; 869), the fourth of the national histories. According to an entry dated 837/7/25 (Jōwa 4), "Emperor Ninmyō went to the rear courtyard, where he ordered the Left Palace Guard Bureau [*sakonoefu*] to play music and juggle balls and knives."[82] There are not many records of juggling in the following centuries, but by the eleventh century it had become a routine part of *sangaku* performances. In the introductory passage to *Shin sarugaku ki*, for example, Akihira lists *shinadama* (knife-and-bell jugglers) and *yatsudama* (ball jugglers) as two types of performers present (see chapter 4). *Shinzei kogaku zu* contains two related illustrations. One, titled *rōgyoku* or "ball play," depicts a juggler whose head is flung up toward the sky as he dances, arms outstretched, beneath a three-legged arc of ten balls (fig. 5.4). Another, titled *rōken* or "sword play," shows a juggler in a similar posture skillfully manipulating several blades (fig. 5.5). Given such a small sample size, it is impossible to generalize about how spectators viewed the practice, but accounts tend to emphasize the virtuosic skill required and in some cases the danger involved.

Kamo no Chōmei (1155–1216), for example, describes a thrilling performance of knife juggling (*katanadama*) by *dengaku* actors in his collection of stories *Hosshinshū* (Collection of the enlightened mind; ca. 1216). In this positive assessment of virtuosic bodily feats, Chōmei emphasizes the assiduousness with which some people, despite it being the "latter days of the law" (*mappō*), still devote themselves to practicing the arts. He writes:

> Also, speaking of things that gather merit and express awe, there are those who perform a dangerous technique called "knife juggling" during *dengaku* performances. If you go and watch, you'll see that there are three people and six knives. The most skilled practitioner stands in the middle, another stands in front of him, and the third stands behind him. These latter two each have three knives, which they throw as fast as they can toward the person in the middle. He catches the knives coming from

82. *Shoku Nihon kōki*, SZKT 3:68.

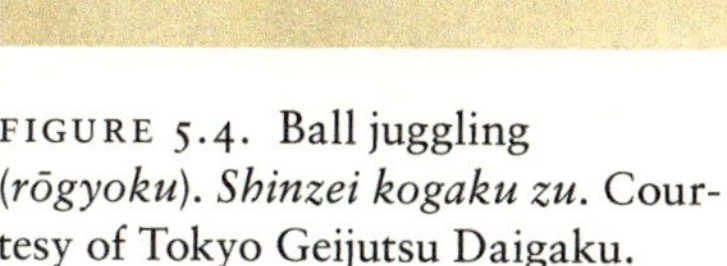
FIGURE 5.4. Ball juggling (*rōgyoku*). *Shinzei kogaku zu*. Courtesy of Tokyo Geijutsu Daigaku.

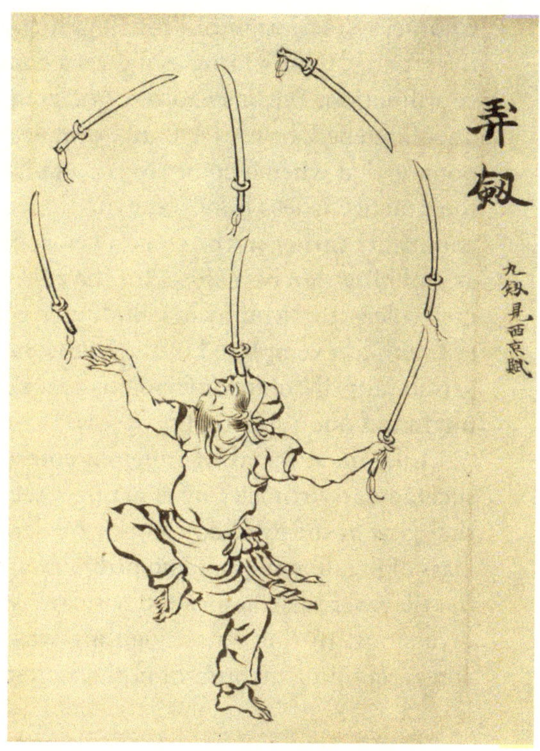

FIGURE 5.5. Sword juggling (*rōken*). *Shinzei kogaku zu*. Courtesy of Tokyo Geijutsu Daigaku.

the front and throws them to the back, and catches the knives coming from the back and throws them to the front. Six knives flying back and forth—this is no ordinary skill. If you heard about this from someone, you simply wouldn't believe it.

But this really isn't so strange. It is simply the result of having accumulated merit. If, for the purpose of spiritual progress, you accumulate merit like this and cultivate an undaunted mind, you will attain perfect awareness in this very body. You will actually see the buddhas and bodhisattvas. The mind can be applied like this to a profitless diversion, whereas [even] virtuous roots will slacken with laziness.[83]

83. *Hosshinshū*, SNKS 5:364–65.

Chōmei's description of knife juggling is one of the most detailed in the archive, highlighting as it does a complex feat requiring speed and coordination. But instead of criticizing the practice as subversive or unenlightened, he uses it as an example of dedication to a pursuit. The point is that when it comes to accumulating merit, the moral status of the practice is less important than one's dedication to it. As Chōmei comments earlier in the story, even something as seemingly immoral as gambling can be a vessel for the cultivation of the mind. Here Chōmei voices the Mahayana Buddhist emphasis on expedient means (*hōben*), as exemplified in the Lotus Sutra, to demonstrate how conventionally dissolute or frivolous practices like gambling and juggling might aid one's spiritual progress.[84]

Like most forms of *sangaku* entertainment, juggling signified a spectacular virtuosity by enacting a seeming suspension of the forces that govern the everyday world. As demonstrated by Chōmei's story, feats of juggling required no ordinary amount of skill and composure, but they were also associated with low-status performers and dissolute diversions. In this sense, juggling was viewed with ambivalence by elites, retaining an aura of both excitement and precarity.

Disciplining Performance: Bodies Beyond Boundaries

In Heian Japan, when performers transgressed expectations or scripted patterns of movement, they ran the risk of facing retaliation in a variety of forms, including incarceration, economic deprivation, and physical violence. An examination of a handful of such incidents will clarify the stakes of transgression as they figured in the lives of *zōgei*, *sangaku*, and *sarugaku* performers.

A recurring tension in the relationship between elites and non-elite performers is the former's inability to accept the improvisational capacity of the latter. As the *ritsuryō* state continued to give way to more decentralized forms of governance, non-elite performance became

84. See especially chapter 2, "Expedient Devices," in *Scripture of the Lotus Blossom*, 22–47.

increasingly deinstitutionalized. This spurred the appearance of new forms, but it also meant performers were subjected unevenly to the pressures accompanying elite patronage and observation. In this section, I explore three examples of boundary breaking that characterize this situation: moments in which performers were criticized, imprisoned, and otherwise censured for acting in ways that did not accord with the wishes of their elite audiences. I read accounts of these moments as attempts by elites to neutralize the nomadic movement that often constituted non-elite performance. Documenting the disorderly was one way to repair breaches of order.

By the turn of the eleventh century, the Heian capital had grown more populous and urban, and an increasing number of unranked attendants were making their presence felt on the streets, especially during the "open festivals" discussed in chapter 1. Some were performers who acted in ways that transgressed elite notions of order. One particularly well-known example is the boisterous actions of a "miscellaneous performer" (*zōgeisha*) named Mukotsu during the Gion *goryōe* in the summer of 999.[85] According to an entry in *Honchō seiki* dated 999/6/14 (Chōhō 1), the final day of the festival, Mukotsu and his fellow performers attracted a crowd by parading around with repurposed materials from the previous year's Daijōe accession ceremony, prompting Fujiwara no Michinaga (then minister of the Left) to dispatch the capital police:[86]

> Today was the Gion Tenjin Festival. A *zōgei* performer has been active in the capital since last year. He appears as a monk and is known as Mukotsu. (His real name is Yorinobu, but he is also referred to as Jinnan.) To draw the attention of the city dwellers, he and his group created

85. The same figure seems to appear in *Shin sarugaku ki*, under the name Jinnan, where he receives a favorable evaluation: "Jinnan, whenever he performs and without fail, earns the admiration of the crowd." "Shin sarugaku ki," NST 8:301 (CJ: 134).

86. The Daijōe or Daijōsai was a harvest ritual (*niinamesai*) that took place during the autumn in years when an emperor acceded to the throne. It involved elaborate displays of products from around the realm, such as regional grains and sake, performances of dances and songs, and the presentation of screen paintings showing local landscapes and inscribed with *waka* poems about those landscapes.

> a pole and brought it to the shrine.[87] As was said, they used the pole just as if they were pulling a *shime* during the Daijōe ceremony.[88] The minister of the Left [Michinaga] was quickly informed about this; he was shocked and issued a directive to stop. As a result, the capital police were summoned and apprised of the situation. They dashed off to where Mukotsu was, and while undertaking his arrest, asked him about what he had done. He ran away and the police returned empty-handed. They then ordered the shrine to get rid of Mukotsu's pole. At this point Tenjin became furious, and a *jushi* exorcist was flung from the dais. An unranked attendant [*genin*] approached the group and delivered an oracle.[89]

Based on this account, Mukotsu seems to earn Michinaga's ire by repurposing objects used in a solemn ritual for the sake of a more spontaneous act of inversion. Intriguingly, the word *mukotsu*, which means "boneless," would later signify a style of rapid dance, often associated with lion dances (*shishimai*) and the activities of *jushi* exorcists.[90] Perhaps Mukotsu's antics left an imprint on the popular imagination and would continue to be associated with quick movement and other acrobatics, resulting in the word shifting to signify a set of bodily practices.[91]

87. Kuroita Katsumi, editor of this edition of *Honchō seiki*, proposes that the character for "village" or "group" (*mura* 村) that appears in the manuscript might be a mistake for the visually similar character for "pole" or "pillar" (*hashira* 柱). *Honchō seiki*, SZKT 9:213. Hayashiya's transcription of the first part of the account contains yet another reading of the character as *zai* 材 or "materials." Hayashiya, *Chūsei geinōshi no kenkyū*, 317. The precise nature of what Mukotsu has created remains unclear.

88. The character for *shime* can also be read *hyō* (marker). This is likely a reference to *shimeyama*, enclosures or "floats" in which tribute goods from selected provinces were displayed during the Daijōe. This is thought by some performance historians to be the earliest mention of the *yama* that would come to characterize the Gion *matsuri*. See Hayashiya, *Chūsei geinōshi no kenkyū*, 317.

89. *Honchō seiki*, SZKT 9:213.

90. This seems to be how Akihira uses it at the beginning of *Shin sarugaku ki* (see chapter 4). In his diary *Kanmon nikki* (1416–1448), Fushiminomiya Sadafusa (1372–1456) briefly describes his encounter with a lion dance that included *mukotsu*. He writes that "they unsheathed their swords, danced *mukotsu*, and went utterly mad. They were skilled beyond belief." *Kanmon nikki*, 261.

91. Wakita, *Chūsei Kyoto to Gion matsuri*, 25.

The order to bring Mukotsu's procession to an end provokes a violent response from Tenjin (also known as Gozu Tennō): a *jushi* exorcist is flung from a dais, and an oracle is then delivered, the contents of which, one imagines, are to reverse the decision. The account shows how unranked attendants were able to transgress elite ideas of order and proper use of materials with unscripted gatherings and spontaneous repurposing. That Michinaga failed to have Mukotsu captured is furthermore a reminder that everything in the Heian capital did not always proceed according to the rules, even if Michinaga would impose his will more effectively during similar incidents in the future.

For example, on 1013/6/14 (Chōwa 2), Fujiwara no Sanesuke related in his diary *Shōyūki* another incident involving Michinaga (still minister of the Left) and a group of *sangaku* performers during the Gion *goryōe*. He wrote, "Moromitsu passed on the following. Today during the Gion *goryōe*, there was a flatbed carriage bearing *sangaku* performers behind the revered carriage. Acting on orders from the minister of the Left, several unranked attendants [*zōnin*] appeared, restrained the *sangaku* performers, and ripped their clothing. In the meantime, the revered carriage came to a stop and was unable to get away. The carriage attendants and spectators alike claimed that this behavior should be censured."[92] Sanesuke wrote this brief report on the fourteenth day of the sixth month: the day of the boisterous procession from the *tabisho* in the capital back to Gion Shrine. Interestingly, it places *sangaku* performers in the procession, something not seen in later depictions (including the illustrations found in *Nenjū gyōji emaki* and discussed in chapter 1). Moromitsu's account does not describe what exactly the performers did to incite Michinaga's anger, but Wakita Haruko speculates that Michinaga may have been attempting to prevent the procession from getting out of hand.[93] As demonstrated by the Great Dengaku of 1096, festivals were often heterotopic spaces in which transgression flourished and social and political

92. *Shōyūki*, ZST 48:115.

93. She also notes that this "flatbed carriage" (*munaguruma*) might be the origin of the floats (*dashi*) that still play a central role in the Gion Festival today. Wakita, *Chūsei Kyoto to Gion matsuri*, 26.

order was contested and reinscribed. In this example, the border crossing plays out across bodies: the proximity of *sangaku* performers conflicts with Michinaga's idea of how the parade should proceed, causing him to dispatch his attendants, who restrain the performers and rip their clothing.[94] The report received by Sanesuke concludes by noting the general displeasure caused by the incident, perhaps indicating the circulation of some resentment toward Michinaga's authority.[95]

Nearly two hundred years later, Fujiwara no Teika (1162–1241), in his diary *Meigetsuki* (Diary of the bright moon; 1180–1235), touched on the fate of a *sarugaku* performer named Menchō, who failed to properly conduct his portion of the annual Shushōe rite at Hosshōji. As mentioned, Shushōe was a penitential rite that took place at the beginning of the year. It was thought to ensure the peace of the realm, an abundant harvest throughout the land, and the prosperity of the people. Although Shushōe was held by all provincial temples for several decades during the Nara period, by the late Heian period, the rite had become especially associated with Tōji, Saiji, Enshūji, and the Six Victory Temples (Rokushōji)—one of which, Hosshōji, was the site of Menchō's transgressive performance. In an entry dated 1202/1/13 (Kennin 2), Teika writes: "This morning the *sarugaku* performer Menchō was taken into custody by Capital Policeman Suekuni. Last night he incurred the disfavor [of the retired emperor] because he did not shout in a loud voice. The cause of this strange incident is being investigated."[96] Menchō was incarcerated because he had apparently upset Retired Emperor GoToba (r. 1183–1198) by not "shouting in a loud voice" (*kyōkan*), a prescribed portion of the Shushōe ritual. *Kyōkan* is usually understood to be an abbreviation of the longer *benyō kyōkan*, or "clapping, dancing, and shouting in a loud voice." These are acts of central ritual importance, since the production of loud sounds played an important role in banishing

94. During the Heian period, clothing was considered a metonymic extension of the physical body, meaning that the tearing of clothing might signify a serious punishment. See Pandey, *Perfumed Sleeves*, 52–54.

95. For Michinaga's many conflicts and how this incident might demonstrate them, see Teeuwen, *Kyoto's Gion Festival*, 32.

96. *Kunchū Meigetsuki*, 481. For a translation into classical Japanese, see *Kundoku Meigetsuki*, 302.

demons and other malign forces, thereby symbolically purifying the realm. As one scholar writes, "It was not a matter of Menchō's performance being good or bad but rather his negligence and the inadequate fervor of his belief."[97] Menchō seems to be the opposite of Chōmei's lauded knife jugglers. Instead of a scripted phonic triumph over the threat of disorder, he causes the ritual to stumble into silence and the authorities to take immediate punitive action. We do not know what became of Menchō (although the fact that he is named implies he was well known), but this incident of unexpected behavior demonstrates the danger of diverging from the ceremonial script.

The transgressive bodily movements and expressions of Mukotsu, Menchō, and the nameless *sangaku* performers demonstrate, in brief, how miscellaneous and minor performances occupied a liminal zone between high and low, order and disorder. By the end of the tenth century, these performances had become a part of both urban festivals and religious rites, a legibility that left performers exposed to censure from capital authorities should they break the rules. More generally, the history of *zōgei*, *sangaku*, and *sarugaku* demonstrates how the excessive capacities of virtuosic bodies could elicit a range of elite responses, from awe to apprehension. With their fugitive energy, these performances thrived on the edges of court culture and were not easily absorbed or negated. If a lingering subversive power is one potential product of ambiguous bodies, the case of *imayō* vocal arts—examined at length in the next chapter—shows that not all bodily practices had the same fate.

97. Takatori, "Minzoku to geinō," 134.

CHAPTER SIX

Bracketed Bodies, Vanished Voices

Imayō, Abstraction, and the Archive

Ever elusive, voice can be understood as sound or music, embodied or disembodied, an expression of aesthetics or an instrument of language. It cannot be reduced to any one of these terms, and yet its conceptual articulation has involved combinations of all of them. In a recent edited volume, Martha Feldman and Judith T. Zeitlin describe the "paradoxical status of voice as something that hovers between embodiment and disembodiment, [thus raising] the uncertainty of determining to whom a voice belongs. [. . .] There's always something more to the voice—a remainder, a gap, a reverb, an echo."[1] In its paradoxical suspension between embodiment and disembodiment, between internal and external, voice becomes a medium for transgression and identification. It is a phenomenon of excess, of "something more," even as it cannot help but vanish into thin air.[2]

Heian-period texts brim with a variety of voices (*koe*), human and nonhuman alike. Should these remainders be understood as embodied, disembodied, or, paradoxically, both? If documents can be used to

1. Feldman and Zeitlin, preface to *The Voice and Nothing More*, xii–xiii.

2. But as Kerim Yasar points out, "Far from being a liability, [voice's] transience endows [it] with an auratic charge. Because the voice is always vanishing, because it cannot be stopped, fixed, and scrutinized, it always occupies a liminal, indeed ghostly, space of absent presence." Yasar, *Electrified Voices*, 5.

grasp the "something more" of the voice, what implications might this have for the other performance practices discussed in this book? In modern Western discourse, voice occupies a privileged position due to its associations with "individual identity, personal agency, collective will, subjectivity, authenticity, [and] style."[3] But in Heian Japan, voice became a central textual concern only when demanded by the pragmatic aspects of performance practice.

One such moment is that occasioned by *imayō* (popular songs), a vocal art performed by non-elite women (*asobi* and *kugutsu*) but also practiced by male aristocrats beginning in the mid-Heian period. The "voice" that emerges in accounts of *imayō* performance is thoroughly material: it is described as youthful, gentle, delicate, and prone to drifting and disappearance. In his treatise on *imayō*, Retired Emperor GoShirakawa writes at length about how his voice changed during his long training—both the technical abilities he honed and the times when his voice ran ragged from singing too often. This treatise and its conception of voice, the song collection it accompanied, and the wider status of *imayō* as vocal performance are the focus of this chapter.

Absent Presence: Disappearance and Mediation in *Ryōjin hishō*

In the fall of 1911, the historian Wada Hidematsu purchased a two-volume text entitled *Ryōjin hishō* at a used bookstore in Tokyo. He passed it to his friend Sasaki Nobutsuna, a well-known scholar of Japanese literature, who verified the text's identity as one of the "lost" volumes of GoShirakawa's twelfth-century collection of *imayō*. In its initial form, *Ryōjin hishō* seems to have spanned twenty volumes: ten devoted to song lyrics and another ten to a lengthy treatise on *imayō*.[4] The extant text is only a fraction of this whole. Of the song collection,

3. Zeitlin, "From the Natural to the Instrumental," 54.

4. In the catalogue *Honchō shojaku mokuroku* (Index of books in Japan; late thirteenth century), the text is included under the heading of "music" (*kangen*, literally "wind and string instruments") and listed as encompassing twenty scrolls. *Honchō shojaku mokuroku*, 35.

there is a fragment of volume 1 and the entirety of volume 2; of the treatise, there is a fragment of volume 1 and the entirety of volume 10. The text that exists today is barely 10 percent of the original.

This story of discovery and fractional recovery evokes the tension between absence and presence that haunts scholarship on the premodern past, especially performance practices transmitted from body to body. Peering back across the vanishing present, scholars depend on those rare tangible artifacts—manuscripts, in this case—to facilitate the imaginative work that interpretation requires. The unexpected "discovery" of new material highlights the fundamental imperfection of scholarly knowledge even as it provides an opportunity to clarify the content of the archive and dream up new ways of understanding.

Sasaki's 1912 transcription and publication of the volume Wada unearthed caused a sensation.[5] In one fell swoop, the archive of late Heian–period song expanded with more than five hundred new examples, and furthermore, due to the text's inclusion of several songs on topics not found in *waka*—female entertainers, puppeteers, gamblers, weasels, snails, and so on—it soon garnered labels like "a second *Man'yōshū*" (*dai-ni no Man'yōshū*) and "the people's song collection" (*shomin kayōshū*).[6] The "discovery," these labels imply, illuminated what had hitherto been lost to history. The thoughts and practices of everyday people who lived in the distant past were now accessible to all.

A text, though, is never simply a straightforward representation of the external world.[7] *Ryōjin hishō*, both the song collection and the treatise taken together, might transmit something of the lived experi-

5. For a revised edition published in 1957, see Sasaki, *Shintei Ryōjin hishō*.

6. Sasaki, "Jo," quoted in Konishi, *Ryōjin hishō kō*, 11; and Niunoya, "Chūseiteki geinō no kankyō," 47.

7. Paul de Man writes, "Literature is fiction not because it somehow refuses to acknowledge 'reality,' but because it is not *a priori* certain that language functions according to principles which are those, or which are *like* those, of the phenomenal world. It is therefore not *a priori* certain that literature is a reliable source of information about anything but its own language." De Man, "The Resistance to Theory," 11. De Man's cautious stripping away of whatever is uncertain about the relationship between language and the phenomenal world is well worth bearing in mind, but this does not mean that texts are entirely cut off from their social contexts.

ences of those who practiced, collected, and performed *imayō*, but it does so through the filter of GoShirakawa's textual apparatus.[8] What Wada discovered was not an unmediated collection of people's voices but instead a product of the retired emperor's long experience with *imayō*, a relationship that in turn was mediated by the unranked professional women who taught him. As much as *Ryōjin hishō* seems to bring to life a lost dimension of the cultural past with its large number of songs about non-elites, the stated fact of these songs' presence often overrides critical engagement with how the songs are situated and presented within the text. In this chapter, I argue that *Ryōjin hishō*, as a textualization of a living performance repertoire, constitutes not a reflection but a composite refraction: performance through text, orality through writing, low (unranked performer) through high (emperor), collective through individual, women through man. This structure of intersecting mediation gives the text a complexity that sustains conflicting interpretations about its nature and function. Is the collection text or performance, writing or oral transmission, high or low, individual or collective, written by one man or transmitted by a lineage of women? I approach *Ryōjin hishō* as a transgressive text, one that crosses composite boundaries even as it enacts new demarcations of social, literary, and religious space.

Mediation entails a doubling—one thing situated in relation to another—and so it is no mistake that *Ryōjin hishō*, as well as *imayō* and non-elite performance more generally, has often been discussed in terms of dualities. Gladys Nakahara, for example, writes, "The fact that aristocrats mixed with and learned from members of the lowest social ranks, such as *asobi* and *kugutsu*, was in itself '*imayô*.' Inter-societal mixing to this degree was unprecedented."[9] Here Nakahara doubles the referential power of *imayō*: it is not only a kind of song but also a mode of interaction. Through this doubling, she intensifies the associations between *imayō* and "mixing"—just as *imayō* songs bear the traces of "inter-societal mixing," so too does "inter-societal mixing" bear the traces of *imayō*.

8. Kawashima, *Writing Margins*, 76–78.

9. Nakahara, *A Translation of "Ryōjinhishō,"* 45.

But this "mixing" and "learning" was far from neutral, and it is difficult to imagine the textualization of *imayō* taking place in what Yung-Hee Kim Kwon calls a "supreme realm of art," in which "social differences are disregarded and replaced by relationships that transcend conventional class distinctions."[10] On the contrary, the text performs a dispossession of *imayō* knowledge and practice, transmitting it from unranked professional women to a powerful member of the imperial family and the courtiers affiliated with him. This particular textualization of *imayō* has continued to exist, at least in fractional form, but *imayō* as an embodied practice has long since vanished into the past.[11] We might hear a voice, but we can hear it only through the presence of the text. This does not deny the reality of *imayō* performance, without which *Ryōjin hishō* could never have existed. But the text does not simply record *imayō*, nor does it record *imayō* simply: GoShirakawa's motivations for writing down the songs and creating the accompanying treatise are more complex, grandiose, and idiosyncratic than those of a momentary act of preservation.

In essence, *Ryōjin hishō* intervenes in the flexible adaptations that characterize the medium of vocal performance by fixing songs into a sequence and replacing the everyday context of singing with a symbolic context of categorization not unlike that of *waka* anthologies. *Ryōjin hishō* is not only a collection of songs or an *aide-mémoire*, though it has at various points been understood as both. I instead argue that the work as a whole—that is, not only the songs but the way in which they are presented, situated, ordered, and interpreted through inscription and collection—transforms *imayō* from a high-context repertoire into a more abstract archive consisting of textual traces of embodied practice.

10. Kwon, "The Emperor's Songs," 266.

11. There have, however, been attempts by modern scholars and performers to resurrect these practices. For example, see Barbara Ruch's ongoing collaborative project "The Songs of Otomae," which seeks to restore "the art of a celebrity singer and her repertory of the popular songs of her day" through performance. Institute for Medieval Japanese Studies, "The Songs of Otomae." Additionally, the modern shamisen player Momoyama Harue's interpretation of twelve *imayō* can be heard on her CD *Asobi o sen to ya umareken: "Ryōjin hishō no sekai."* I thank Katherine Whatley for directing me to Momoyama's recordings.

What Was *Imayō*?

To understand the mechanics of this transformation, it is first necessary to touch on the history of *imayō*, its social contexts, and its assimilation into aristocratic spaces. Literally meaning "present style," the popular songs known as *imayō* were from an early date associated with *asobi* and *kugutsu*, entertainers who were skilled in a variety of arts.[12] Starting in the mid-Heian period, the songs were also recited by male courtiers during parties and other gatherings, and by the end of the Heian period, they were performed by *shirabyōshi*, professional female entertainers who dressed in men's clothing and sang and danced to the accompaniment of drums or the rapping of a closed fan.[13] The broad popularity of *imayō* by the twelfth century is epitomized by GoShirakawa's voluminous collection, but it was not unusual for courtiers in the eleventh and twelfth centuries to organize gatherings in which they mixed with professional performers of song and dance, including *imayō*.[14]

In contrast to *saibara* (folk songs set to *gagaku*), *imayō*'s assimilation into elite court culture took place relatively late, meaning that it retained an aura of otherness. This was likely intensified by the form's domination by female performers and its formal associations with vocal prowess and even excess.[15] Sei Shōnagon, for example, dismissed *imayō* as being "long" (*nagaute*) and having "unusual melodies" (*kusetzuitari*).[16] Around the same time, Murasaki Shikibu (b. ca. 970) described in her diary an amusing situation in which an older courtier tried to join a group of young courtiers who were singing *imayō*, only to give up once it became clear that his voice did not mix well with their "youthful and charming" (*wakau wokashiku*) sound.[17] *Imayō*'s unconventional melodies and connection with youthful voices

12. For a detailed summary of modern scholarship on *asobi*, see Tsuji, *Chūsei no yūjo*, 12–33.

13. For more on *shirabyōshi*, see Okimoto, *Ranmai no chūsei*, 42–72; and Strippoli, *Dancer, Nun, Ghost, Goddess*, 26–49.

14. Tsuji, *Chūsei no yūjo*, 57–88.

15. Strippoli, *Dancer, Nun, Ghost, Goddess*, 41.

16. *Makura no sōshi*, SNKBZ 18:418.

17. *Murasaki Shikibu nikki*, SNKBZ 26:213.

indicate a certain otherness and specificity of function within the court, to say nothing of its gendered associations. Okimoto Yukiko notes that depictions of aristocratic women singing are rare in court literature and, as a result, are typically presented as strange or unusual.[18] Singing, it seems, was risky for court women, which perhaps made female song all the more strongly associated with unranked women like *asobi* and *kugutsu*, the entertainers who ensured the broad dissemination of *imayō*.

A passage from *Sarashina nikki*, the diary of Sugawara no Takasue's daughter, suggests the general contours of how *asobi* figured in *monogatari* (tale literature) during the mid-Heian period.[19] While staying in a hut in the forests near Mount Ashigara (on the border of the provinces of Sagami and Suruga), the narrator and her entourage encounter a group of three *asobi*, who seem to "come out of nowhere" (*itzuku yori tomo naku idekitari*). The group, which consists of a woman in her fifties and two younger women, one about twenty years old and the other fourteen or fifteen, proceeds to sing for the travelers. The narrator comments on the performers' astounding beauty and the charm of their singing voices, which are "without comparison as they rise up into the sky" (*koe subete niru mono naku, sora ni sumi noborite*). But soon the performance is over, and the *asobi* "wander back into the fearsome mountains" (*osoroshige naru yamanaka ni tachite yuku*). The narrator becomes sad and lonely, wishing the splendid entertainers could have stayed longer.

This brief anecdote introduces several tropes often found in descriptions of *asobi*. First, they are not residents of urban centers but rather travelers who move through the countryside in search of work. The episode emphasizes this itinerant quality by noting that the *asobi* emerge from, and return to, the dark and threatening expanse of forest

18. Okimoto, *Imayō no jidai*, 152–55. Her examples include the "old-style" singing of the elderly nun in the "Tenarai" chapter of *Genji monogatari* (The tale of Genji; ca. 1010) and a similar scene in *Sagoromo monogatari* (The tale of Sagoromo; late eleventh century). One could add another example from *Genji*: that of Gen no Naishi, whose beautiful singing voice initially titillates Genji, but when he encounters it again years later, he instead hears "a toothless, puckered voice tinged with anxiety." *Genji monogatari*, SNKBZ 21:483.

19. The following summarizes *Sarashina nikki*, SNKBZ 26:287–88.

that stretches across the foothills. Another aspect stressed by the narrator is the prodigious beauty and exceptional singing voices of the *asobi*, something they share with *miko* (female spirit mediums). She describes them as "without comparison" twice during her narration of the encounter, emphasizing their remarkable quality.

In Terry Kawashima's analysis, the narrator's evocation of the memorable meeting is noteworthy for not mentioning the *asobi*'s "sinful" association with prostitution that figures so centrally in male-authored literary Sinitic works on the topic.[20] Kawashima argues that the narrator and other female authors who depicted *asobi* did not necessarily stand in solidarity with the non-elite female entertainers they described and that their depictions instead generally emphasize the *asobi*'s proficient musical performance above all else.[21] Such texts can still be understood as participating in "marginalizing processes" in relation to *asobi*, but in ways that are inconsistent with those of male authors.[22] The result is a different kind of otherness, one articulated as a virtuosic resonance that crossed boundaries of space and class.

Resonant Sounds: *Miko*, *Imayō*, and *Ryōjin hishō*

Evocations of *asobi* and other female performers, such as *miko*, often emphasize their ability to produce resonant sounds, be they virtuosic vocalizations or thunderous drumbeats. In *Yūjo no ki* (An account of asobi; ca. late eleventh century), for example, Ōe no Masafusa writes of *asobi* that "their voices arrest the clouds in the valleys, and their rhythms float along the water's surface."[23] Texts like this imagined the female voice as an exceptional extension of the body that was able to

20. Kawashima, *Writing Margins*, 69. Roberta Strippoli makes a similar point about the episode and furthermore emphasizes that the narrator recounts it with a rare enthusiasm—a striking contrast with the chiding tone she often directs at her younger self. Strippoli, *Dancer, Nun, Ghost, Goddess*, 22.

21. Kawashima, *Writing Margins*, 69–70.

22. Kawashima, *Writing Margins*, 72.

23. "Yūjo no ki," NST 8:307 (CJ: 154). For a full translation of the text, see Kawashima, *Writing Margins*, 295–97.

travel far and wide, and affect both other humans and natural phenomena.

In an essay on sound in the medieval period, Amino Yoshihiko argues that loud sounds (*kōshō*) were generally treated in two different ways. On the one hand, prohibitions against speaking in a loud voice were frequently issued, especially in religious contexts. But there are also several accounts and stories that dramatize the importance of loud noises in gaining the attention of the gods and buddhas. Sonic excess is thus ambiguous, alternately an object of regulation and an instrument of awe.[24] More generally, loud sounds played an important role in the realm of religious rites and festivals in premodern Japan, as evident in texts concerning the vocal performances and sonic significance of *miko*, women whose activities encompassed a wide range of ritual performance. *Ryōjin hishō* includes several songs about *miko*.

Lori Meeks argues that the place of *miko* within the history of religion has been largely ignored by contemporary anglophone scholars despite receiving ample attention in recent Japanese scholarship.[25] Although I am specifically interested in records depicting *miko* as musical performers, they did a great many things and occupied a wide range of social roles. Meeks writes that they constitute

> a large spectrum with *miko* employed at large shrines like Kasuga at one end, and entirely itinerant *arukimiko* who relied upon the donations of individual patrons on the other. In the middle were *miko* who enjoyed stable employment at small shrines [. . .], *miko* who worked as professional dancers outside official shrine employ, and a whole range of other women who specialized in some combination of musical performance and divine service. In short, *miko*, like Buddhist monks, occupied a number of different social roles.[26]

Yet unlike Buddhist monks, *miko* have been largely excluded from the secondary scholarship, not least because of the nontextual nature of their practices and the methodological difficulties this poses.

24. Amino, "Kōshō to biin," 31–34.
25. Meeks, "The Disappearing Medium," 209–10.
26. Meeks, "The Disappearing Medium," 224.

Miko were thought to be endowed with the power to give voice to the divine and to summon the attention of gods, spirits, and humans alike. Indeed, descriptions of *miko* often emphasize their superior skill in song, dance, and instrumental music. As virtuosic performers, they attracted audiences from far and wide, but as unranked professionals, they sometimes incited feelings of ambivalence or even outright distain. For example, as mentioned in chapter 1, the monk Jien described how after GoShirakawa died, several women associated with him were convinced they had become possessed by his vengeful spirit and called for the establishment of a memorial shrine. According to Jien's interpretation, though, these women had come under the spell of *miko* and other "mad people" (*kuruhimono*) who were acquainted with GoShirakawa.[27] As Tsuji Hirokazu shows, GoShirakawa indeed visited *miko* on several occasions, especially later in life during his frequent visits to Imagumo Shrine and Shin Hiyoshi Shrine, where he traveled to receive oracles. Tsuji further notes that there are both contemporary records of and later stories about GoShirakawa singing *imayō* for *miko* and having *miko* sing *imayō* for him.[28] Whatever Jien's agenda, it is clear the retired emperor, as someone who spent decades developing a commitment to *imayō*, interfaced with *miko* for both religious and instructional reasons.

Approximately a century before GoShirakawa started assiduously practicing *imayō* and spending time with *miko*, *asobi*, *kugutsu*, and other professional performers, Fujiwara no Akihira included a *miko* in *Shin sarugaku ki* as the lieutenant's fourth daughter—one of the audience members gathered to watch the *sarugaku*. Her substantial musical abilities attract crowds from far and wide:

> The wife of the fourth son is a female spirit medium [*kamunagi*].
>
> She is skilled at divination [*ura*], sacred songs and dances [*kagura*], summoning spirits by plucking a catalpa bow [*yotsura*], and giving voice to those spirits [*kuchiyosuru*].

27. *Gukanshō*, NKBT 86:292.
28. Tsuji, *Chūsei no yūjo*, 102–3.

When she dances, her sleeves flutter about like those of an immortal;
her singing voice, gentle and elegant, is like the cry of the paradisal *kalaviṅka.*

The atonal sound of her *koto* brings forth manifestations of the land deities [*chigi*];
the unrhythmic sound of her drum without fail makes foxes [*yakan*] perk up their ears.[29]

As a result, the men and women of the realm come in droves,
with near and far, high and low, forming markets [*ichi o nashite*].

There is no way to take in all the offerings of polished rice,
and no time to collect and count all the paper offerings.[30]

In describing the fourth daughter, the narrator contrasts the "gentle and elegant" quality of her voice with the "atonal" and "unrhythmic" sounds of her instruments. The dissonance indexes the *miko*'s ability to appeal to both humans and a range of supernatural creatures like spirits, gods, and foxes. As a *miko*, the fourth daughter can summon spirits by plucking a catalpa bow and then communicate the words of those spirits to a listening audience. But her other performances are also characterized in terms of religious appeal. Her singing voice, for example, is compared to the call of the *kalaviṅka*, a mythical bird

29. My translation of this passage follows Ōsone Shōsuke and Shigematsu Akihisa, who both interpret it as a description of the sounds produced by the *miko*'s instruments. See "Shin sarugaku ki," NST 8:139; and *Shin sarugaku ki, Unshū shōsoku*, 24. Kawaguchi Hisao, however, offers a different gloss: "Even though there are no sounds of the tonal *koto*, manifestations of the land deities appear; although there are no sounds of the rhythmic drum, foxes tilt their ears [in audition] without fail." *Shin sarugaku ki*, ed. Kawaguchi, 85. In Kawaguchi's reading, the land deities and the foxes are called to attention despite the absence of *koto* playing and drumming. Extant manuscripts of *Shin sarugaku ki* indicate disagreement from early on about the correct interpretation. For high-quality reproductions of three manuscripts (the *Kōanbon*, the *Koshōbon*, and the *Kōeibon*) held by Sonkeikaku Bunko, see *Shin sarugaku ki*, Sonkeikaku Zenpon Eiin Shūsei 42.

30. "Shin sarugaku ki," NST 8:302 (CJ: 139).

thought to reside in Amida Buddha's Pure Land.[31] The *kalaviṅka*'s own voice was often said to resemble that of the Buddha, so the bird is conventionally associated with enlightenment.[32] The *miko*'s plucking of her atonal *koto* strings summons land deities, who appear in temporary form (*yōgō*), and her unrhythmic drumming causes foxes (*yakan*) to perk up their ears. It might seem like this noise would repel human listeners, but the narrator makes a clear connection ("as a result") between the irregular sounds and the throng of men and women who surround her. The space she forges through her virtuosic vocal and instrumental performances transgresses ontological boundaries, drawing human and nonhuman together.[33]

As discussed in chapter 4, *Shin sarugaku ki* is a textualization of the urban space of the capital, the avenues of which mediated contact and exchange between people from a wide variety of social groups. The *miko*'s appeal can be read as an evocation of one such site of exchange. Those who "come in droves" to see the *miko* do not simply watch but "form markets" (*ichi o nashite*), presumably to purchase her oracular services and the services of other skilled urban workers. As Komine Kazuaki notes, it is no mistake that Akihira couples the *miko* with a husband who is a smith by profession (his name is Kanatsume Momonari, which literally means "metal-gathering one hundred creations") and also serves as the headman of the area south

31. Later in *Shin sarugaku ki*, Akihira mentions that the sixteenth daughter, an *ukareme* or prostitute, "has the voice of a *kalaviṅka* and the face of a heavenly maiden." "Shin sarugaku ki," NST 8:305 (CJ: 147). The sonorous voice of the *miko* and *ukareme* contrasts with that of the fourteenth daughter's husband, an "uncomposed idiot of the first order. He brags about himself in the most exaggerated fashion and disparages others despite his inferiority. He blathers on and on in a loud voice [*kōshō*]: a loquacious man with a plump face." "Shin sarugaku ki," NST 8:305 (CJ: 145).

32. The association is evident, for example, in Genshin's (942–1017) *Ōjō yōshū* (The essentials of rebirth in the Pure Land; 985). The text includes a story about how King Aśoka (ca. 268–232 BCE) did not convert to Buddhism until he heard the song of the *kalaviṅka*, which "bore an astounding resemblance to the voice of the Buddha." *Ōjō yōshū*, 366.

33. The anthropologist Rodney Needham has observed a broad connection between percussion and transition (communication with the "other world"). Needham, "Percussion and Transition." Although not percussion in a strict sense, the atonal noise produced by the *miko*'s *koto* can also be understood as acoustically complementary to her unrhythmic drumming.

of Shichijō.[34] Both figures would have been indispensable—the smith materially, the *miko* ritualistically—to the livelihood of the Eastern Market (Higashi no ichi), which occupied four blocks north of Shichijō.[35] With her magnetic voice and noisy instruments, we can imagine this *miko* as an agent who mediates relationships between humans and spirits, buyers and sellers, and is herself integrated into the vibrant craft economy located in the southeastern sector of the capital.

Given the associations with vocal performance shared by *miko* and *asobi*, it is no surprise that *miko* (and their male counterparts, *otoko miko*) appear in several of the songs collected in *Ryōjin hishō*, including three that highlight their ability to produce highly resonant sounds.[36] The second volume of the song collection, which consists of 545 songs, is divided into three main sections that each contains a different type of song.[37] In order, these are (1) *hōmonka* (220 songs about buddhas, priests, sutras, and other Buddhist topics), (2) *shiku no kamiuta* (204 "four-line god songs," which cover a wide range of material, including summoning gods [*jinbun*], buddhas, sutras, monks, miraculous occurrences, and "miscellaneous"), and (3) *niku no kamiuta* (121 "two-line god songs," which consist mostly of unclassified songs in addition to songs about shrines). To read this volume of the collection in sequence is to move from the highly textual and referential world of Buddhist thought to the more local imaginary of vernacular and often nontextual practices. It is the latter two sections that demonstrate the social breadth of the collection, with songs featuring a range of characters including woodcutters, gamblers, performers, children, and grannies.

Song 265 (a four-line god song from the "summoning gods" subsection) depicts one particular *miko* as a virtuosic performer whose spectacular labor produces a sense of awe within the listening community:

34. "Shin sarugaku ki," NST 8:302 (CJ: 139).

35. Komine, *Setsuwa no koe*, 108–9. For more on the Eastern and Western Markets, see Stavros, *Kyoto*, 22–23.

36. Yung-Hee Kim notes that there are "some twenty songs about *miko*" in the text. Kim, *Songs to Make the Dust Dance*, 5.

37. For an overview of the three types of songs found in *Ryōjin hishō*, see Kim, *Songs to Make the Dust Dance*, 46–58.

On Golden Peak[38]
The *miko* strikes her drum.
Striking high, striking low,
How wonderful!
Why don't we go there?
The echo of her drum—
teitontō, it cries and cries.
How does she strike it like that?
Surely this sound will never end.

kane no mitake ni aru miko no utsu tsuzumi
uchiage uchioroshi omoshiroya warera mo mairabaya
teitontō tomo hibiki nare hibiki nare utsu tsuzumi
ikani utebaka kono oto no taesezaruramu[39]

The song both describes and performs. It details the *miko*'s exceptional performance and her skill in producing a communal auditory experience: the sound of her drum resounds throughout the hills and mountains of the sacred landscape of Yoshino, drawing listeners to her just like the *miko* in *Shin sarugaku ki.* The emphasis on noise recalls the thunderous drums used in *dengaku* performance, but here the immediacy of the sonic excess pulls in more than it pushes away. It is furthermore clear that the song lyrics play with the capacity of language to communicate sensory experience. This is especially audible in the word *teitontō*, a *giseigo* (animate phonomime) that signifies iconically, rather than conventionally, the sounds produced by the *miko*'s drums—an attempt to transpose something of the drum's real-world sound into the song's lyrics. As a result, a recitation of the song both describes an experience of communal audition and performs a sonic transposition of some of the nonverbal elements that make up the *miko*'s music. When one sings the song, the textual representation of the *miko*'s music and the sensory experience of hearing it redouble in iteration.

38. A reference to Mount Kinpusen in Yoshino, an important center of *shugendō* practice long associated with the semi-legendary ascetic En no Gyōja. Wakita notes that this was the highest peak in the area and emphasizes its religious significance: it had connections to Zaō Gongen and was thought to symbolically evoke the inner pavilion of Tuṣita Heaven, one of the six heavens in Buddhist cosmology. Wakita, *Josei geinō*, 31.

39. *Ryōjin hishō*, SNKBZ 42:255.

The song's ability to communicate experience sensorially is further strengthened by the lexical echoes that resonate throughout it. These echoes can be heard, for example, in the repetition of *hibiki nare, hibiki nare*. They are also apparent when the *miko* "strikes her drum" (*utsu tsuzumi*) in the first and third line of the Japanese transcription of the song, and when the second syllable of the word "strike" (*utsu*) is immediately echoed by the first syllable of the word "drum" (*tsuzumi*). These echoes mimic the imagined reverberations of the *miko*'s drum, which, as suggested by the final line, will continue unabated. The gesture to an everlasting resonance emphasizes the divine and virtuosic aspects of the *miko*'s performance; it also signals that the song is itself about song and sound.

Two additional songs in *Ryōjin hishō* suggest the taxing physical labor required by such performances. Song 324 (also a four-line god song, from the "miscellaneous" subsection) is addressed to a *miko* named Tōta who struggles to stay in form:[40]

> Tōta *miko*, should you shake your bells like that?
> Bells are meant to be shaken above the eyes,
> swayed back and forth and thrust upward.
> When you shake your bells below the eyes,
> the gods will get angry and call you lazy. How scary!
>
> *suzu wa saya furu Tōta miko   me yori kami ni zo suzu wa furu*
> *yura yura to furiagete   me yori shimo nite suzu fureba*
> *ketai nari tote   yuyushi   kami haradachi tamafu*[41]

These bells (*suzu*), typically associated with *miko* performance and certain types of *kagura*, are better understood as "bell trees," hand-held rods on which small bells have been attached to a metal frame in

40. The editors of the SNKBZ edition note that although Tōta is generally a male name, here they understand the *miko* to be a woman. *Ryōjin hishō*, SNKBZ 42:271n324.2. In Akihira's *Meigō ōrai*, the suffix "-tōta" appears in the names Naitōta and Hakutōta, who play the flute and perform *sarugaku*, respectively, during the Inari Festival. "Unshū shōsoku," 192. See chapter 1 for a discussion of this passage.

41. *Ryōjin hishō*, SNKBZ 42:271.

FIGURE 6.1. *Miko* perform. The figure in the middle dances with a bell tree, while the six figures flanking her sing and strike the *tsuzumi. Nenjū gyōji emaki*, scroll 11. Courtesy of National Diet Library.

the shape of a pyramid.[42] (See figure 6.1 for an illustration from *Nenjū gyōji emaki* of *miko* performing with bell trees and other instruments.) That Tōta does not seem able to shake them in the proper manner—above, not below, her eyes—evokes the exhaustion induced by a performance consisting of the same motions repeated for long periods of time. Song 471 (an unclassified two-line god song) also references the

42. De Ferranti, *Japanese Musical Instruments*, 50.

demanding nature of this labor, albeit in a different register—first with annoyance and then with a touch of sympathy:

> It's the drum that wakes everyone up!
> Her hand must be so tired from striking it—how pitiful.
>
> *netaru hito uchi odorokasu tsuzumi ka na*
> *ikani utsu te no tayukaruran itohoshiya*[43]

Here the resonant echo of the *miko*'s drum (song 265) becomes an unwelcome noise that draws people out of their slumber. But the second line reverses course, speculating about the strain incurred by the hand that strikes the drum and offering a word of sympathy. The paradoxical tone suggests that *miko* performance was received with a certain amount of ambivalence.

Wakita contextualizes the demanding labor of *miko* performance with her own tactile experience with the bell trees used by Korean *mudang* (female shamans), which she notes are "considerably tough" to shake above the eyes. The difficult work of shaking instruments like these, she proposes, can be understood as a technique for dissolving the self and accelerating contact with the gods.[44] In this sense, song 324 both reflects the reality of the difficult bodily work performed by *miko* and, by referencing the anger of the gods, conveys the consequences of ritual failure. A high-stakes mode of contact with the gods and spirits, *miko* performance was both revered and policed.

As performers who bridged the human world and the spirit world, *miko* possessed the ability to produce extraordinary sounds and movements. Atonal *koto* playing and nonrhythmic drumming would have otherwise prompted censure from observers, but in the context of *miko* performance, these were awesome sounds that attracted listeners. In this sense, acoustic irregularity can be understood as a form of rule breaking that transports the listener to a liminal space in which communication with the gods is possible. The sounds of the *miko*'s

43. *Ryōjin hishō*, SNKBZ 42:311.
44. Wakita, *Josei geinō*, 32.

instruments echo from up on high, calling to attention humans, deities, and spirits alike. Numinous and auspicious, these sounds reverberate throughout the realm, imbuing it with the sacred and situating it within a wider cosmological order.

Writing the Material Voice in *Ryōjin hishō kudenshū*

The songs of *Ryōjin hishō* encompass a wide swath of social terrain and several different performance practices. In addition to *asobi* and *miko*, there are *kugutsu*, *jushi* actors, dancers, and even a group of dancing and instrument-playing animals. Because *imayō* were performed by professional female entertainers, it makes sense that the content of the songs in the collection would speak, in a variety of ways, to the world of performance in which they lived and labored. Reading *Ryōjin hishō*, it is difficult not to be struck by its glorious range of sounds, including musical performance, sutra recitations, crashing waves, fulling clothes, and the sound of silence.

As a vocal art, *imayō* encompassed both the semantic and the sonic, and the question of how to understand the function of *imayō* motivates much of the song collection's accompanying treatise, *Ryōjin hishō kudenshū*. GoShirakawa uses the treatise to anchor the history, significance, and ontology of *imayō* according to particular desires and sensibilities. The treatise can hence be read not only as an essay on *imayō* but also as a document of its author's investment in appropriating the practice of *imayō* for his own political, cultural, and religious aims.

The treatise, of which only the tenth and final volume is fully extant, begins with an introduction and a brief description of GoShirakawa's lifelong dedication to performing *imayō*. He notes that although several treatises (*zuinō*, *uchigiki*) have been written about *waka*, his is the first on the topic of *imayō*.[45] He then discusses his

45. *Ryōjin hishō*, SNKBZ 42:343. GoShirakawa singles out Minamoto no Toshiyori's (1055–1129) work of *waka* poetics *Toshiyori zuinō* (Toshiyori's poetic essentials; ca. 1115) as a model for his own treatise. In the preface to his work, Toshiyori laments

tutelage under the *kugutsu* Otomae (1086?–1169) before transitioning into a lengthy treatment of Otomae's professional lineage, her vocal prowess, her interactions with competing lineages, and various anecdotes about other *asobi*.[46] The next section, also of considerable length, consists of GoShirkawa's evaluations of the singing capabilities of several courtiers, some of whom are his disciples. He then recounts several stories about pilgrimages to temples and shrines, highlighting how *imayō* can be an efficacious medium for summoning the attention of the gods and buddhas. The treatise concludes with an endorsement of the idea of attaining rebirth in the Pure Land through *imayō* (*imayō ōjō*, memorably described by Kawashima as "discursive insurance"), a few thoughts about the transient nature of vocal performance, and finally speculation about whether his lineage of *imayō* performance will live on or disappear.[47]

The retired emperor's comments about the precarious ontological status of vocal performance illuminate how he conceived of *imayō* and sought to make use of it. He writes, "Because those who create Chinese poetry, sing *waka*, and practice calligraphy write down their works, these live on into the future without degrading in the slightest. The sad thing about vocal art [*koewaza*] is that once I pass away, there will be no way to record it. As a result, I have decided to create the first ever oral transmission [*kuden*] of *imayō* so that people can look at them after I am gone."[48] Here GoShirakawa locates the justification for his text in the ephemerality of vocal performance. He describes an intent to use text to arrest performance before its inevitable disappearance. Once enshrined in this new medium, the "oral transmission" (*kuden*) will remain "so that people can look at them after

---

the decline of *waka*: "How sad it is that the Way [of *waka*, *kono michi*] is perishing before my very eyes!" Quoted in Shibayama, "Ōe no Masafusa and the Convergence of 'Ways'" 315. For the original, see *Toshiyori zuinō*, SNKBZ 87:17. *Toshiyori zuinō* was an influential text, prompting a marked increase in the production of poetic treatises (*karon*), so it is no surprise that GoShirakawa would reference it in this manner. But it is likely that Toshiyori's efforts to reinvigorate the academic study of poetry also resonated with how GoShirakawa conceived of his own project.

46. On Otomae, see Strippoli, *Dancer, Nun, Ghost, Goddess*, 41–43.

47. Kawashima, *Writing Margins*, 95.

48. *Ryōjin hishō*, SNKBZ 42:380.

I am gone" (*nakaramu ato ni hito miyo tote*) even when they can no longer hear the performer's voice. Furthermore, GoShirakawa uses *imayō*'s dearth of material traces to differentiate it from elite cultural practices. In contrast to aristocratic pursuits like Chinese poetry, *waka*, and calligraphy, *imayō* lacks an inherent inscriptional dimension, and as a result also lacks a standardized framework that enables transfer from performance to text, repertoire to archive. This passage, and in a sense the entirety of the treatise, functions as a rationale for the creation of a new discourse that attempts to elevate *imayō* to the level of established aristocratic pursuits and thereby preserve it for posterity.

Such a project revolves around the evocation of *imayō* as a "vocal art" or "vocal practice" (*koewaza*).[49] In Heian Japan, as in "traditional Chinese discourse," voice rarely figured as a central concern in understandings of music's function and meaning.[50] But because *imayō* is a preeminently vocal practice, GoShirakawa's treatise resounds with observations about the voices of *asobi* and *kugutsu* (including that of his teacher Otomae, who taught him for ten years), the voices of courtiers who practiced *imayō*, and his own voice. This largely stems from the text's interest in establishing a lineage of transmission, such that discrete styles of singing can be marked and charted. But there is also a consistent component of evaluation, which transforms what would otherwise remain a conceptual voice into a material one.

This discursive act not only seeks to textualize performance and heighten the low but also to individualize the collective and assert ownership. GoShirakawa devotes a considerable amount of space in the treatise to describing communities of *imayō* performers, both professional women and aristocratic men, but he consistently returns to his own experience with singing, sometimes providing an extremely fine level of bodily detail. Toward the beginning of the treatise, he writes, "I have lost my voice three times. Twice I continued to

49. For a genealogy of *koewaza* from the eighth through twelfth centuries, see Abe, *Seija no suisan*, 61–85.

50. Zeitlin, "From the Natural to the Instrumental," 54. Zeitlin's chapter provides a useful overview of the emergence of different models of the voice throughout Chinese history.

sing according to the proper method and managed to produce a voice. If I strained too much, my throat became inflamed. Swallowing warm water had no effect, but I composed myself and kept on singing. I started by singing seven, eight, fifty, or even one hundred days in a row, after which I continued for even a thousand days. Although there were times when I did not sing during the day, not a single dawn broke without a song."[51] Losing his voice three times, continuing to sing even after losing his voice, singing for a thousand days in a row: the rapid multiplication of these figures seems designed to impress upon the reader the depths of the retired emperor's devotion to the performance of *imayō*. A second passage toward the end of the treatise makes this even more apparent:

> When on pilgrimage to shrines, I have often encountered divine manifestations while singing *imayō*. When I think about these instances, I do not understand why I should receive the gods' consideration: my voice is insufficient [*tarazu shite*] and devoid of any real skill [*tahe naru koto*]. Is it perhaps because of the many years I have devoted to practice? Or is it due to the power of faith [*shinriki*] particularly evident in my singing? All told I have spent more than forty years in fond devotion to *imayō*. Very few, even those of old, have committed themselves so resolutely. Despite my fondness, my voice is rough [*koe kohaku*] and faint [*tatazu shite*]; despite my deep regret, I am powerless to address these deficiencies.[52] But because of my years of practice, and regardless of my shockingly insufficient voice [*asamashiki fusoku no koe*], even competing with an abundant and splendid voice that cannot be surpassed, or with a woman's unapproachably high voice—in competition with both of these, my voice has never been discarded as unworthy. Due to my years of practice, even a soaring voice or a difficult low pitch are not difficult to produce.[53]

51. *Ryōjin hishō*, SNKBZ 42:344.

52. The verb *tatsu* (literally "to stand") means something like "resonant," "booming," or "fully formed" when used in relation to sound or music. My "faint" translates the verb when combined with a negative verb suffix.

53. *Ryōjin hishō*, SNKBZ 42:377–78.

Looking back on the decades he has spent singing *imayō*, GoShirakawa questions the religious utility of his voice, given its evident deficiencies. He alternately criticizes his voice as insufficient, devoid of skill, rough, and faint, but at the end of the passage, he emphasizes its range and flexibility, which ultimately seem to be a result of his long training. By describing his own voice in minute detail and stressing its imperfection but basic functionality, GoShirakawa demonstrates how his vocal practice aligns with Pure Land ideas about the strong connection between sincerity and rebirth. As far as his religious aspirations go, devotion seems to matter more than perfection.

Yung-Hee Kim Kwon has referred to the treatise as a "portrait of [GoShirakawa] as a private individual."[54] I would add that the portrait is shaded by descriptions of voice and vocal practice and their attendant connotations of immediacy, intimacy, and ephemerality. The treatise is a text about voice—how it works, what it enables and requires—even though it fundamentally lacks voice: it cannot transmit, beyond a crude representation, the vocal performances it describes, transcribes, and spins into stories. The tension between rhetorical presence and sensorial lack animates the treatise, even as it destabilizes its formal possibility.

What emerges through this tension is a thematization of GoShirakawa's own voice as something that links him with a wider performance community, be it *asobi* or the gods and buddhas. This is highly unusual given that, prior to the twelfth century, the emperor rarely sang. Okimoto Yukiko comments that by "intoning his 'voice' clearly, [GoShirakawa] brings individuality and humanity to the surface, revealing a living body [*namami*]."[55] In revealing this living body through detailed descriptions of his voice and vocal practices, the retired emperor claims the tactile physicality of *imayō* as a decisive component of a constructed cultural identity, one that distinguishes him from other members of the imperial family and contributes to, according to Kawashima, a "uniqueness and possibly 'renegade'

54. Kwon, "The Emperor's Songs," 262.
55. Okimoto, *Imayō no jidai*, 134.

quality."[56] In this way, GoShirakawa uses *imayō* to tell a story of transgressive engagement with bodily practices that flaunt conventions designed to regulate his social and symbolic interactions. The treatise does not signify the overcoming of differences of class and gender through a transcendent experience with art (note, for example, the recurrence of comparison and competition in the passage just discussed), nor is it one powerful elite's straightforward appropriation of peripheral practices or the triumph of peripheral performers in transmitting their culture into elite spaces. It is, instead, a transgressive and transactional fashioning, a flexible adaptation and abstraction designed to further a politico-religious agenda even as it transmits aspects of nontextual practices and lives.

GoShirakawa's treatise, as a self-identified *kuden* or "oral transmission" in textual form, and its fraught relationship with the wider community of *imayō* performers, embody the sociopolitical tensions between writing and orality in a broader ontological sense. Paul Zumthor's analysis of the differences between writing and orality in terms of scale, space, and lifespan will help draw out further some of the tensions that mark the treatise:

> In principle, if not always in fact, the oral message is offered up to public consumption: writing, in contrast, isolates. This notwithstanding, orality functions only in the midst of a limited sociocultural group: the need to communicate that sustains it does not spontaneously look toward universality, whereas writing, split between so many individual readers, buttressed on abstraction, moves freely only at the broad, social, level, if not at the universal. [. . .] Thus orality interiorizes memory, the same as it spatializes it: voice is deployed in a space whose dimensions are measured at its acoustic range [. . .] but that it never exceeds. Writing, certainly, is spatial as well, but in another way. Its space is the surface of a text: geometry without depth, pure dimension [. . .] while the indefinite repetitiveness of the message, in its intangible identity, assures its triumph over time. The text as a result is completely pliable: I read

56. Kawashima, *Writing Margins*, 93. Tsuji Hirokazu detects a similar facet of GoShirakawa's behavior, explaining it as the result of his lack of formal training as an emperor (he was not initially expected to succeed to the throne). Tsuji, "GoShirakawa to 'toshimin,'" 27.

it, reread it, cut it apart, put it back together, put it down or take it up as I will. It presents itself, in stone or on paper, as a whole and is perceptible as such.[57]

For Zumthor, orality lives and dies in a particular bounded social space, whereas writing, "buttressed on abstraction," opens toward the universal in its potentially limitless interactivity and repurposing. This depends in the narrow sense on the existence of objects—stone, paper—without which there could be no fixing of the whole, no twenty-first-century interpretation of a twelfth-century text. In this sense, despite its fashioning as a *kuden* and its obvious debt to generations of embodied transmission, GoShirakawa's song collection and the accompanying treatise should be approached first of all as writing, as something that can be picked up or put down, performed or read silently, reproduced or rearranged.

Does this mean that vocal performance as a phenomenon remains forever locked within its own sociotemporal space, impervious to probes from other times, places, and media? There are methods of conjuring what has been lost: for example, R. Murray Schafer's use of what he calls "earwitness accounts" to articulate in the present the contours of premodern soundscapes.[58] But in the end, perhaps it is most productive to approach disappearance as something to engage rather than overcome. In its material existence, *Ryōjin hishō* seeks to escape from the ephemerality of *imayō* performance through abstraction, with GoShirakawa putting brush to paper in an attempt to fill the gap ("there are no *imayō* treatises") before it becomes impossibly wide ("once I pass away, there will be no way to record it"). A preemptive sense of loss suffuses the treatise, a mood that brings about not acceptance but resistance to the inevitability of disappearance, resulting in a catalogue of *imayō*'s multitudinous uses. But something deeper is arguably lost in this drive to preserve. As Peggy Phelan writes, "the act of writing toward disappearance, rather than the act of writing toward preservation, must remember that the after-effect of disappearance is

57. Zumthor, *Oral Poetry*, 28–29.
58. Schafer, *The Soundscape*, 8.

the experience of subjectivity itself."[59] GoShirakawa deposited in his treatise countless details about his long practice and performance of *imayō*, details that have survived the ineluctable modalities of time and space. They survive, though, not as "an experience of subjectivity itself" but as something "split between so many individual readers," a collection of signs that do not exist altogether in the same world of embodied transmission as the songs and practices he would have them transmit. *Ryōjin hishō* and *Ryōjin hishō kudenshū* do not facilitate a direct experience with bodies and voices but instead remain as artifacts of textual mediation.

The "discovery" of these texts in the early twentieth century fundamentally changed how scholars understand the songs' formal and semantic scope, as well as the broader history of song of the late Heian period. If volume 2 of *Ryōjin hishō* enabled an expansion of the collective repertoire, volume 10 of *Ryōjin hishō kudenshū* facilitated a deeper engagement with GoShirakawa's idiosyncratic approach to his collection, an approach that largely revolves around his embodied abilities and experiences, and his anxieties about the transience of voice. The many voices audible throughout the collection of songs—those of *miko*, instruments, insects, animals, buddhas, gods, and humans—cannot be separated from the rough, faint, inflamed, and profoundly imperfect living voice of GoShirakawa. The two, just like the other forms of mediation discussed in this chapter, remain impossible to untangle. In the end, it is this messy and bounded relationality that an engagement with the text enables most of all.

59. Phelan, *Unmarked*, 148. Charlotte Eubanks uses this same passage to open a discussion of "the fluid relationship between body and text" within the corpus of medieval *setsuwa*. Eubanks, *Miracles of Book and Body*, 99.

CHAPTER SEVEN

Between Bodies

Performance, Identification, Illness, and Contagion

At the beginning of part 2, I briefly discussed the interrelatedness of crowds and bodies, despite their separation into the two parts that constitute this book. In this chapter, I explore this relationality further by focusing on how the two have been intertwined through the notion of contagion and its related discourses of excess and suggestibility. These discourses, observable in diary entries, accounts, histories, and literary texts, construed bodies as inherently susceptible to the movements and actions of other bodies, especially if those movements and actions were deemed aberrant or unorthodox. Because of this, in elite writings, there is a recurring association—sometimes overt, other times implied—between the otherness of non-elite performance and the abnormality of illness. Illness was often identified as a breakdown in normative performance (acts of excess, a lack of energy), and non-elite performance was at times apprehended as a kind of illness (rapidly spreading, immobilizing). The merging of the two indicates how they share a structural similarity as social experiences that intensify with density and proximity, as can be observed in the urban environment of the Heian capital. Both were seen as "other" states of being, alterities that triggered responses ranging from phobic distancing to curious attraction.

Modern allopathic medicine has tended to view illness as a biological phenomenon, much to the exclusion of social and psychological contexts.[1] But even the germ theory of disease takes for granted the centrality of social factors like density and proximity. Zoonotic diseases—including cholera, smallpox, mumps, measles, influenza, and chicken pox—were spawned in early states due to crowding brought on by agriculture and urbanism.[2] Without the dense congregation of humans and animals in sedentary societies, these diseases would never have flourished. Far from aberrations, outbreaks of epidemic and pandemic disease are reminders of the regular cost wrought by sedentary life and its attendant array of microbes.

It was not so long ago that scholars were able to consign such outbreaks to other times and places. For example, Wakita Haruko began her 1999 study of the Gion *goryōe* by noting the impossibility of imagining just how terrifying past epidemics would have been for those living through them—after all, she writes, we live after the discovery of antibiotics.[3] Reading this passage in August 2022, more than two years into the COVID-19 pandemic, I was struck by how quickly and how decisively our sense of the present's relationship to the past can change. The year 1999 may as well have been a different epoch, one in which something like the spread of COVID-19 would have seemed impossible, despite the 1918 influenza pandemic, the 2003 SARS outbreak, and other similar events in recent history. Contrary to Wakita's sensitive appeal to the limits of the historical imagination, it now requires all too little imagination to recall and inhabit the fear, uncertainty, and wide-scale suffering brought on by the global spread of a virus that confounded modern medicine.

Another factor often excluded by biological approaches to illness is the mind, specifically its capacity to impact the body. This exclusion is diametrically opposed to the Heian-period understanding, which saw body and mind as intimately connected, as discussed at the beginning of part 2. Today we speak colloquially of "psychosomatic" illnesses or disorders; the current psychiatric language is "somatic symptom disorders," which are "characterized by the prominent focus on somatic concerns and their initial presentation mainly in medical

1. O'Sullivan, *The Sleeping Beauties*, 8.
2. Scott, *Against the Grain*, 102.
3. Wakita, *Chūsei Kyoto to Gion matsuri*, 3.

rather than mental health care settings."[4] These are situations where behavior is disordered (months-long unconsciousness, repetitive seizures, unstoppable laughter) but without any identifiable biological or environmental causes. Perceiving something wrong—with one's body, with a community—but not being able to diagnose it, let alone fix it, is a form of apprehension that constitutes a broad layer of experience throughout history and certainly captures the fragile tenor of many records of illness and performance in premodern Japan.[5]

The notion of contagion has already surfaced in these pages, most directly in chapter 3, where I examined how elites emphasized the rapid "spread" and unknown provenance of the crowd performances that made up the Great Dengaku of 1096, a discourse that depends on an underlying metaphor of disease. I begin this chapter by tracing *dengaku* beyond the Heian period, focusing in particular on an early fourteenth-century record that speaks of a "*dengaku* illness" (*dengakubyō* or *dengaku no yamai*) sweeping through the realm. I argue that this shift from an implicit metaphor to an overt association of performance with illness suggests the appearance of a more discriminatory attitude toward *dengaku*. I use this shift in attitude as a point of departure to consider broader changes in how elites identified with social others, describing a three-stage movement from assimilation (seventh through ninth century) to apprehension (tenth through twelfth century) to rejection (beyond the twelfth century but starting especially in the fourteenth century). Having tracked the history of elite identification with non-elite performance, I conclude the chapter, and the body of this book, with an inversion: a discussion of a handful of non-elite acts of identification found in stories from the twelfth-century *Konjaku monogatari shū*.

4. American Psychiatric Association, *Diagnostic and Statistical Manual*, 310. The previous (fourth) edition of the manual used the term "somatoform disorders." Related terms often found in studies of similar phenomena include "conversion disorder" and "mass psychogenic illness."

5. For a captivating study of illness and illegibility in the "Kashiwagi" chapter of *Genji monogatari* and its related picture scroll, see Jackson, *Textures of Mourning*, 93–151.

Dengakubyō: Illness and Performance Beyond the Heian Period

In the spring of 1311, the aristocrat Tōin Kinkata recorded a remarkable convergence of illness and performance in his diary *Entairyaku*. On 1311/3/8 (Engyō 4), he wrote, "I've felt exhausted since this morning and have a cold-like cough. But other than a fever, I feel active. Food won't go down and I've struggled all night. Lately there has been an illness popularly referred to as the *dengaku* illness. It is said to be similar to the two- or three-day affliction. Perhaps this is what I've caught."[6] By this point, the association between *dengaku* and illness had long been established. As discussed in chapter 1, performances of *dengaku* regularly took place during the Gion *goryōe*, a festival designed to entertain and send away deities thought to cause illness. But Kinkata's locution marks a different kind of relationship: here *dengaku* is not an apotropaic performance that protects against the spread of illness, but illness (*byō* or *yamai*) itself. After centuries of proximity to rapidly spreading epidemics, *dengaku* here becomes the very thing it was intended to avert. If chapters 2 and 3 explore the transgressive ambivalence *dengaku* provoked in elites, in acts both textual and performed, Kinkata's invocation of *dengakubyō* registers a more direct othering in which non-elite performers become objects of fear and discrimination.[7]

Kinkata's brief record can be put into dialogue with other references to the 1311 epidemic. The chronicle *Buke nendai ki* (Chronology of the warrior house; a chronicle of events from 1180 to 1499), for example, states that the illness spread rapidly from Chinzei (Kyushu) to Ōshū (northeastern Honshū) between the third and fifth

6. Quoted in Iwasaki, "Sarugaku no setsuwa to oni," 39. For the original, see *Entairyaku*, 94. A slightly different and much abbreviated version is found in the chronicle *Zokushi gushō* (Foolish selections of history, continued; late eighteenth century): "An epidemic is spreading. It is known popularly as the *dengaku* illness." *Zokushi gushō*, SZKT 13:408.

7. Bialock notes that Kinkata elsewhere in his diary refers to *dengaku* as "*tenma no shoi*, or 'acts of demonic possession.'" Bialock, *Eccentric Spaces*, 231, 383n47.

months, that few avoided it, and that it resulted in the era name being changed.[8] Here the affliction is referred to as the "three-day illness" (*mikkabyō*), a name that suggests the duration of symptoms. Nakamura Akira has collected references to this illness from the medieval archive and argues that it can be understood in contemporary terms as a rapidly spreading cold or flu.[9] As a chronicle spanning a vast period of time, *Buke nendai ki* does not provide as much detail as Kinkata about how the disease was popularly understood: it offers a more distant view, whereas Kinkata's diary reproduces the chatter on the street.

The chaotic events of the spring of 1311 are memorialized most famously by section 50 of Kenkō's miscellany *Tsurezuregusa* (Essays in idleness; ca. 1330s). In his narrative, the illness bears a different name: "something that afflicted people for two or three days" (*futsuka mika hito no wazurafu koto*).[10] Just like the *Buke nendai ki*, Kenkō does not draw a connection between *dengaku* and the outbreak of illness but instead offers a different explanation in the unchecked circulation of a rumor (*soragoto*) about a demon. He tells the story of a woman from Ise who has been brought to the capital after turning into a demon. For twenty days, people go to see the demon and talk of little else except its whereabouts. According to Kenkō, no one reports a direct sighting, yet no one says it is an outright lie. One day he encounters a group of people who claim the demon is at Ichijō and Muromachi. He follows them and sees, from a distance, a large crowd of people near the retired emperor's viewing gallery (ordinarily used to watch the Kamo Festival), but after making inquiries, Kenkō learns that, once again, there are no eyewitnesses. He watches the spectators until nightfall; fights break out and other shocking things happen. Kenkō concludes with the following interpretation: "Around that time, the populace was afflicted with a two- or three-day illness, prompting

8. Quoted in Nakamura, "Chūsei no ryūkōbyō 'mikkayami,'" 309. For the original, see "Buke nendai ki," 154. Initially, 1311 began as the year Engyō 4, but due to the epidemic, the era name was changed, resulting in the new year of Ōchō 1.

9. Nakamura, "Chūsei no ryūkōbyō 'mikkayami,'" 308.

10. *Tsurezuregusa*, SNKBZ 44:121.

people to say, 'Those rumors [*soragoto*] about the demon were a portent [*shirushi*] of this illness.'"[11]

Up until this point, the narrative has tracked the spectacle of the "demon woman" and the boisterous crowds she attracted, but here Kenkō pivots and establishes a causal link between the rumors and the epidemic. As implied earlier in the story, the "demon woman" is not the issue, since after all Kenkō cannot find anyone who has actually seen her. What he does see is the frenzied behavior of suggestible crowds, a phenomenon made legible by linking it to the epidemic. Besides amounting to a form of prognostication, the passage's conclusion also registers the structure of contagion that is shared by rumors and epidemics: both spread rapidly from body to body, and both cause bodies to act in ways they otherwise would not. In one narrative, *dengaku* is illness; in another, rumors portend illness. In both cases, illness is rendered visible through crowd and performance behavior that spreads contagiously.

The springtime epidemic of 1311 took place more than a century after the end of the Heian period, the core temporal focus of this book. I start here not only to gesture toward *dengaku*'s transformation into an unambiguously malign force in the fourteenth century, but also because it vividly introduces the relationship between performance, contagion, and excess that had been burgeoning for centuries prior.[12] Resonances between them can be found in many of the documents already discussed, including visual depictions of open festivals (chapter 1) and records of the *dengaku* craze of 1096 (chapter 3). In this chapter, I use these associations to think more deliberately about the history and range of identification, and the varied forms of relationality between elites and non-elites, signified by such acts.

11. *Tsurezuregusa*, SNKBZ 44:121.

12. As Amino Yoshihiko has shown, prior to the Nanbokuchō period (1333–1392), peripheral populations were often understood as embodying a kind of sacrality, an association that conjured an ambivalent mixture of fear and awe. See Amino, *Igyō no ōken*, esp. 23–36. Amino makes this argument throughout his monograph in reference to a variety of cultural practices, from clothing styles to stone throwing (*tsubute* or *inji-uchi*).

Contagion and Identification

As suggested by the stories and accounts circulating with and around the "three-day illness," performance and illness triggered similar anxieties about contagion and control. Broadly speaking, illness is often thought to involve intrusion by an external force, be it a virus, bacterium, or something more ambiguous. It is for this reason that Italians in the eighteenth century described the viral infection now commonly known as the flu as *influenza* or "influence"—the idea was that an "influence of unknown origin (probably the stars)" caused the sickness.[13]

An "influence of unknown origin" could just as easily describe the several rapidly spreading crowd performances discussed in this book. Masafusa, for example, echoed such rhetoric at the outset of his account of the Great Dengaku of 1096 by noting that "there were many *dengaku* performances in the capital, but no one knows where they began."[14] Nearly forty years later, in an entry dated 1133/5/8 (Chōshō 2), Munetada extended the trope of uncontrollable influence to the performing body when he saw a particularly jarring performance of *dengaku* as part of the Uji Shrine Festival (Uji rikyū sai):

> Today was the Festival of the Guardian Deity of the Uji Detached Palace. This is celebrated by the unranked attendants [*genin*] from the environs around Uji. I arrived around the Hour of the Sheep [2:00 p.m.] at an open corridor of the Byōdōin to watch. There were a few *miko* and youths parading on horses [*umaosa*], and *dengaku* and *sarugaku* performers who, attired as priests [*hōshi*], executed a series of miscellaneous performances [*zōgei*]. It was impossible to count the onlookers: several thousands of unranked attendants watched from boats, which looked like a line of roof tiles. There was no end to the performances of the *dengaku* priests. They played no set pieces on their flutes, instead leaving it to their mouths; they struck no set rhythms on their drums, instead

13. Flu was known in French as *la grippe* (from *gripper*, to attack or to seize), which suggests an even more aggressive challenge to the body. "Statement Regarding Influenza," 3366.

14. "Rakuyō dengaku ki," NST 23:219 (CJ: 218).

> leaving it to their hands. Such clamorous drumming and fluting shocked people's ears and eyes.[15]

Munetada was perturbed by the sounds he encountered because they seemed to issue from bodies acting directly on and through instruments, without recourse to the mediating authority of a set melody or rhythmic pattern. In "leaving it" (*makasu*) to their hands and mouths, the performers produced music that was illegible to listeners who expected a more regulated sound. In contrast to this sonic disorder, the literary Sinitic prose Munetada employed to register his critique makes use of an ordered and symmetrical parallelism (the three "couplets" have character counts of 4–3, 4–3, and 4–4). There is hence a gap between sensory experience and written representation, one that exemplifies the broader tensions between the disorienting influence of performance and the conventional ordering of writing. As this entry demonstrates, the fear of suggestion often prompts a reimposition of order.

The problem for Masafusa, Munetada, and other elites who found themselves peering at and sometimes participating in cultural contact zones can be productively understood in terms of identification.[16] How did they attempt to make sense of unfamiliar practices? Did they appropriate them for their own political gain, or did they use them to diagnose or to prognosticate? The history of the modern concept of identification offers some clues for unpacking the various kinds of relationality that inhere in these records.

In her study of identification, Diana Fuss examines Sigmund

15. *Chūyūki*, ZST 15:42. This entry is the earliest extant description of the festival. Uji Shrine had long been a site of ancestor worship for the imperial family, and with Fujiwara no Yorimichi's (992–1074) strong connections to Uji, by the twelfth century the site had become a familiar retreat for aristocrats. On the history of Uji Shrine and its relationship to performance, see Hayashiya, *Chūsei geinōshi no kenkyū*, 327–42. For a more detailed study of the festival, see Yamaji, *Uji sarugaku to rikyū sai.*

16. On contact zones, see Pratt, "Arts of the Contact Zone," 34.

Freud's articulation of the concept and the centrality of two "dominant metaphorics," ingestion and infection.[17] She observes:

> Unlike the ingestion model of identification, which stresses the subject's annihilation of the Other through oral incorporation, this other kind of identification works more like a case of contagious infection in which it is the subject who is vulnerable to invasions from without. [This latter] disease model of alterity depicts the subject as peculiarly vulnerable, even *susceptible*, to sudden invasions from the Other. It represents alterity as an infectious agent that can spread through unseen currents of "mental infection," putting every subject at potential risk.[18]

If "ingestion" is an active and punctual form of identification, then "infection" is passive and durative, such that "every subject" is potentially "susceptible" at all times. Importantly, the metaphoric shift from ingestion to infection within Freud's theory of identification tracks the expansion of his psychoanalytic project from the individual to the group: identification becomes predominantly passive and infectious when the individual's relationship to the broader social unit is highlighted.[19]

In premodern Japan, the modalities of elite identification with non-elite performance practices similarly delineate a diachronic move from ingestion to infection, active to passive. The centralized *ritsuryō* state that formed in the seventh and eighth centuries, with its investment in cultural assimilation and territorial expansion, viewed difference as something to be absorbed and integrated. Even heterodox practices like *sangaku* and *zōgei* were housed, at least for a time, within the official bureaucracy. But a shift in governance away from centralization and assimilation, well underway by the eleventh century, meant that the imperial family was only one entity in a wider field of institutions in which performers plied their trade. For courtiers and scholars like Munetada and Masafusa, this heralded a more passive relationship to social others: the court—and, by extension, the capital—were no

17. Fuss, *Identification Papers*, 40.
18. Fuss, *Identification Papers*, 40–41 (emphasis in original).
19. Fuss, *Identification Papers*, 40.

longer sites of cultural integration but rather heterogeneous spaces that mediated a range of identifications, some of which seemed to spread uncontrollably. It was not until the fourteenth century that such passive identifications became dominant and phobic discourses of discrimination emerged.

Suggestible Bodies: Another View of Identification

Records of performance are, inevitably, imbued with the values of those writing them. There are no emic records from the Heian period produced by non-elite performers for the simple reason that they could not write. As I have argued throughout this book, performers' inability to leave their own marks on the written record does not mean that they did not influence the actions of elites or transmit their practices from body to body. The written record can be selective, especially regarding phenomena that impinge on the social order's core fragilities and anxieties. But there are exceptions to this basic archival pose, and they often come in the form of "literature"—that is, texts that suspend questions of factuality and historicity in favor of an appeal to truthfulness, the workings of which cannot be reduced to positivism or scientific rationalism.

In chapter 2, I explored a story from *Konjaku monogatari shū* (28:7) in which the monk Kyōen has a shocking encounter with a group of noisy *dengaku* musicians who had been assembled due to an official's misunderstanding. In that story, the articulation of the performing crowd conformed to prevailing elite perceptions that stressed the crowd's otherness and illegibility, therefore reinscribing elite anxieties about *dengaku*. But because *Konjaku* runs the gamut in terms of content as well as tone and perspective, it should come as no surprise that its stories encompass various treatments of non-elite performance.

Consider "The Matter of Governor of Izu Ono no Itsutomo's Deputy" (28:27), another story from the twenty-eighth volume, which, as noted in chapter 5, centers around humor.[20] In it, an unnamed pro-

20. The following is a summary of the story as found in *Konjaku monogatari shū*, SNKBZ 38:222–25. For an English translation, see Dykstra, *Buddhist Tales of India*,

vincial deputy governor, formerly a *kugutsu* puppeteer, encounters and identifies with the embodied practices he no longer performs. But unlike Kyōen's momentary confrontation with the *dengaku* crowd and the jolt of abjection it provokes, in this case the narrative perspective stays close to the puppeteer as he tries to make sense of how his life has changed. As Terry Kawashima notes, the story offers a "counter-narrative to the seemingly monolithic discourse of the 'nomadic kugutsu,'" as seen in Masafusa's account and other Heian-period literary Sinitic treatments.[21] The story portrays the former puppeteer's social mobility as a function of his bodily and intellectual skills, but body and mind are also what link him inexorably to his past as a performer. Revolving around how the man's *kugutsu* past clings to his present, the story provides an extraordinary account of non-elite identification.

It all begins with a staffing issue: Ono no Itsutomo, the governor of Izu Province in eastern Japan, needs a deputy. He hears of someone in Suruga Province, which borders Izu to the west, who is "intelligent, savvy with official business, and has good penmanship" (*zai kashikoku wakimahe arite, te nado yoku kaku*). Pleased, Itsutomo summons him. When he arrives, the governor sees before him "a greatly overweight man of around sixty years who seemed composed and experienced" (*toshi rokujū bakari no wonoko no, ohoki ni futorite shikutokuge nari*). The man furthermore "makes a sour face, with no hint of a smile" (*uchi wemi taru ke mo nakute, ke nikuge naru kaho shitareba*). Itsutomo thinks to himself that this man would make an excellent deputy, and has him demonstrate his writing ability. His skills are not spectacular, but his "light brushwork" (*fude karokute*) befits that of a deputy.[22] The governor next tests the man's clerical skills by giving him a jumble of tax documents and asking him to calculate the income. He produces counting sticks and easily completes the calculation. "I cannot tell if he is a trustworthy person [*kokoro wa*

China, and Japan, 921–22.

21. Kawashima, *Writing Margins*, 41n41.

22. The description of his brushwork as "light" perhaps channels the broader approbation for lightness and speediness in *sangaku* and related forms. If so, the description can be read as foreshadowing the reveal of the deputy's past identity.

shirazu]," thinks Itsutomo, "but he sure is good at clerical work." The governor appoints him as deputy, and for the next two years, Itsutomo keeps him close by and delegates to him all manner of business. Not once does the man go against Itsutomo's wishes; he simply takes care of everything properly and quickly. Greatly pleased with his performance, the governor grants him bonus resources from within the province. The deputy lets none of this go to his head and, as a result, earns the trust and respect of both the province's officials and its people. His reputation as a wise man spreads even to neighboring provinces.

But one day, as the deputy sits in front of the governor while working on documents and affixing the provincial seal to them, several *kugutsu* puppeteers arrive at the compound and gather before the men. They sing songs, play the flute, and dance with great skill. Itsutomo feels somehow transported by the fascinating spectacle, but glancing at the deputy, he notices that whereas the man had previously sealed documents properly, he now "presses the seal in a three-beat rhythm according to the puppeteers' fluting and singing" (*kono kugutsu domo no fukiutafu hiyaushi ni shitagahite, sando hiyaushi ni in o sashinu*). Thinking this strange, the governor looks closely and sees the deputy's broad shoulders moving to the same rhythm. Observing the same phenomenon, the puppeteers sing, play their flutes, strike rhythmically with added vigor, and hasten the tempo. All of a sudden, the deputy "belts out in a deep, throaty voice" (*futoku karabitaru koe o uchi dashite*) and joins them in song. The governor looks on in shock and wonders what is going on. The deputy, still sealing documents, says, "It is hard to forget the past [*mukashi no koto*]," and he quickly stands up and starts dancing, causing the puppeteers to play with even greater intensity.

Seeing this, the other officials in the compound laugh at and mock the deputy, who, now feeling ashamed, tosses away his seal and runs off. Thinking the whole thing strange, the governor asks the puppeteers what in the world is going on. The man, they tell him, used to be their attendant, and having heard he became a deputy, they figured he might not have forgotten about his "old heart" (*mukashi no kokoro*), and so they decided to visit. From the puppeteers' explanation, the governor and the gathered officials learn the truth of the deputy's past identity. Afterward, the officials in the compound and all the people in the province label him the "puppeteer deputy" (*kugutsu mokudai*) and have a good laugh. The deputy's reputation suffers, but the governor takes pity on him and retains his services. We are told that despite purposefully forgetting about his past, the deputy still retains the heart of a *kugutsu*. The narrator concludes the story by noting that people in the province think the deputy has been possessed by the puppeteer god (*kugutsugami*).

The story relies for its effect on tensions of contact and characterization. On a basic level, it dramatizes a contact zone forged by the encounter of provincial officials with the puppeteers who have come to the compound to perform. The climactic reveal, of course, is that the deputy is a former puppeteer, or at least someone who spent ample time as an attendant to the puppeteers. But his past has been buried by the single-minded seriousness with which he pursues his official duties. The governor quickly determines that the man possesses the temperament, deportment, and skills needed to succeed as a deputy, and everything about him seems solid and dependable—except for his "light brushwork," which might foreshadow his former identity.

The moment of contact between the puppeteers and the officials quickly turns into a vector of contagious identification. The rhythm of the music triggers the deputy's embodied, unconscious memories, and before he realizes what is happening, his actions have synchronized with those of the puppeteers. The idea that the deputy now seals his documents in a "three-beat rhythm according to the puppeteers' fluting and singing" is probably meant to be amusing, but it also suggests the power of sound and vibration in exhuming forgotten experiences and techniques. In this moment of embodied remembering, the deputy becomes a fusion of past and present as he performs his present official labor in a style that belongs to his past. The "infection" spreads from the deputy's hand to his shoulders, which begin to move to the beat, and when the puppeteers intensify the tempo, he adds his "deep, throaty" voice to the song and joins in the dancing. His hand, shoulders, voice, and, finally, entire body are "possessed": the deputy's memories surge forth in an irresistible wave of kinetic energy that suppresses his more recently acquired clerical comportment.

Despite appearing in a tale collection that often avoids psychological characterization (as in the famous story of the thief who encounters a dead woman in Rashōmon gate, which depicts bare lives of precarity with hardly any reference to feeling, emotion, or state of mind), this story revolves around the affective implications of forgetting and remembering for one's sense of self.[23] The deputy's sudden identification with a forgotten past, triggered by a chance encounter with the puppeteers' music, exposes him to ridicule and shame. He forgets himself, even as his self is revealed to be something other than what it seemed to be. The band of puppeteers anticipate this: they decide to visit the compound because they have heard their former attendant is there. They wonder if his "old heart" might still be receptive to the rhythms it once knew. The narrator confirms this dynamic at the end of the story by stating that the deputy "retained the heart of a *kugutsu*" despite having "forgotten about his past." Redeemed by the governor in no small part due to his years of good service, the deputy continues to deputize—but the encounter marks him as identifying with the puppeteers and their distinctive bodily practices, even if he had forgotten about them. The story proposes the idea that practices like these survive not only in textual records or through intentional embodied transmission but also as a kind of muscle memory, latent and noncognitive, poised to replicate given the right circumstances.[24]

The story never explains why the music has such immediate power over the deputy or why he has forgotten about his past relations with the puppeteers. He is already in his sixties when the governor decides to employ him, and there is no information about how he made a living before this. With details like these omitted, the story materializes like scaffolding over a gaping hole. This makes the climax, with its scene of sudden conversion of work to performance, even more dramatic. It is also worth noting that the centrality of absence aligns with psychoanalytic understandings of trauma, whereby forgetting often signifies

23. For "How a Thief Who Climbed to the Upper Story of Rashōmon Gate Saw a Dead Person" (29:18), see *Konjaku monogatari shū*, SNKBZ 38:346–47. For an English translation of the story, see Dykstra, *Buddhist Tales of India, China, and Japan*, 985.

24. The automaticity with which the deputy's forgotten memories return recalls Richard Dawkins's meme theory of cultural transmission, which sees longevity, fecundity, and copying fidelity as the main criteria for successful cultural replication. Dawkins, *The Selfish Gene*, 245–60.

ongoing repression, which in turn may indicate a past trauma.[25] As mentioned in chapter 3, *kugutsu* lived precarious lives that bore little resemblance to Masafusa's idealized image of them. Unlike his account, this story's thematization of forgetting, remembering, and identification allows the reader to apprehend the deputy's experiences and personal history. The tight narrative focus on the deputy strengthens this sense: the story is not about puppeteers in general but rather about the life of a single former puppeteer who negotiates the eruption of the past into the present. As a result, the story affords a more intimate look at how identification works for a low-ranking functionary, a remarkable and rare phenomenon made possible by the breadth of *Konjaku*'s social imaginary and folkloric narrative perspective.

The connection between psychological distress and suggestibility hinted at by the *Konjaku* story is a common trope in narratives concerning inexplicable and often excessive bodily acts, especially those that seem to spread through contagion. The trope is evident, for example, in the accounts of the Shidarajin Incident of 945 and the Great Dengaku of 1096, in the records of the Yasurai Festival of 1154, in the entangling of rumor and performance during the epidemic of 1311, in the outlawing of communal dancing in the streets of Kyoto in the early sixteenth century, and in the postwar scholarly interpretation of the *ee ja nai ka* ("Isn't it great?") parades and dances of 1867.[26] It furthermore persists throughout world history, in premodern and modern times alike. For example, consider the outbreaks of choreomania in medieval Europe, such as the dancing plague that gripped Strausburg in 1518, which John Waller argues was "spread not by foul breath, vermin, or dirty water, but through the equally potent forces of sight and suggestion."[27] More recent phenomena include the epidemic spread of laughter among schoolgirls in Tanganyika following Tanzania gaining independence in 1961 and Sweden's "sleeping children epidemic," in

25. See, e.g., Freud, "Fixation to Traumas," 338–42.

26. On the Yasurai Festival, see Kawane, *Chūsei hōken shakai*, 55–93; and Bialock, *Eccentric Spaces*, 227–31. On communal dancing in Kyoto in the sixteenth century, see Berry, *The Culture of Civil War*, 55. On the *ee ja nai ka* parades and dances, see Miura, *Agents of World Renewal*, 109–10.

27. Waller, *The Dancing Plague*, 108.

which hundreds of children granted asylum to the country since the 2000s have become bedridden with "resignation syndrome."[28]

These varied examples all consist of bodies collectively behaving in ways that exceed the boundaries of conventional structures of diagnostic knowledge. Simply put, they are phenomena that cannot be easily explained or ignored, and as a result, they trigger crises of interpretation. Masafusa's "spirit foxes" and Munetada's "strange spirits," for example, are attempts to reframe the illegible and unnamable within a more familiar ontological order. But as demonstrated by the story about the *kugutsu* deputy, identification need not be about interpretation and can indeed signify the practices that constitute embodied transmission. Though literate elites tended to transpose seemingly strange movements into writing as a way to stymie the capacity of transgression, performers (sometimes including elites) allowed the kinetic contagion to inhabit their bodies, transforming into vectors of viral transmission. This, too, is identification: welcoming the suspension of the boundary between self and other and allowing one's body to be moved.

Raucously Dancing in the Mountains

To further articulate the notion of embodied identification, I conclude this chapter with a discussion of one last *Konjaku* story—in fact, the very next story in the collection, entitled "How Nuns Went to the Mountains, Ate Mushrooms, and Danced" (28:28).[29] This memorable story begins with a group of woodcutters who have become lost in the hills of the Kitayama area north of the capital. Four or five "raucously dancing" (*imijiku mahikanadete*) nuns suddenly emerge from the depths of the mountain, and the woodcutters wonder what they are looking at—surely not people, they initially think, but perhaps *tengu*

28. For the laughter epidemic, see Hempelmann, "The Laughter." For the sleeping children epidemic, see O'Sullivan, *The Sleeping Beauties*, 13–39.

29. *Konjaku monogatari shū*, SNKBZ 38:226–28. For an English translation of the story, see Dykstra, *Buddhist Tales of India, China, and Japan*, 922–23.

or other supernatural beings (*onigami*). As the nuns get closer, the woodcutters, despite being "intensely afraid" (*imijiku osoroshi*), ask why they are dancing so deep in the mountains. The nuns acknowledge the frightfulness of the scene and offer an explanation. They came to the mountains to pick flowers for offerings to the Buddha but before long lost their way. Discovering some mushrooms, they figured it would be better to eat than die of starvation, so they cooked the mushrooms and found them to be exceedingly delicious, though now they found themselves "dancing involuntarily" (*kokoro narazu maharu nari*). The woodcutters are shocked by the nuns' story, but they too figure it is better to eat the mushrooms than die of starvation, so they do just that and soon find themselves dancing as well. And so the nuns and the woodcutters dance together and laugh. After some time has passed, they feel as if they have awoken from drunkenness, and without knowing where they are going, both groups leave. This, the narrator concludes, is why the mushrooms are called *maitake* (literally, "dancing mushrooms"), though not all who eat them start dancing.

True to form for much of this part of the *Konjaku* collection, the story has a simplistic and amusing veneer: some nuns and woodcutters eat mushrooms and dance, and as it happens, this is the story that provides a folk etymology for the word *maitake*. The narrator explains at the outset why the nuns and the woodcutters are in the forest, but leaves much unstated. Why are both groups fearful of starving when there is no indication that they have been lost for a substantial period of time? And just what kind of mushrooms are these? The "involuntary" (*kokoro narazu*) and "raucous" (*imijiku*) nature of the dancing suggests that these are not the *maitake* widely available in supermarkets today but instead another name for psilocybin mushrooms, which typically trigger hallucinations, laughter, and euphoria when ingested. But this too is unclear; perhaps similar sensations would be produced by eating nontoxic mushrooms if one were hungry enough.

The point of the story is not the *maitake* themselves, despite their crucial role in the coming together of the two groups, but the way the remote forest becomes a transgressive space as the nuns and woodcutters join together in laughter and wild dancing. Just as Munetada described the *dengaku* musicians acting directly on their instruments without recourse to musical conventions at the Uji Shrine Festival, here the two groups submit to the mushrooms' effects and enter a liminal space of boisterous performance and suspended social conventions. In this moment of excess, identities slip away and the woodcutters, who moments earlier were shocked and amazed by the nuns' behavior, engage in collective exultation. This annihilation of the self cannot last, however, and before long they return to the social order "as if waking from intoxication" (*yoi no sametaru ga gotoku shite*). Other than a brief note about each group returning to their respective homes, there is no indication about the aftermath. From beginning to end, the narrative remains tightly trained on what happened in the forest in the hills to the north of the capital.

This carnivalesque scene recalls *utagaki* (or *kagai*), which in early Japan seem to have consisted of people gathering at "geographic extremities"—places like forests, mountains, capes, markets, and shrines—to sing, dance, and pursue unconventional sexual relationships.[30] The *fudoki* gazetteers (eighth century), which provide the earliest records of these festivals, describe men and women heading up to the mountains during moments of seasonal transition (in spring when flowers blossomed and in fall when leaves changed color) to sing, dance, play music, and eat.[31] Benito Ortolani describes *utagaki* as "a kind of primitive carnival without masks," but he notes their eventual assimilation, as group dances and songs, into politically central spaces (such as the Nara court) and mainstream cultural practices (such as *hanami* and the *bon-odori* festival).[32] Similarly, Herbert E. Plutschow views the *utagaki*'s original "orgiastic" character as indicating a certain "ritual freedom from ordinary social bonds."[33]

There is nothing overtly sexual about the woodcutters' encounter with the nuns. There are, however, more general echoes of *utagaki* throughout the story, as the forest becomes a space in which social identities dissolve and communal acts of singing, dancing, and eating

30. Plutschow, *Chaos and Cosmos*, 119.

31. Nakahara, *A Translation of "Ryōjinhishō,"* 52–53.

32. Ortolani, *The Japanese Theatre*, 9. For a more detailed discussion of this assimilation, see Plutschow, *Chaos and Cosmos*, 123, 127.

33. Plutschow, *Chaos and Cosmos*, 122, 120, respectively.

flourish. This *Konjaku* story, like the one that precedes it and like the wider archive of non-elite performance, demonstrates the attractive force of performance and the abiding appeal, even if involuntary, of experiencing something else, something lost, something forgotten.

Dengaku, *sangaku* and *sarugaku*, *imayō*, *kugutsu*, and the diverse repertoires of singing, dancing, acting, and musicking they embodied and transmitted, formed a collection of transgressive practices that drew high and low together and prompted negotiations along intersecting lines of class, culture, and cosmology. These negotiations took place in both social and symbolic spaces: directly on the streets of the capital and at temples and shrines; and indirectly within the discursive space of elite records, accounts, and picture scrolls. Viewed from a remove, such moments of contact lay bare modalities of identification and enable a granular understanding of how the embodied practices of non-elites contributed to broader cultural shifts. Non-elite performance was a vibrant component in, to borrow Carol Fisher Sorgenfrei's words, the "reversible, transformative processes [by which] the self and the double exist simultaneously."[34] Far from being treated as isolated distractions or simplistic entertainments, the performances analyzed throughout this book occupied a central, constitutive position in the elite imaginary, in the Heian period and beyond.

34. Sorgenfrei, "Reversibility," 170–71.

CONCLUSION

The Performance in the Document

Throughout this book, I have used archival documents—histories, diary entries, literary texts, images—to explore the form, content, and context of past performances. I have argued that these works depict, in various ways and for countless purposes, performance's ability to mediate a transgressive relationality between elites and non-elites. Performances of *dengaku*, *sangaku* and *sarugaku*, *imayō*, and *kugutsu* constitute a robust repertoire of boundary crossing and negotiation, and they demonstrate the breadth and diversity of Heian culture.

The mechanics of transgression and social fluidity suggested by these primary sources has led me to reflect on my own practices of research and writing, which similarly delineate patterns of shuttling between here and there, now and then, experience and document. In which forms, venues, and modes have I encountered past objects? How has my archival research been inflected by experiences like attending and documenting contemporary folk performances (*minzoku geinō*) in Japan? What, in the end, has my work taught me about apprehending the past in the present?

First Frozen, Then on Fire: Documenting Contemporary *Kagura* and *Dengaku*

Memories from the Flower Festival: the damp cold, the dry smell of freshly cut wood and paper, steam from the cauldron, an array of trucker hats, LED lights flooding from NHK cameras, the entangled rhythms and melodies of flutes, voices, and bell trees ferrying me through cycles of shallow sleep, the ocean of the dawn sky as it slowly turns from charcoal blue to white.

I spent the 2011–2012 academic year studying at the University of Tokyo with the noh scholar Matsuoka Shinpei and his graduate students. In addition to learning how to read Zeami's *Sarugaku dangi* (Talks on sarugaku; ca. 1430) and a variety of other texts related to medieval performance, I attended several performances of noh at the Kanze Nōgakudō in Tokyo, participated and presented in the *Kanmon nikki* reading group, and on two occasions traveled far from the metropolis to see rural folk performances.

It was a full year, but the two trips to see *kagura* and *dengaku* were particularly memorable. In a sense they bookended my time in Japan, with the first coming a few months into my stay, once I had gotten used to the rhythms of life as a research student in the department, and the second coming mere days before I returned to the United States to finish my dissertation.

The first trip took place in early December. My fellow graduate students and I piled into a car and drove four hours to Nakashitara ward in the town of Tōei-chō in Aichi Prefecture, the site of the annual *hana matsuri* (flower festival). Most of the drive was spent on the Tōmei Expressway, a congested freeway that feels more like an overland concrete tunnel than a perch from which to admire the countryside. This made for a sudden and dramatic ascent into the mountains once we exited the freeway toward the end of our journey.

The Nakashitara *hana matsuri* is one of several performances of *kagura* that take place annually in northeastern Aichi Prefecture. In 1976, it was designated an "important intangible folk cultural property" (*jūyō mukei minzoku bunkazai*) by the Japanese government, currently one of thirty-eight *kagura* to have received this recognition.[1] There are several types of extant *kagura*, which typically feature music, dance, and theater performed as entertainment for visiting *kami* (and gathered audiences). The Nakashitara *hana matsuri* lasts three days (Saturday, Sunday, and Monday) and consists of a series of different performances bracketed by opening and closing rituals. As a type of Ise *kagura*, the focal point is the concluding purification ritual that involves practitioners spraying onlookers with boiling water from a large cauldron.[2]

We arrived in the late afternoon, after the sun had started to set, and the hills were shrouded in a dark blue mist. We were met by the food stands that are ubiquitous at contemporary *matsuri*, and there were groups of people hurrying this way and that in preparation for the night's events. The building where the performances were to take place was entirely open on one side and featured two interior raised platforms: one across from the opening and a second to the right. The first was for spectators, and the second was occupied by a shrine and, in front of it, the musicians who played the bamboo flutes and *taiko* drums that continued through the night. The ceiling was adorned with countless sheets of white paper that had been cut into various designs. The walls displayed records of donations by companies and organizations, a list of the different acts that would make up the night's entertainment, and even a bright painting of the festival donated in 2000. In the center of the floor was a small platform where the cauldron would eventually be placed. It was adorned with branches from a *sakaki* tree, which in turn were decorated with white paper streamers (*gohei*) in the usual Shinto fashion.

The star of the first night was the deity Sarutabiko, who appears in *Kojiki* during the mythical emperor Ninigi's descent to Takachiho. In the text, Sarutabiko proclaims to Ame no Uzume, the deity whose performance helped lure Amaterasu out of her cave, his desire to serve

1. On this designation and the law that underpins it, see Thornbury, *The Folk Performing Arts*, 67–74.

2. Ise *kagura* is also referred to as *yudate kagura* (boiling water *kagura*). For an overview of the different types of *kagura*, see Lancashire, *An Introduction to Japanese Folk Performing Arts*, 21–35.

Ninigi. Sarutabiko and Ame no Uzume thereby become associated, and *Kojiki* explains this as the origin of the Sarume clan, which consisted of female performers who interacted with spirits during imperial ceremonies and rituals. Other than noting that he drowned after a giant clam snapped shut over his head, *Kojiki* does not say anything else about Sarutabiko.[3] But Gustav Heldt notes that in *Kogo shūi* (Gleanings of ancient words; 807), the deity is depicted as "a tall, long-nosed, and fiery-eyed guardian of the road with shining buttocks."[4]

A few hours after we arrived, we caught a glimpse of Sarutabiko and his long nose, and we followed him out along the road as he visited residences to perform ritual dances of purification and receive offerings. We were invited into one home to watch: as Sarutabiko swung his axe and stomped rhythmically, a little girl of no more than three became increasingly agitated and before long was crying, a humorous sight for her parents, who had perhaps gone through the same experience decades earlier.

We returned to the main building and watched a variety of dances. The climax of the night occurred close to 1 a.m., when Sarutabiko made his way back to the main building. Guided by attendants wearing hard hats and blue *happi*, he pushed his way through the crowd and into a small pocket of space next to the cauldron, where he was immediately swallowed by a hundred or more revelers. There was a fraught moment of tense anticipation, and then the crowd exploded into the trademark *hana matsuri* song: *tē ho he te ho he!* (fig. C.1). Cued into action, Sarutabiko wildly swung his axe and vigorously stomped his feet. The attendants formed a circle around him, making sure he had enough space to dance without bludgeoning anyone with the axe. The performance lasted only a few minutes, but there was so much kinetic energy that it felt like the roof was going to blow clear off. Perched on the raised platform, my back to the wall, I could feel the strong, pulsing movement as it rippled through the crowd and ricocheted around the building. And then, just as quickly as he had started, Sarutabiko steadied his axe and glided back out into the night.

3. *Kojiki*, SNKBZ 1:115–19. For an English translation, see *The Kojiki: An Account of Ancient Matters*, 49–51.

4. *The Kojiki: An Account of Ancient Matters*, 230.

FIGURE C.1. A tense moment during the Nakashitara *hana matsuri* as the crowd eagerly awaits Sarutabiko's performance. Photograph courtesy of the author, 2011.

The entertainments continued with one dance after another, and the night deepened. I looked out at the crowd: animated faces among winter coats, puffs of steam as people chattered away. My eyelids became increasingly heavy, and I soon entered the liminal space between dreaming and waking. Every now and then, I would unfold my stiff body and walk out to the bonfire to warm up. An old man was sitting next to it, as he had been all night, his back turned to the performances. He was wearing a pair of blue work pants and a faded black leather jacket. He had a handful of liver spots on his face and wore a black baseball cap that had the words "New York" written in bold lettering across the brim. We had chatted with him earlier in the evening; I remember the feeling of my mind chasing after his strong dialect. At one point he reached into his jacket pocket and pulled out a package of instant ramen. Unsealing it, he produced a stack of photographs. As he spread them out before us, I saw images of a dilapidated shack in the forest and blurry close-ups of a series of stone fragments. "This," he told us, "is the remains of the tomb of Emperor Kazan. He died right around here."

The collective exuberance of the crowd and the solitary figure talking history by the bonfire—I have continued to revisit these two memories over the years. The former is one of a set of experiences that I relied on to concretize phenomenologically the past performances I write about in this book. I am still unpacking the latter: a story of a dead emperor told by an elderly outsider and supplemented by several pieces of documentary evidence. Emperor Kazan (r. 984–986) was known for his poetic skill and his odd and eccentric behaviors. In later times, he was remembered as insane.[5] Although it seems highly unlikely that his tomb would be in the mountains of what is now Aichi Prefecture, he was known for his pilgrimages to mountainous areas after he took the tonsure. Nowadays I think especially of the old man's photographs (and my photographs of his photographs), which, as images of a purported memorial site for an emperor who lived elsewhere a millennium ago, tangle time and compress space.

Cut to July 14, 2012. This time I am on my own, hiking up the steep slopes of Mount Nachi in Wakayama Prefecture on the Kii Peninsula. I have come to see Nachi *dengaku*, which takes place on a raised stage in the courtyard of Kumano Nachi Taisha, as part of the annual fire festival (*Nachi no hi matsuri*). Compared to the rustic small-town feel of Nakashitara, the area models grandeur: the massive shrine and temple structures, the famous waterfall that plunges uninterrupted for 133 meters, the dizzying expanse as you gaze at the hills that tumble into the ocean.

Just like the Nakashitara *hana matsuri*, Nachi *dengaku* was also recognized as an "important intangible folk cultural property" in 1976. Months after I saw it performed, it was inscribed by UNESCO on its Representative List of Intangible Cultural Heritage of Humanity.[6] The origins of Nachi *dengaku* are murky, but the authors of the

5. See, for example, several anecdotes in *Ōkagami* (The Great Mirror; late eleventh century). *Ōkagami*, SNKBZ 34:193–201. English translations can be found in *Ōkagami, The Great Mirror*, 148–52.

6. For the inscription, see "Decision of the Intergovernmental Committee."

UNESCO nomination file describe a timeline marked by disappearance and reappearance. In 1581, the costumes, instruments, and other equipment were destroyed in a fire, but the performance was revived in 1599. In the late nineteenth century, it faded away with the anti-Buddhist *haibutsu kishaku* movement triggered by the Meiji (1868–1912) government's modernization policies, but it was once again reinvigorated by stakeholders in 1921.[7] Nachi *dengaku* does not so much transfer acts from the past as it reenacts performances that have disappeared.

The *dengaku* takes place in the morning and, as Terence A. Lancashire notes, is eclipsed by "the more publicized afternoon rituals where men, brandishing fire torches, confront another group of men carrying 12 long, red, perpendicular *ōgi mikoshi* (fan portable shrines)."[8] This was my experience as well. Earlier in the morning, the bearers of the *ōgi mikoshi* practiced hoisting up their unwieldy objects, and they did so right in front of the *dengaku* stage. After they finished their dry run, most of the spectators wandered off, perhaps hoping to get a good spot by the waterfall, where the blazing confrontation would later take place.

There were still some onlookers present for the *dengaku* when it began. I watched as the performers danced, struck drums, waved elegant golden *binzasara*, and played flutes. Their costumes, complete with the typical *ayaigasa* hats, were bright and festive (fig. C.2). But the overall experience was a far cry from Sarutabiko's dramatic movements among the crowd during the *hana matsuri*, and other than superficial similarities, it had little in common with the raucous performances of *dengaku* documented by Munetada and Masafusa some nine hundred years earlier.[9] The most jarring part of the experience was the presence of a simultaneous audio commentary, delivered through speakers placed behind the stage, which in a loud yet flat voice

7. "Nomination File No. 00413," 4.

8. Lancashire, *An Introduction to Japanese Folk Performing Arts*, 44.

9. Lancashire has a similar take on the *dengaku* performed as part of the contemporary Onmatsuri in Nara. He writes that "it is difficult to become excited by the slow ambulations of aged men where the only highlight, if it can be called such, is the tossing of short sticks into the air." Lancashire, *An Introduction to the Japanese Folk Performing Arts*, 45.

FIGURE C.2. A *dengaku* performer at Nachi Taisha snaps his golden *binzasara* as he executes a stomp. Photograph courtesy of the author, 2012.

narrated what we were watching. This commentary syncopated with the rhythms of the drums and *binzasara*, making it difficult to focus on one or the other. I remember feeling aggrieved at the time, but in hindsight the entanglement of these two signals enables a clearer understanding of what I experienced in that moment: not a repertoire that had somehow survived the ravages of time but instead a present reenactment of practices from the past.

Performing Documentation: Non-identity, Reactivation, Syncopation

While researching and writing this book, I have learned that the past is something to be apprehended not all at once or as fully formed but instead at irregular intervals and across countless discontinuous objects and contexts. Academic studies of the past, though, risk smoothing over this profoundly uneven engagement: objects are selected and interpreted in service of a specific argument, within the bounded spatiotemporal dimensions of a book or an article and through a narrative form that relies on and reproduces communicative norms. The smaller the gaps between scholarly subject, object of study, and reader, the more complete the illusion of seamlessness becomes.

But my encounters with the objects, texts, and performances that make up the raw material of this book demonstrate discontinuity more than anything else. My attention has been pulled in different directions at different times, my arguments have shifted from when I first started researching and writing, and my manner of engaging with and thinking about past performances has changed. The fields that provide the immediate context for the intellectual shape of this book have also changed, and there are ever more interpretations of the artifacts, documents, and repertoires I write about here. At a more basic level, this proliferation of interpretations is structured by the everyday work of scholarship, which involves returning to "the past object," again and again. Michael Shanks understands the past object as something that:

> exists in its non-identity, a condition which requires me to use my imagination to come to an understanding of it, following its connections and differences, open to its possibilities. But not just anything can be invented of this thing I have found. A responsibility (to the object, and its maker or user) requires me to respect its empirical otherness. [. . .] This responsibility is a demand that the object be respected. So the rules of my engagement with the past are not laid down in method or in a theory of knowledge, but in an ethic which maintains that I acknowledge I do not know but can learn from the past, that the past is ineffable in its difference.[10]

In its "non-identity," the past object possesses no transcendent meaning on its own; meaning emerges only through the relationality produced by repeated contact. Throughout his monograph, Shanks argues that the past is neither inherent in objects (the rational scientific approach, in which the scholar is effaced in favor of the positivist truth)

10. Shanks, *Experiencing the Past*, 138.

nor simply whatever one desires it to be (the idealist approach, seen, for example, in nationalist ideology). It is instead to be found in an ethical recognition of the past's otherness, an encounter with which enables relational becoming.

Given his emphasis on experience in making sense of encounters with the past, Shanks's approach can be understood as broadly phenomenological. In a recent book of essays, Philip Auslander delineates a similarly phenomenological approach to the past, as accessed through the specific format of performance documentation across a variety of media including texts, photographs, and films. As I discussed in the introduction, performance studies scholars often understand performance as a phenomenon of copresence. Peggy Phelan brackets documentation as "something other than performance," and Diana Taylor stresses that a "live performance can never be captured or transmitted through the archive."[11] In his book, Auslander develops the concept of "reactivation" to argue for the document's central role not only in preserving performance but also in constituting performance as such. Reactivation, he writes, is "a way of understanding how we experience performances through documentation as unfolding in our perceptual present, even as we acknowledge their connections to events that probably occurred elsewhere and in another time."[12] Auslander defines reactivation as something that binds the beholder's "perceptual present" together with the "elsewhere" and "other time" in which the performance took place, emphasizing phenomenological encounter over ontological veracity. This encounter doubles time and space: I am here but also there, I am now but also then.[13] Such relational entangling recalls Shanks's careful preservation of the past's non-identity, which—in its distance and difference—structures present encounters with it.

Auslander sources the term "reactivation" from Walter Benjamin's well-known essay "The Work of Art in the Age of Mechanical Reproduction" (1935). The term appears toward the end of the second section, after Benjamin outlines his concept of aura but before he explores

11. Phelan, *Unmarked*, 146; and Taylor, *The Archive and the Repertoire*, 20.
12. Auslander, *Reactivations*, 45.
13. Auslander, *Reactivations*, 15.

the political possibilities of the mass-produced aesthetic object. He writes:

> Technical reproduction can put the copy of the original into situations which would be out of reach for the original itself. Above all, it enables the original to meet the beholder halfway, be it in the form of a photograph or a phonograph record. The cathedral leaves its locale to be received in the studio of a lover of art; the choral production, performed in an auditorium or in the open air, resounds in the drawing room. [. . .] One might generalize by saying: the technique of reproduction detaches the reproduced object from the domain of tradition. By making many reproductions it substitutes a plurality of copies for a unique existence. And in permitting the reproduction to meet the beholder or listener in his own particular situation, it reactivates [*aktualisiert*] the object reproduced.[14]

This is from Harry Zohn's 1968 translation of the essay, in which he renders the German *aktualisiert* as "reactivates." The 2002 translation of the essay's expanded "second version" renders the same word more straightforwardly as "actualizes."[15] While both translations work, Zohn's "reactivates" neatly captures the spatiotemporal doubling implicit in the beholder encountering the reproduction.[16] This doubling is important for Benjamin because reactivation is first and foremost an effect of mechanical reproduction. It is what happens when an image or a sound is transported across time and space to meet "the beholder halfway." Reactivation jeopardizes the object's authenticity because it exists in this "halfway," as opposed to "the domain of tradition."

For Benjamin, it is the photograph and the phonograph that enable viewers and listeners to experience something elsewhere and in a manner not bound by the object's initial context. For those of us living in the twenty-first century, it is also the audio or video recording that

14. Benjamin, "The Work of Art in the Age of Mechanical Reproduction," 220–21.

15. Benjamin, "The Work of Art in the Age of Its Reproducibility," 104.

16. I thank my colleague Joseph Metz for his help with Benjamin's German.

digital cameras and, later, camera phones have made ubiquitous. I can watch the video recordings I made of the 2012 Nachi *dengaku* on my computer monitor or on my phone while sitting at a café, and I can do so for two minutes or twenty, in chronological order or discontinuously. Benjamin argues that when I do this, I experience an object (the performance) detached from the domain of tradition (Nachi Taisha and the broader social and historical environment) and reactivated through an encounter with my own perceptual time and space. Meeting the original halfway means that neither past nor present unilaterally dictates the encounter. Just as the past has no ontologically static meaning waiting to be uncovered, the conditions of the present do not fully delimit the potential meanings of the past. Through reactivation, our engagement and experience with past performances necessarily happen in the present, but they happen "without effacing the performance's pastness."[17]

One of the most appealing aspects of Auslander's approach to documentation is its pedagogical pragmatism. If documentation did not, in the end, communicate something about the event of a past performance, then a course like Theater and Performance in Japan would simply be shorthand for Textual and Visual Depictions of Theater and Performance in Japan. When I read *Rakuyō dengaku ki* with my students, we of course discuss Masafusa's literary Sinitic language and the structure of the account, but on a more fundamental level, we approach it as a document that can help us imagine some aspect of the past. We mentally reconstruct, in our present moment, the event based on the fine level of detail Masafusa provides about costumes, instruments, dances, music, who performed what, and rumors about how the event started. We furthermore supplement this imagining with objects that reactivate the past otherwise, such as the two *binzasara* I bought several years ago in Japan for 3,000 yen each. As we consider what Masafusa does and does not include in his account and why, a dry rasp syncopates the classroom's soundscape, transporting the sonic past into the present.

Benjamin dwells on the spatial dislocation of reactivation, but reactivation also involves a tangling of multiple times. "Then"

17. Auslander, *Reactivations*, 53.

becomes "now," just like in the conventional opening line of so many of the stories in *Konjaku monogatari shū*: "Now it is the past" (*ima wa mukashi*). Rebecca Schneider's work on reenactment is full of insights about performance's persistent temporal zigzagging. But unlike Auslander via Benjamin, she emphasizes how the present is always already composed of and by other times:

> Is the live really only a matter of temporal immediacy, happening only in an uncomplicated now, a "transitory" present, an immediate moment? Is a "maniacally charged present" not punctuated by, syncopated with, indeed charged by other moments, other times? That is, is the present really so temporally straightforward or pure—devoid of a basic delay or deferral if not multiplicity and flexibility? Does it not take place or become composed in double, triple, or multiple time—especially if performance and the "sedimented acts" that comprise the social are already a matter of "twice-behaved behavior"?[18]

In this barrage of interlaced questions, Schneider interrogates the assumption of "an uncomplicated now" that somehow remains insulated from echoes, delays, deferrals, and folds. The idea of a "straightforward" and "pure" present recalls the studio and the drawing room evoked by Benjamin as places where reactivation happens: the beholder who meets the object halfway is, one imagines, comfortably ensconced in the stillness of domestic space. But whereas Benjamin sees reproduction as the cathedral and the chorale stepping out of the authenticity of past tradition and into the modern home, Schneider sees reenactment (and performance in general) as a challenge to "any neat antinomy between appearance and disappearance, or presence and absence."[19] In its relentless repetition, performance necessarily transgresses the boundary between present and past.

In this conclusion, I have thought through two kinds of encounter with the past: contemporary performances (repertoire) and performance documentation (archive). Both make appeals to sensing bodies: the vibrations I felt in my feet when the drums were struck, the smooth

18. Schneider, *Performing Remains*, 92.
19. Schneider, *Performing Remains*, 102.

feel of the page as my finger traced the words. Both create: contemporary performances renew or generate bonds with and between communities, publics, and gods; and documentation meets the beholder halfway in a unique encounter. Lastly, both are phenomena of the present, which, as Schneider points out, is uneven, discontinuous, and inflected with a multiplicity of different temporalities. A phenomenological approach to scholarship reminds us that our encounter with the past can only ever happen through a variety of sensory modalities and in the jumbled temporality that is the present moment.[20] The present moment *is* the sensorium of the archive as we research, the fugitive mental images we construct when reading and thinking, and the ethics demanded by the "non-identity" of the past that meets us halfway. Past objects are not traces or fragments of some impossibly coherent historical reality, but instead they are things that "speak to us now in a way that makes us wish to engage with them."[21] And it is this desire for engagement that brings us to the past and the past to us, again and again.

20. As Schneider puts it, "Think of it this way: the same detail of information can *sound*, *feel*, *look*, *smell*, or *taste* radically different when accessed in radically different venues or via disparate media (or when *not* told in some venues but told in others)." Schneider, *Performing Remains*, 104 (emphasis in original).

21. Auslander, *Reactivations*, 17.

APPENDIX 1

Translations of Selected Texts

An Inquiry into Sangaku

"An Inquiry into Sangaku"
Emperor Murakami

I ask. The history of *sangaku* is long. An actor once went to the State of Lu to perform and had his foot severed as punishment. Comic actors came to our realm and made audiences laugh so hard their jaws dislocated. Revisiting old performance techniques and reflecting on current practices, we see that [our contemporary] *sangaku* has no connection to what the *Zhou li* says the standard-bearers taught, nor to what the Han records say the barbarians presented as tribute.[1]

1. The relevant entry in the *Zhou li* reads, "The standard-bearers teach the dances of *sanyue* and barbarian [foreign] music." Quoted in *Honchō monzui*, SNKBT 27:29n16. For the "Han records," editors point to an entry in the *Hou Han shu* that reads, "In the first year of Yongning [120], the barbarians in the southwest paid tribute to the Shan King with musicians and magicians. They excelled in breathing fire, making their limbs disappear, and changing their heads into those of oxen and horses." Quoted in *Honchō monzui*, SNKBT 27:29n17. But since the passage indicates *kanten* or "Han records" in general, it is possible this refers to a different instance of "barbarian performance." For example, Shigeta Michi argues that it simply points back to the same passage in the *Zhou li* already cited. Shigeta, "*Honchō monzui* shoshū 'Ben sangaku,'" 7.

People told beautiful stories about Senta's [Yoshimi's] New Mohe dances and praised as captivating Uomaro's [Mochizane's] Shiluoguo dances.[2] [Our own *sangaku*] is questionable. Boarding a half-lattice carriage, whip cracking—in what direction does he run away? Approaching a pillar with a quiver slung on his back—for whose sake is he so dressed? It is difficult to know who will pass on [the skill of] wrestling now that Anchokushi [Anhonchū] has grown old, and I am curious about Rihō-ō's [Tōshūjin's] novel hidden technique of puppetry. The chamberlains' stories about styles changing every month—are these true or false? The story told by the middle captain of the Inner Palace Guards about light shining above the circular mats—does this speak well or ill [of *sangaku*]? You have transmitted the Confucian teachings throughout the generations and enriched the garden of floral language. You should study well the rare form of a monkey in a gorge and not get used to waterfowl walking on land.[3]

"Answer Provided by Lord Hada no Ujiyasu, Graduate Student of Sangaku, Functionary of the Ancillary Guard Senior Sixth Upper Rank"

(It is said that chamberlain and graduate student of letters Fujiwara no Masaki wrote this.)

I answer. When you consider it intently, people's natures can be divided into wise and foolish. The feeling of enjoyment [likewise] differs between past and present. When one's nature shifts between happiness, anger, pathos, and enjoyment, it is called emotion. When sounds respond to differences between instability, peace, order, and disorder, it is called music. Accordingly, when there is a wise ruler, those endowed with virtue involuntarily dance with their hands and stomp with their feet. When the realm is devoid of problems, those filled with benevolence express in words what they feel in their hearts. This

2. Unlike Mohe, the location of Shiluoguo is unknown. Shigeta Michi discusses some possibilities in Shigeta, "*Honchō monzui* shoshū 'Ben sangaku,'" 4.

3. Here Emperor Murakami exhorts Masaki to answer the questions by drawing on his considerable knowledge and displaying his scholarly talent.

emotion must not always be unbending; this nature must not always be pliable. The wise seek to follow the mysterious and sacred shape of the world, just as water fits the shape of a vase; the foolish, not knowing whether to proceed or retreat, entrust themselves to the ruler's influence. Even the truly ignorant are filled with kindness, saturated by virtue, and carefully guided. Possessed of an unsophisticated nature, they watch dances, listen to songs, and share in the ruler's musical diversions. Taking Mochizane [Uomaru] as their model, the nobles of the purple-laced golden seal flip their sleeves; in deference to Yoshimi [Senta], the high-ranking officials of the State Academy flutter their clothes. They do this only in the palace and take care to abstain when elsewhere.

Here is what I know. Half-lattice carriages do not take the place of horses; how could attendants make them move by cracking their whips? Quivers are martial vessels; why would warriors carry them toward pillars? This should of course be understood as nonsense uttered by young boys holed up together. It is difficult to have a conversation when everyone is spouting rumors. The joke of offering wine to the senior captain of the Palace Guards transmits Anhonchū's [Anchokushi's] wrestling. Making offerings of dried meat and delighting in sitting in front of the blinds of the Shōkyōden teaches the puppetry of Tōshūjin [Rihō-ō]. As for the styles, they follow the changing months and the circular mats become bright; if one were to completely change the style of formal documents, then unfortunately it would be useless to try to teach people. If light is skillfully emitted [from the circular mats] and said to be the same as the appearance [of the Buddha], wouldn't this constitute the sin of equating it with the Buddha? Works of baseless fancy spring from the rumors of the loquacious. Inducing laughter to the point of dislocating jaws—how can this be the main occupation of the *sangaku* performer?

At times our realm returns to being plain and simple, matching the customs of Huaxu.[4] All people divert themselves with music and

4. This mythical utopia is described in the "Yellow Emperor" section of *Liezi* (The writings of Master Lie; ca. fifth century BCE). The mythic emperor falls asleep and dreams of a "place which you cannot reach by boat or carriage or on foot, only by a journey of the spirit. In this country there are no teachers and leaders; all things follow their natural course. The people have no cravings and lusts; all men follow their natural course. They are incapable of delighting in life or hating death, and therefore none of

enjoy various performances in all places. Even the sun of Emperor Yao's virtue pales [in comparison to that of Emperor Murakami]. Emperor Shun composed songs about the early-summer breeze, but they have not yet fully exerted their good [in shaping the people through virtue]. [Those in the realm] enjoy [performance and music] naturally, and not excessively, which also praises the gods. Though the diminutive men who make their bodies lightweight during the *kagura* held on snowy nights might seem strange, we secretly detest the nobles who remain silent during the *tōka* dances held under spring skies. I have done my best to answer, despite my lack of ability.[5] I agonized over this study and for years endured extraordinary hardship; my answers are different from what I have read or heard [up until now], and I still have not reached an understanding of the writings on *sangaku*. I humbly submit my answer.[6]

Hyakurenshō, Entries About the Great Dengaku of 1096

1096/7/12

Courtier attendants held a *dengaku* performance. As of late, practically everyone, the high and the low alike in various places, has been

---

them dies before his time. They do not know how to prefer themselves to others, and so they neither love nor hate. They do not know how to turn their faces to things or turn their backs, go with the stream or push against it, so nothing benefits or harms them. There is nothing at all which they grudge or regret, nothing which they dread or envy. They go into water without drowning, into fire without burning; hack them, flog them, there is no wound nor pain; poke them, scratch them, there is no ache nor itch." Graham, *The Book of Lieh-tzŭ*, 34.

5. Literally, "I have borrowed falsehoods and sought names, executing my duties toward what there is not and criticizing what there is."

6. My translation follows the version found in *Honchō monzui*, SNKBT 27:174–75 (CJ: 29–33). For help reading this difficult text, I have consulted Shigeta Michi's *kundokubun* and Modern Japanese overview. See Shigeta, "*Honchō monzui* shoshū 'Ben sangaku,'" 2–6. I have also referenced Liwen Tu's recent doctoral dissertation, which includes a translation of Murakami's question and a wider analysis of *Ben sangaku*. See Tu, "Fujiwara no Akihira," 49–57.

performing *dengaku*. The palaces of the emperor and retired emperor were brought to a standstill as attendants, Confucian scholars, and low-ranking bureaucrats were tasked with performances.

1096/8/7

Ikuhōmon'in passed away. (She was twenty-two years old, the first daughter of the retired emperor and the older sister of the emperor.)

1096/8/9

The retired emperor took the tonsure, as he was deeply grieved by the loss of his daughter.[7]

Kojidan 1:83

The Great Dengaku of Eichō 1. According to the records of a certain person (Lord Suenaka's diary):[8]

Seventh month, twelfth day. I was at the palace to attend the council on shrine offerings for this year's Five Cereals rite. Today the courtiers performed *dengaku*—more than thirty people total, it was said. (The secretary controller [Minamoto no Moroyori] did not participate due to illness.) The costumes had been determined in advance. Their crimson hanging robes and gathered trousers were extravagantly adorned, and they wore the lids of headgear boxes as broad hats. By imperial decree, Chamberlain Junior Counselor Narimune performed *The Head of the Field*. Long-handled parasols displayed unparalleled extravagance with their eye-catching canopies.[9] This was all prepared in the Chamberlains' Office.

7. *Hyakurenshō*, SZKT 11:43.

8. Fujiwara no Suenaka was a high-ranking noble who at the time held the position of grand controller of the Left.

9. This is a tentative translation of a sentence that is difficult to understand. For potential readings, see *Kojidan*, SNKBT 41:104n12.

Pole hopping: Akimasa
Kaketsuzumi: Tsunetada
Stilt walking: Munesuke
Kaketsuzumi: Director of Repairs Lord Akisue, Right Controller Lord Munetada, Left Captain Lord Akizane, Vice-Director of the Palace Guards Sanetaka, Chamberlain Moroshige, Assistant Kanesue.
Small cymbals: Former Vice-Director of the Palace Guards Lord Nagatada, Right Junior Controller Tokinori, Senior Assistant Minister of Population Affairs Yukinobu, and Senior Assistant Minister of Civil Affairs Atsukane.
Sasara: Vice-Director of the Palace Guards Morotoki, Lieutenant Akimichi, Minister of the Left Bureau of Horses Morotaka, Governor of Inaba Nagazane, Governor of Suō Tsunetada, Chamberlain Moriie.
Small *tsuzumi*: Acting Controller Lord Shigesuke, Acting Assistant Director of the Bureau of Horses Iesada, Acting Senior Assistant Minister of Population Affairs Motokane, Governor of Misaka Mototaka, et al.
The flute [*fue*] was played by Minister of the Right Bureau of Horses Lord Kanezane and Chamberlain Aide to the Ministry of Ceremonial Munenaka.

They performed for some time at the Shishinden and then spent several hours playing songs in the Imperial Apartments. After nightfall, they withdrew to Ichijō Palace.[10] They then returned to the palace after midnight. I secretly had a look at the performances: it was like a dream. The things that happen in the world are difficult to predict and difficult to understand; they must be seen [to be believed].

Thirteenth day. Today Retired Emperor Shirakawa's courtiers performed *dengaku*. A group including Emperor Horikawa's courtiers was not allowed to join them, except for Nagazane and Tsunetada—these two were able to enter the palace due to their skill in performing. Each

10. This appears to be a mistake. The author likely intended to write either Rokujōin (the location of Retired Emperor Shirakawa's residence) or Ichiin, which also referred to the retired emperor (the "first" *in*, in contrast to his daughter, who also possessed the title of *in* [*nyoin*]).

of the costumes displayed utter extravagance. It is said they stayed holed up in the palace performing *dengaku* all through the night.

Four senior nobles concluded the performances: Captain of the Left Palace Guards Mototada, Minister of Civil Affairs Michitoshi, Captain of the Right Palace Guards Masatoshi, and Consultant Captain Munemichi. It is said they all wore ordinary clothing and grasped poles topped with fans, and that paper inscribed with the word "abstinence" was attached. In this way, day and night, here and there, all the princes and members of the imperial family, and the lords, regent, and members of the Chamberlains' Office all performed *dengaku* in the various towns and villages. Some performed for elite audiences; others made pilgrimages to shrines.[11]

Entries from *Ranshōshō*

"Sumiyoshi Shrine"

Kahō 3 [1096], third month, seventh day. The Head of Sumiyoshi Shrine Tsumori no Kunimoto [planned to] hold a service at a private devotion hall. Acting Lesser Prelate Keichō was to preside. On the day of the ceremony, groups of believers gathered and overran the premises. Meanwhile, Capital Policeman and Lieutenant of the Left Outer Palace Guards Norikata came to meet his granddaughter's husband. While using the forces under his command to suppress the disturbance, several people flung themselves into the pond. Thirty-eight people died. The court musician Kiyotaka, who had been exposed to this contamination [*shokue*] entered the palace, and Norikata went to see the former grand minister. As a result, all important shrine affairs were canceled.

"Attendants' Dengaku"

On the twelfth day of the seventh month of Kahō 3, there was a performance in the imperial palace. Those ranked lower than controller and minor counselor were to attend, but the two head chamberlains

11. *Kojidan*, SNKBT 41:105–6 (CJ: 104–5).

did not pay any mind. They did not wear ordinary clothing. They drummed and danced gleefully and visited places like the retired emperor's palace. Perhaps this was the custom at that time. Due to [head of Sumiyoshi Shrine Tsumori no] Kunimoto's serious contamination during this past third month, the Matsu-no-o Festival was postponed. A prophetic song [*wazauta*] [circulated]: "The deity will not abide by this." As a result, those remaining competed [in *dengaku* performances], and the situation developed into what it is now. It was said the shrine would be visited.[12]

Koji ruien, "Dengaku"

Dengaku likely has its origins in the rice-planting activities of the classical period [*chūko*], during which time people played flutes, struck drums, sang, and danced to allay the strain of labor [*rō o nagusameshi*]. It replicates the conditions of rice planting. Performances include sword juggling, stilt walking, and pole hopping, and the instruments used include the *koshitsuzumi*, *furitsuzumi*, small cymbals, and *binzasara*. In earlier times, *dengaku* performances thrived among high and low. Especially famous was the Great Dengaku of Eichō 1 [1096] during the reign of Emperor Horikawa. During the time of the Kamakura shogunate, it became wholly associated with the skills of monks. Known as *dengaku* monks [*dengaku hōshi*], they established two groups: the Main Troupe and the New Troupe. Among them were skilled performers of dramas like *Possession by the Deity of Kitano* and *The Woman's Revenge Killing*. In brief, during the time of the Ashikaga shoguns, this art [*gei*] prospered along with *sarugaku* but gradually declined. Later it could be seen only rarely, during shrine festivals at places like Kasuga, Sumiyoshi, and Nikkō.[13]

12. *Ranshōshō*, 336.
13. *Koji ruien*, 687.

APPENDIX 2

Timeline of Selected Performances and Events

Date	Era and year	Place	Description	Source
675/2/1	Tenmu tennō 4	Kiyomihara Palace	Singers, dwarf dancers, and acrobats ordered to be sent to the capital	*Nihon shoki*
685/9/15	Tenmu tennō 14	Kiyomihara Palace	Singers and flute players ordered to transmit their skills to descendants	*Nihon shoki*
735/5/5	Tenpyō 8	Heijō Palace	Spear-twirling viewed by Emperor Shōmu	*Shoku Nihongi*
782/7/11	Enryaku 1	Heijō Palace	Sangaku Division abolished	*Shoku Nihongi*
832/4/14	Tenchō 9	Urin Pavilion	Fujiwara no Junshi observes farming customs	*Nihon kiryaku zenpen*
861/6/28	Jōgan 3	Heian Palace	Oldest record of *sangaku* being performed during the annual Wrestling Rite	*Nihon sandai jitsuroku*
863/5/20	Jōgan 5	Shinsen'en	*Goryōe* first held in capital	*Nihon sandai jitsuroku*
864/2/25	Jōgan 6	Somedono	Rice-planting rite viewed by Emperor Seiwa	*Nihon sandai jitsuroku*
865/6/14	Jōgan 7	Heian Palace	*Goryōe* ceremonies officially banned	*Nihon sandai jitsuroku*

Date	Era and year	Place	Description	Source
865/7/23	Jōgan 7	Heian Palace	"One hundred feats" (*hyakugi*) viewed by Emperor Seiwa	*Nihon sandai jitsuroku*
866/i3/1	Jōgan 8	Somedono	Rice-planting rite viewed by Emperor Seiwa	*Nihon sandai jitsuroku*
880/7/29	Gangyō 4	Heian Palace	*Sangaku* performed during the annual Wrestling Rite	*Nihon sandai jitsuroku*
922	Engi 22	Ōtori Shrine (Izumi Province)	*Dengaku* appears along with parades and *kagura* as entertainment during the shrine's annual festival	*Heian ibun*, vol. 7 (document no. 218, "Settsu no kuni Ōtori jinja ryū-kichō")
945	Tengyō 8	Various Kinai locations	Shidarajin Incident	*Honchō seiki*; *Ribu ōki*
958/4	Tentoku 2	Tōdaiji	Thirteen *dengaku hōshi* perform	*Tōdaiji miseikan monjo*
963	Ōwa 3	Heiankyō	Emperor Murakami and Fujiwara no Masaki write the two components of *Ben sangaku*	*Honchō monzui*
965/8/2	Kōhō 2	Heian Palace	Emperor Murakami views *sarugaku* in front of the Seiryōden (oldest recorded instance of the word *sarugaku*)	*Nihon kiryaku kōhen*
988/8/19	Ei'en 2	Heian Palace	*Sangaku* performed during the annual Wrestling Rite	*Shōyūki*
999/4/10	Chōhō 1	Matsu-no-o Shrine	*Dengaku* performed at the Matsu-no-o Festival	*Nihon kiryaku kōhen*
999/6/14	Chōhō 1	Streets of Heiankyō	Mukotsu performs on the eve of the Gion *goryōe*	*Honchō seiki*

Date	Era and year	Place	Description	Source
1005/7/29	Kankō 2	Heian Palace	*Sangaku* performed during the annual Wrestling Rite	*Shōyūki*
1012/2/8	Chōwa 1	Mount Funaoka and Murasakino	Shidarajin worshippers arrive in the capital from Kyushu	*Hyakurenshō*
1012/12/4	Chōwa 1	Heian Palace	Fujiwara no Michinaga is said to compare court proceedings to a *sangaku* performance	*Shōyūki*
1013/8/1	Chōwa 2	Heian Palace	*Sangaku* performed during the annual Wrestling Rite	*Shōyūki*
1019/7/28	Kannin 3	Heian Palace	*Sangaku* performed during the annual Wrestling Rite	*Shōyūki*
1023/5	Jian 3	Tsuchimikado Palace	*Dengaku* performed during Fujiwara no Michinaga's rice-planting rite	*Eiga monogatari*
1023/7/28	Jian 3	Heian Palace	*Sangaku* performed during the annual Wrestling Rite	*Shōyūki*
Early 1060s		Heiankyō	Fujiwara no Akihira writes *Shin sarugaku ki*	*Shin sarugaku ki*
1088/7/27	Kanji 2	Heian Palace	*Sarugaku* (including *zōgei*) performed during the annual Wrestling Rite	*Chūyūki*
1094/5/20	Kahō 1	Streets of Heiankyō	Minamoto no Ietoshi and his band of *dengaku* performers attack a group of courtiers	*Chūyūki*
1094/8/8	Kahō 1	Kyōgokuji	*Dengaku* performed in front of the State Academy during the Sekiten Festival	*Chūyūki*

Date	Era and year	Place	Description	Source
1095/8/1	Kahō 2	Heian Palace	*Sarugaku* and *zōgei* performed during the annual Wrestling Rite	*Chūyūki*
Summer of 1096, esp. 6/12, 6/14, 7/12, 7/13, 7/19	Eichō 1	Heiankyō, various locations	The Great Dengaku of 1096	*Chūyūki*; *Rakuyō dengaku ki*; *Imakagami*; *Kojidan*; *Hyakurenshō*; *Ranshōshō*
1099–1103	Kōwa 1–5	Onjōji	*Dengaku* performed as part of the Hachiman Festival	*Jimon kōsō ki*
1102/9/4	Kōwa 4	Tōdaiji	*Dengaku* performed as part of an enshrinement festival	*Chūyūki*
1102	Kōwa 4	Ōyamadera (Hōki Province)	*Dengaku* performed as part of an impromptu festival put on by the governor of Hōki	*Hōki Daisenji engi emaki*
1103/6/8	Kōwa 5	Toba Villa	Retired Emperor Shirakawa attends a *dengaku* performance	*Chūyūki*
1104/5/15	Chōji 1	Toba Villa	*Dengaku* performed during a rice-planting rite	*Chūyūki*
1104/7/29	Chōji 1	Heian Palace	*Sarugaku* performed during the annual Wrestling Rite	*Chūyūki*
1105/6/14	Chōji 2	Heiankyō	Performances of *dengaku* turn violent near Princess Reishi's residence, causing the capital police to get involved	*Chūyūki*
1106/6/13	Kajō 1	Heiankyō	Munetada laments the outbreak of "inauspicious" and "uncontrollable" *dengaku* performances among the lower ranks	*Chūyūki*

Date	Era and year	Place	Description	Source
1127/5/14	Daiji 2	Toba Villa	*Dengaku* performed during a rice-planting rite	*Chūyūki*; *Hyakuren-shō*
1127/6/14	Daiji 2	Heiankyō	*Dengaku* and other performances take place during the Gion *goryōe*	*Chūyūki*
1129/5/10	Daiji 4	Heiankyō	Bifukumon'in abruptly leaves during a *dengaku* performance	*Chōshūki*
1133/5/8	Chōshō 2	Uji	*Dengaku* performed during the Uji Shrine Festival	*Chūyūki*; *Hyōhanki*
1133/6/14	Chōshō 2	Heiankyō	*Dengaku* performed during the Gion *goryōe*	*Chūyūki*
1134/5/8	Chōshō 3	Uji	An assortment of performances take place at the Uji Shrine Festival	*Chūyūki*
1136/9/17	Hōen 2	Kasuga Wakamiya Shrine	*Dengaku*, *sarugaku*, and more performed as part of the first instance of the Wakamiya Festival (today know as Onmatsuri)	"Wakamiya sairei-ki" (in *Kasuga*)
1147/6/15	Kyūan 3	Gion Shrine, Heiankyō	Taira no Kiyomori organizes a *dengaku* performance during the Gion *goryōe*. He and his attendants enter the shrine armed; they are restrained, and fighting breaks out	*Honchō seiki*
1150/8/24	Kyūan 6	Hosshōji	A temple festival features *dengaku* performances, which for the author recall the Gion *goryōe*	*Honchō seiki*

Date	Era and year	Place	Description	Source
1153/4/15	Ninpei 3	Uji	*Dengaku* and *sangaku* performed during the Uji Shrine Festival; presence of performance guilds (*za*) in Uji and Shirakawa mentioned	*Hyōhanki*
1154/3	Kyūju 1	Murasakino Shrine	Yasurai Festival	"Ryōjin hishō kudenshū, Volume 14
1164/5/6	Chōkan 2	Kitano Tenmangū Shrine, Chikugo Province	The shrine appoints a new overseer of *dengaku* performances	*Heian ibun*, vol. 7 (document no. 3357 "Chikugo no kuni Kitano Tenmangū dengaku matsuridc koro shoku no kotc
1178/11/10	Jishō 2	Heiankyō	*Dengaku* performed as a prayer for fertility	*Sankaiki*
1179/6/8	Jishō 3	Uji	*Dengaku hōshi* perform at a rice planting festival and are awarded clothing by the regent	*Kujōke-bon Gyokuyō*
1183/4/19	Juei 2	Kumano	Senior nobles and courtiers perform *dengaku*	*Hyakurenshō*
1185	Bunji 1	Jingoji	As part of a divine appeal, Mongaku asks that *jushi*, *sarugaku*, and *dengaku* performers be denied access to the temple because they get in the way of devotional activities	*Heian ibun*, vol. 9 (document no. 489 "Sō Mongaku no kishōmon")
1187/5/2	Bunji 3	Imperial Palace	The retired emperor watches *dengaku*	*Kujōke-bon Gyokuyō*
1188/6/1	Bunji 4	Ōhime's residence	Rice-planting rite held	*Azuma kagami*
1199/5/9	Shōji 1	Hie Shrine	*Dengaku* attended in secret by Retired Emperor GoToba	*Inokuma kanpaku ki*

SOURCE: Adapted in part from Suzuki, *Nōgaku shi nenpyō*, 2–9; and Katō, "Dengaku shiry nenpyō."

Bibliography

Abbreviations are as listed in the front matter. Primary sources are arranged by title for ease of reference and in recognition of the uncertainties of premodern authorship.

Abe Yasurō. "Geinō ō no tōjō: Koewaza no teiō GoShirakawa-in." In *Tennō to geinō*, 106–32. Tennō no Rekishi 10. Tokyo: Kōdansha, 2011.

———. *Seija no suisan: Chūsei no koe to wokonaru mono*. Nagoya, Japan: Nagoya Daigaku Shuppankai, 2001.

"An Account of the New Monkey Music." By Fujiwara no Akihira. Translated by Joan R. Piggott. In *Traditional Japanese Literature: An Anthology, Beginnings to 1600*, edited by Haruo Shirane, 491–97. New York: Columbia University Press, 2007.

Addiss, Stephen, Gerald Groemer, and J. Thomas Rimer, eds. *Traditional Japanese Arts and Culture: An Illustrated Sourcebook*. Honolulu: University of Hawai'i Press, 2006.

Adolphson, Mikael S. *The Gates of Power: Monks, Courtiers, and Warriors in Premodern Japan*. Honolulu: University of Hawai'i Press, 2000.

Adolphson, Mikael, and Edward Kamens. "Between and Beyond Centers and Peripheries." In *Heian Japan: Centers and Peripheries*, edited by Mikael Adolphson, Edward Kamens, and Stacie Matsumoto, 1–11. Honolulu: University of Hawai'i Press, 2007.

Akiyama Kiyoko. *Chūsei kuge shakai no kūkan to geinō*. Tokyo: Yamakawa Shuppansha, 2003.

American Psychiatric Association. *Diagnostic and Statistical Manual of Mental Disorders*. 5th edition. Washington, DC: American Psychiatric Publishing, 2013.

Amino Yoshihiko. *Igyō no ōken*. Tokyo: Heibonsha, 2013.

———. "Kōshō to biin." In *Kotoba no bunkashi: Chūsei 1*, edited by Amino Yoshihiko, Kasamatsu Hiroshi, Katsumata Shizuo, and Satō Shin'ichi, 10–37. Tokyo: Heibonsha, 1988.

———. *Nihon chūsei no hinōgyōmin to tennō*. Tokyo: Iwanami Shoten, 1984.

———. *Nihon chūsei no minshū zō: Heimin to shokunin*. Tokyo: Iwanami Shoten, 1980.

———. *Rethinking Japanese History*. Translated by Alan S. Christy. Ann Arbor: Center for Japanese Studies, University of Michigan, 2012.

Angles, Jeffrey. "Watching Commoners, Performing Class: Images of the Common People in *The Pillow Book of Sei Shōnagon*." *Japan Forum* 13 (2001): 33–65.

Arai Tsuneyasu. *Nihon no matsuri to geinō*. Tokyo: Gyōsei, 1990.

Auslander, Philip. *Liveness: Performance in a Mediatized Culture*. London: Routledge, 2008.

———. *Reactivations: Essays on Performance and Its Documentation*. Ann Arbor: University of Michigan Press, 2018.

Azuma kagami. SZKT 33. Tokyo: Yoshikawa Kōbunkan, 2004.

Babcock, Barbara A., ed. *The Reversible World: Symbolic Inversion in Art and Society*. Ithaca, NY: Cornell University Press, 1978.

Bakhtin, Mikhail. *Rabelais and His World*. Translated by Hélène Iswolsky. Bloomington: Indiana University Press, 1984.

Ban Dainagon ekotoba. Edited by Komatsu Shigemi. Nihon Emaki Taisei 2. Tokyo: Chūō Kōron, 1977.

Batten, Bruce L. *To the Ends of Japan: Premodern Frontiers, Boundaries, and Interactions*. Honolulu: University of Hawai'i Press, 2003.

Benjamin, Walter. "The Work of Art in the Age of Its Reproducibility." In *Walter Benjamin: Selected Writings*, vol. 3, *1935–1938*, edited by Howard Eiland and Michael W. Jennings, 101–33. Cambridge, MA: Harvard University Press, 2006.

———. "The Work of Art in the Age of Mechanical Reproduction." In *Illuminations: Essays and Reflections*, translated by Harry Zohn, 217–51. New York: Schocken Books, 2007.

Berry, Mary Elizabeth. *The Culture of Civil War in Kyoto*. Berkeley: University of California Press, 1994.

Bialock, David. *Eccentric Spaces, Hidden Histories: Narrative, Ritual, and Royal Authority from "The Chronicles of Japan" to "The Tale of the Heike."* Stanford, CA: Stanford University Press, 2007.

———. "From *Heike* to *Nomori no kagami*: Onmyōdō and the Soundscapes of Medieval Japan." *Cahiers d'Extrême-Asie* 21 (2012): 165–99.

Bloch, Marc. *The Historian's Craft*. Translated by Peter Putnam. New York: Vintage Books, 1953.

Borgen, Robert. *Sugawara no Michizane and the Early Heian Court.* Honolulu: University of Hawai'i Press, 1994.
Brightwell, Erin L. *Reflecting the Past: Place, Language, and Principle in Japan's Medieval "Mirror" Genre.* Cambridge, MA: Harvard University Asia Center, 2020.
"Buke nendai ki." In *Kamakura nendai ki, uragaki; Buke nendai ki, uragaki; Kamakura ōnikki*, 67–186. Edited by Takeuchi Rizō. Zōho Zoku Shiryō Taisei. Kyoto: Rinsen Shoten, 1978.
Burns, Susan L. *Kingdom of the Sick: A History of Leprosy and Japan.* Honolulu: University of Hawai'i Press, 2019.

Canetti, Elias. *Crowds and Power.* Translated by Carol Stewart. New York: Farrar, Straus and Giroux, 1984.
"Chiteiki." By Yoshishige no Yasutane. In *In Praise of Solitude: Two Japanese Classics of Reclusion*, translated and edited by Matthew Stavros, 27–55. Vicus Lusorum, 2022.
Chōshūki. By Minamoto no Morotoki. ZST 16. Kyoto: Rinsen Shoten, 1989.
Chōya gunsai. Compiled by Miyoshi Tameyasu. SZKT 29. Tokyo: Yoshikawa Kōbunkan, 1999.
Chūyūki. By Fujiwara no Munetada. 7 vols. DNK. Tokyo: Iwanami Shoten, 1993–2005.
Chūyūki. By Fujiwara no Munetada. 7 vols. ZST, vols. 9–15. Kyoto: Rinsen Shoten, 1965.

Daigo zuihitsu. By Nakayama Sanryū. In Zoku Nihon Zuihitsu Taisei 10, 1–60. Tokyo: Yoshikawa Kōbunkan, 1980.
Dawkins, Richard. *The Selfish Gene.* Oxford: Oxford University Press, 2016.
De Ferranti, Hugh. *Japanese Musical Instruments.* Oxford: Oxford University Press, 2000.
De Man, Paul. "The Resistance to Theory." In *The Resistance to Theory*, 3–20. Minneapolis: University of Minnesota Press, 1986.
"Decision of the Intergovernmental Committee: 7.COM 11.19." UNESCO, 2012. Accessed February 5, 2025. https://ich.unesco.org/en/decisions/7.com/11.19.
"A Dedicatory Proclamation for *The Tale of Genji.*" By Chōken. Translated by Michael Jamentz. In *Reading The Tale of Genji: Sources from the First Millennium*, edited by Thomas Harper and Haruo Shirane, 188–91. New York: Columbia University Press, 2015.
Deleuze, Gilles, and Félix Guattari. *A Thousand Plateaus: Capitalism and Schizophrenia.* Translated by Brian Massumi. Minneapolis: University of Minnesota Press, 1987.

Dolby, William. *A History of Chinese Drama*. London: Paul Elek, 1976.
Dykstra, Yoshiko. *Buddhist Tales of India, China, and Japan: Japanese Section; A Complete Translation of the Konjaku Monogatarishū*. Honolulu: Kanji Press, 2014.

Ebersole, Gary L. *Ritual Poetry and the Politics of Death in Early Japan*. Princeton, NJ: Princeton University Press, 1989.
Eiga monogatari. Vol. 2. Edited by Yamanaka Yutaka, Akiyama Ken, Ikeda Naotaka, and Fukunaga Susumu. SNKBZ 32. Tokyo: Shōgakukan, 1997.
Entairyaku. By Tōin Kinkata. Vol. 7. Edited by Saiki Kazuma, Kurokawa Takaaki, and Atsuya Kazuo. Shiryō Sanshū 76. Tokyo: Zoku Gunsho Ruijū Kanseikai, 1986.
Eubanks, Charlotte. *Miracles of Book and Body: Buddhist Textual Culture and Medieval Japan*. Berkeley: University of California Press, 2011.

Farris, William Wayne. *Japan to 1600: A Social and Economic History*. Honolulu: University of Hawai'i Press, 2009.
Faure, Bernard. *Gods of Medieval Japan*, vol. 3, *Rage and Ravage*. Honolulu: University of Hawai'i Press, 2022.
Feldman, Martha, and Judith T. Zeitlin. Preface to *The Voice as Something More: Essays Toward Materiality*, edited by Martha Feldman and Judith T. Zeitlin, xi–xv. Chicago: University of Chicago Press, 2019.
Freud, Sigmund. "Fixation to Traumas—The Unconscious." In *Introductory Lectures on Psycho-Analysis*, translated by James Strachey, 338–53. New York: W. W. Norton, 1966.
Fukazawa Tōru. *Chūsei shinwa no rentanjutsu: Ōe no Masafusa to sono jidai*. Kyoto: Jinbun Shoin, 1994.
Fukushima Masaki. *Nihon chūsei no rekishi 2: Insei to bushi no tōjō*. Tokyo: Yoshikawa Kōbunkan, 2009.
Fukuyama Toshio. "*Nenjū gyōji emaki* ni tsuite." In *Nenjū gyōji emaki*, edited by Fukuyama Toshio, 3–23. Tokyo: Kadokawa Shoten, 1978.
Fusō ryakki. SZKT 12. Tokyo: Yoshikawa Kōbunkan, 1999.
Fuss, Diana. *Identification Papers*. New York: Routledge, 1995.
Futsū shōdōshū. Compiled by Ryōki. Edited by Murayama Shūichi. Tokyo: Hōzōkan, 2006.

Gamō Mitsuko. "Tōka." In *Kokushi daijiten*. Tokyo: Yoshikawa Kōbunkan. Online version. Accessed January 12, 2025. https://japanknowledge.com/psnl/display/?lid=30010zz337720.

Genji monogatari. By Murasaki Shikibu. Vol. 2. Edited by Abe Akio, Akiyama Ken, Imai Gen'e, and Suzuki Hideo. SNKBZ 21. Tokyo: Shōgakukan, 1995.

Gōke shidai. Compiled by Ōe no Masafusa. Vol. 2. Kaitei Zōhō Kojitsu Saisho. Tokyo: Meiji Tosho Shuppan, 1993.

Gomi Fumihiko. *Inseiki shakai no kenkyū*. Tokyo: Yamakawa Shuppansha, 1984.

GoNijō Moromichi ki. By Fujiwara no Moromichi. Vol. 3. DNK. Tokyo: Iwanami Shoten, 1958.

Goodwin, Janet R. *Selling Songs and Smiles: The Sex Trade in Heian and Kamakura Japan*. Honolulu: University of Hawai'i Press, 2007.

Graham, A. C. *The Book of Lieh-tzŭ*. Frome, England: Butler & Tanner, 1960.

Groner, Paul. "Annen, Tankei, Henjō, and Monastic Discipline in the Tendai School: The Background of the *Futsū jubosatsukai kōshaku*." *Japanese Journal of Religious Studies* 14, nos. 2–3 (1990): 129–59.

Gukanshō. By Jien. Edited by Okami Masao and Akamatsu Toshihide. NKBT 86. Tokyo: Iwanami Shoten, 1967.

Hama Kazue. *Nihon geinō no genryū: Sangaku kō*. Tokyo: Kadokawa Shoten, 1968.

Hardacre, Helen. *Shinto: A History*. New York: Oxford University Press, 2017.

Hare, Tom. *Zeami: Performance Notes*. New York: Columbia University Press, 2008.

Harootunian, Harry. *Overcome by Modernity: History, Culture, and Community in Interwar Japan*. Princeton, NJ: Princeton University Press, 2000.

Hashimoto Hiroyuki. *Engi no seishinshi: Chūsei geinō no gensetsu to shintai*. Tokyo: Iwanami Shoten, 2003.

Hatakayama Kazuhiro and Yasuda Tsuguo. *Sairei de yomitoku rekishi to shakai: Wakamiya Onmatsuri no kyūhyaku nen*. Tokyo: Yamakawa Shuppansha, 2016.

Hayashiya Tatsusaburō. *Chūsei geinōshi no kenkyū: Kodai kara no keishō to sōzō*. Tokyo: Iwanami Shoten, 1966.

Heian ibun. Edited by Takeuchi Rizō. 13 vols. Tokyo: Tōkyōdō Shuppan, 1963–1974.

Hempelmann, Christian F. "The Laughter of the 1962 Tanganyika 'Laughter Epidemic.'" *Humor: International Journal of Humor Research* 20, no. 1 (2007): 49–71.

Hérail, Francine. *Emperor and Aristocracy in Heian Japan: 10th and 11th Centuries*. Translated by Wendy Cobcroft. CreateSpace Independent Publishing Platform, 2013.

Hirama Michiko. *Kodai Nihon no girei to ongaku, geinō: Ba no ronri kara sōgaku no myakuraku o yomu*. Tokyo: Bensei Shuppan, 2023.

Honchō monzui. Compiled by Fujiwara no Akihira. Edited by Ōsone Shōsuke, Kinpara Tadashi, and Gotō Akio. SNKBT 27. Tokyo: Iwanami Shoten, 2007.

Honchō seiki. Compiled by Fujiwara no Michinori. SZKT 9. Tokyo: Yoshikawa Kōbunkan, 2003.

Honchō shojaku mokuroku. Center for Open Data in the Humanities. Accessed January 13, 2023. http://codh.rois.ac.jp/pmjt/book/200019785/.

Hosshinshū. By Kamo no Chōmei. Edited by Miki Sumito. In SNKS 5, 41–385. Tokyo: Shinchōsha, 1976.

Hyakurenshō. SZKT 11. Tokyo: Yoshikawa Kōbunkan, 2004.

Hyōhanki. By Taira no Nobunori. Vol. 2. ZST 19. Kyoto: Rinsen Shoten, 1965.

Imakagami zenchūshaku. Edited by Kawakita Noboru. Tokyo: Kasama Shoin, 2014.

Inokuma kampaku ki. By Konoe Iezane. Vol. 1. DNK. Tokyo: Iwanami Shoten, 1972.

Inoue Mitsurō. "Eichō gannen no dengaku sōdō: Insei shoki no bunka to seiji." *Geinōshi kenkyū* 36 (January 1972): 1–18.

Institute for Medieval Japanese Studies. "The Songs of Otomae." Accessed January 20, 2025. https://www.imjs-jchi.org/songs-of-otomae/.

Ishii Kōsei. *"Monomane" no rekishi: Bukkyō, warai, geinō*. Tokyo: Yoshikawa Kōbunkan, 2017.

Itō Isojūrō. *Dengaku shi no kenkyū*. Tokyo: Yoshikawa Kōbunkan, 1986.

Itō Masahiro. "'Hyakki yagyō dan' ge." *Denshō bungaku kenkyū* 31 (1985): 115–23.

———. "'Hyakki yagyō dan' jō." *Denshō bungaku kenkyū* 30 (1984): 107–14.

Iwahashi Koyata. *Geinōshi sōsetsu*. Tokyo: Yoshikawa Kōbunkan, 1975.

Iwasaki Masahiko. "Sarugaku no setsuwa to oni." *Nōgaku kenkyū* 26 (2002): 37–82.

Jackson, Reginald. "*Midare* Performance and the Ethics of Decomposition." PhD diss., Princeton University, 2007.

———. *Textures of Mourning: Calligraphy, Mortality, and "The Tale of Genji Scrolls."* Ann Arbor: University of Michigan Press, 2018.

Jimon kōsō ki. In Zoku Gunsho Ruijū, 28 *ge*, 26–571. Tokyo: Zoku Gunsho Ruijū Kanseikai, 1943.

Jinno Kiyokazu. *Ritsuryō kokka to senmin*. Tokyo: Yoshikawa Kōbunkan, 1986.

"Kairaishi no ki." By Ōe no Masafusa. Edited by Ōsone Shōsuke. In *Kodai seiji shakai shisō*, NST 8, 157–59, 308. Tokyo: Iwanami Shoten, 1979.

Kanmon nikki. By Fushiminomiya Sadafusa. Vol. 2. Edited by Kunaichō Shoryōbu. Tokyo: Meiji Shoin, 2004.

"Kansō jūshu." By Sugawara no Michizane. Edited by Kawaguchi Hisao. In *Kanke bunsō, Kanke kōshū*, NKBT 72, 259–65. Tokyo: Iwanami Shoten, 1966.

Kasuga. Shintō Taikei Jinja-hen 13. Tokyo: Seikōsha, 1985.

Kataoka Kōhei. "Eichō no daidengaku no dōkō: Nihon chūsei tennō no ken'i ni tsuite no ichi kōsatsu." *Hisutoria* 206 (2007): 34–57.

Katō Saburō. "Dengaku shiryō nenpyō." *Matsuri* 6 (1963): 48–52.

Kawane Yoshiyasu. *Chūsei hōken shakai no shuto to nōson*. Tokyo: Sanyōsha, 1984.

Kawashima, Terry. *Writing Margins: The Textual Construction of Gender in Heian and Kamakura Japan*. Cambridge, MA: Harvard University Asia Center, 2001.

Kim, Yung-Hee. *Songs to Make the Dust Dance: The "Ryōjin hishō" of Twelfth-Century Japan*. Berkeley: University of California Press, 1994.

Koji ruien. Vol. 43. Tokyo: Koji Ruien Kankōkai, 1931.

Kojidan. Compiled by Minamoto no Akikane. Edited by Kawabata Yoshiaki and Araki Hiroshi. In SNKBT 41, 1–600. Tokyo: Iwanami Shoten, 2005.

Kojiki. Edited by Yamaguchi Yoshinori and Kōnoshi Takamitsu. SNKBZ 1. Tokyo: Shōgakukan, 1997.

The Kojiki: An Account of Ancient Matters. Translated by Gustav Heldt. New York: Columbia University Press, 2014.

Kokinshū: A Collection of Poems Ancient and Modern. Translated by Laurel Rasplica Rodd and Mary Catherine Henkenius. Boston: Cheng & Tsui, 1996.

Kokin wakashū. SNKBZ 11. Edited by Ozawa Masao and Matsuda Shigeho. Tokyo: Shōgakukan, 1994.

Kokon chomonjū. By Tachibana no Narisue. Edited by Nishio Kōichi and Kobayashi Yasuharu. SNKS 76. Tokyo: Shinchōsha, 1986.

Komatsu Shigemi. "*Nenjū gyōji emaki* tanjō." In *Nenjū gyōji emaki*, edited by Komatsu Shigemi, Nihon Emaki Taisei 8, 106–28. Tokyo: Chūō Kōron, 1977.

Komine Kazuaki. *Inseiki bungaku ron*. Tokyo: Kasama Shoin, 2006.

———. "Inseiki no bunka to jidai: 'Miru' koto no seiji bunka gaku." In *Inseiki bunka ronshū*, vol. 1, *Kenryoku to bunka*, edited by Inseiki Bunka Kenkyūkai, 8–28. Tokyo: Shinwasha, 2001.

———. *Setsuwa no koe: Chūsei sekai no katari, uta, warai.* Tokyo: Shinyōsha, 2000.

Konishi Jin'ichi. *Ryōjin hishō kō.* Tokyo: Sanseidō, 1942.

Konjaku monogatari shū. 4 vols. Edited by Mabuchi Kazuo, Kunisaki Fumimaro, and Inagaki Taiichi. SNKBZ 35–38. Tokyo: Shōgakukan, 1999–2002.

Kōnoshi Takamitsu. "Constructing Imperial Mythology: *Kojiki* and *Nihon shoki.*" Translated by Iori Joko. In *Inventing the Classics: Modernity, National Identity, and Japanese Literature*, edited by Haruo Shirane and Tomi Suzuki, 51–67. Stanford, CA: Stanford University Press, 2000.

"Kujō ujōshō ikai." By Fujiwara no Morosuke. Edited by Ōsone Shōsuke. In *Kodai seiji shakai shisō*, NST 8, 116–122, 296–97. Tokyo: Iwanami Shoten, 1979.

Kujōke-bon Gyokuyō. By Kujō Kanezane. Vol. 6. Edited by Kunaichō Shoryōbu. Tokyo: Meiji Shoin, 2000.

Kumakura Isao. "Joron 2: Geinōshi no shiten." In NG 1, 73–117. Kyoto: Hōsei Daigaku Shuppankyoku, 1996.

Kunchū Meigetsuki. By Fujiwara no Teika. Vol. 1. Edited by Inamura Eiichi. Tokyo: Matsue Imai Shoten, 2002.

Kundoku Meigetsuki. By Fujiwara no Teika. Vol. 1. Edited by Imagawa Fumio. Tokyo: Kawade Shobō Shinsha, 1977.

Kuramoto Kazuhiro. *Fujiwara Michinaga no nichijō seikatsu.* Tokyo: Kōdansha, 2013.

———. *Heiankyō no kakyū kannin.* Tokyo: Kōdansha, 2022.

Kurata Minoru. *Zukan Mono kara yomitoku ōchō emaki.* 3 vols. Tokyo: Kachōsha, 2024.

Kuroda Hideo. *Nihon chūsei kaihatsushi no kenkyū.* Tokyo: Azekura Shobō, 1984.

Kwon, Yung-Hee Kim. "The Emperor's Songs: Go-Shirakawa and *Ryōjin Hishō Kudenshū.*" *Monumenta Nipponica* 41, no. 3 (Autumn 1986): 261–98.

LaMarre, Thomas. *Uncovering Heian Japan: An Archaeology of Sensation and Inscription.* Durham, NC: Duke University Press, 2000.

Lancashire, Terence A. *An Introduction to Japanese Folk Performing Arts.* London: Routledge, 2016.

Law, Jane Marie. “Of Plagues and Puppets: On the Significance of the Name Hyakudayū in Japanese Religion.” *Transactions of the Asiatic Society of Japan* 4, no. 8 (1993): 107–31.

———. *Puppets of Nostalgia: The Life, Death, and Rebirth of the Japanese Awaji Ningyō Tradition*. Princeton, NJ: Princeton University Press, 1997.

Lazarus, Ashton. “Folk Performance as Transgression: The Great Dengaku of 1096.” *Journal of Japanese Studies* 44, no. 1 (2018): 1–23.

———. “Performing Culture: Representations of Commoner Performance in Early Medieval Japan.” PhD diss., Yale University, 2014.

LeBon, Gustave. *The Crowd: A Study of the Popular Mind*. Translated by Robert K. Merton. New York: Viking Press, 1960.

Lee, Sherman E. *A History of Far Eastern Art*. Upper Saddle River, NJ: Prentiss Hall, 1994.

Li, Michelle Osterfeld. *Ambiguous Bodies: Reading the Grotesque in Japanese Setsuwa Tales*. Stanford, CA: Stanford University Press, 2009.

Lim, Beng Choo. “They Came to Party: An Examination of the Social Status of the Medieval Noh Theatre.” *Japan Forum* 16, no. 1 (2004): 111–33.

Lowenthal, David. *The Past Is a Foreign Country*. Cambridge: Cambridge University Press, 2015.

Makura no sōshi. By Sei Shōnagon. Edited by Matsuo Satoshi and Nagai Kazuko. SNKBZ 18. Tokyo: Shōgakukan, 1997.

Malm, William P. *Japanese Music and Musical Instruments*. Tokyo: Charles E. Tuttle, 1959.

Matsumoto Shinpachirō. “Chūsei no shisō.” In *Iwanami kōza Nihon rekishi*, vol. 7, *Chūsei* 3, 203–54. Tokyo: Iwanami Shoten, 1963.

Matsuo Kōichi. *Girei kara geinō e: Kyōsō, hyōi, dōke*. Tokyo: Kadokawa Gakugei Shuppan, 2011.

Matsuoka Shinpei. *Chūsei geinō o yomu*. Tokyo: Iwanami Shoten, 2002.

———. *Embodied Performance: Warriors, Dancers, and the Origins of Noh Theater*. Translated by Janet Goff. New York: Columbia University Press, 2024.

———. *Utage no shintai: Zeami kara basara e*. Tokyo: Iwanami Shoten, 2004.

———. “Vinayaka kō.” In *Oni to geinō: Higashi Ajia no engeki keisei*, edited by Matsuoka Shinpei, 222–52. Tokyo: Shinwasha, 2000.

McPhail, Clark. *The Myth of the Madding Crowd*. New York: Aldine de Gruyter, 1991.

Meeks, Lori. “The Disappearing Medium: Reassessing the Place of *Miko* in the Religious Landscape of Premodern Japan.” *History of Religions* 50, no. 3 (2011): 208–60.

Mezaki Tokue. "Fujiwara no Yoshifusa." In *Kokushi daijiten*. Tokyo: Yoshikawa Kōbunkan. Online version. Accessed January 12, 2025. https://japanknowledge.com/psnl/display/?lid=30010zz419960.

Midorikawa, Machiko. "Reading a Heian Blog: A New Translation of *Makura no Sōshi*." *Monumenta Nipponica* 63, no. 1 (Spring 2008): 143–60.

Mills, D. E. *A Collection of Tales from Uji: A Study and Translation of "Uji Shūi Monogatari."* Cambridge: Cambridge University Press, 1970.

Miura, Takashi. *Agents of World Renewal: The Rise of Yonaoshi Gods in Japan*. Honolulu: University of Hawai'i Press, 2019.

Momoyama Harue. *Asobi o sen to ya umareken: "Ryōjin hishō" no sekai*. Japan Victor Foundation, VZCG-168, 1981, compact disc. Reissued by Nihon Dentō Bunka Shinkō Zaidan, 2000.

Monzen. Compiled by Xiao Tong. Vol. 1. Edited by Obi Kōichi and Hanabusa Hideki. Zenshaku Kanbun Taikei 26. Tokyo: Shūeisha, 1974.

Moriya Takeshi. *Chūsei geinō no genzō*. Kyoto: Tankōsha, 1985.

———. "Geinō to wa nani ka." In NG 1, 19–72. Tokyo: Hōsei Daigaku Shuppankyoku, 1996.

Morris, Mark. "Sei Shōnagon's Poetic Catalogues." *Harvard Journal of Asiatic Studies* 40, no. 1 (1980): 5–54.

Murasaki Shikibu nikki. By Murasaki Shikibu. Edited by Nakano Kōichi. In SNKBZ 26, 115–272. Tokyo: Shōgakukan, 1994.

Nagai Kumiko. "Hizō sareta 'toshizu': *Nenjū gyōji emaki* shinkō." *Chōiki bunka kagaku kiyō* 6 (2001): 134–55.

Nakagawa Shin. *Heiankyō: Oto no uchū*. Tokyo: Heibonsha, 1992.

Nakahara, Gladys E. *A Translation of "Ryōjinhishō," a Compendium of Japanese Folk Songs (*Imayō*) from the Heian Period (794–1185)*. Lewiston, NY: Edwin Mellen, 2003.

Nakamura Akira. "Chūsei no ryūkōbyō 'mikkayami' ni tsuite no kentō." *Nihon ishigaku zasshi* 33, no. 3 (July 1986): 308–15.

Nakazawa Shin'ichi. *Seirei no ō*. Tokyo: Kōdansha, 2008.

Narimichi-kyō kuden nikki. By Fujiwara no Narimichi. In Gunsho Ruijū 19, 392–405. Tokyo: Gunsho Ruijū Kanseikai, 1941.

Needham, Rodney. "Percussion and Transition." *Man* 2, no. 4 (1967): 606–14.

Nellhaus, Tobin, ed. *Theatre Histories: An Introduction*. London: Routledge, 2016.

Nenjū gyōji emaki. Edited by Komatsu Shigemi. Nihon Emaki Taisei 8. Tokyo: Chūō Kōron, 1977.

Nichūreki. Edited by Kondō Heijō. Kaitei Shiseki Shūran 23. Tokyo: Kondō Shuppanbu, 1907.

Nihon kiryaku kōhen. SZKT 11. Tokyo: Yoshikawa Kōbunkan, 2000.

Nihon kiryaku zenpen. SZKT 10. Tokyo: Yoshikawa Kōbunkan, 2000.

Nihon ryōiki. Compiled by Kyōkai. Edited by Nakada Norio. SNKBZ 10. Tokyo: Shōgakukan, 1995.

Nihon sandai jitsuroku. SZKT 4. Tokyo: Yoshikawa Kōbunkan, 2005.

Nihon shoki. Vol. 2. Edited by Kojima Noriyuki, Naoki Kojirō, Nishimiya Kazutami, Kuranaka Susumu, and Mōri Masamori. SNKBZ 2. Tokyo: Shōgakukan, 2006.

"Nikyoku santai ningyō zu." By Zeami. In *Zeami, Zenchiku*, edited by Omote Akira and Katō Shūichi, NST 24, 121–32. Tokyo: Iwanami Shoten, 1974.

Niunoya Tetsuichi. "Chūseiteki geinō no kankyō." In *Chūsei no sairei: Chūō kara chihō e*, edited by Amino Yoshihiko, Ōsumi Kazuo, Ozawa Shōichi, Hattori Yukio, Miyata Noboru, and Yamaji Kōzō, 9–50. Taikei Nihon Rekishi to Geinō 4. Tokyo: Heibonsha, 1991.

———. *Zōho Kebiishi: Chūsei no kegare to kenryoku*. Tokyo: Heibonsha, 2008.

Nōgaku shi nenpyō: Kodai chūsei hen. Edited by Suzuki Masando. Tokyo: Tōkyōdō Shuppan, 2007.

"Nomination File No. 00413 for Inscription on the Representative List of the Intangible Cultural Heritage of Humanity in 2012." Intergovernmental Committee for the Safeguarding of the Intangible Cultural Heritage. Seventh Session, Paris, December 2012. Accessed February 5, 2025. https://ich.unesco.org/doc/src/17067-EN.doc.

Nose Asaji. *Nōgaku genryū kō*. Tokyo: Iwanami Shoten, 1958.

Ōjō yōshū. By Genshin. Edited by Ishiba Mizumaro. Genten Nihon Bukkyō no Shisō 4. Tokyo: Iwanami Shoten, 1991.

Ōkagami. Edited by Tachibana Kenji and Katō Shizuko. SNKBZ 34. Tokyo: Shōgakukan, 1996.

Ōkagami, The Great Mirror: Fujiwara Michinaga (966–1027) and His Times. Translated by Helen Craig McCullough. Princeton, NJ: Princeton University Press, 1980.

Okimoto Yukiko. *Imayō no jidai: Hen'yō suru kyūtei geinō*. Tokyo: Tokyo Daigaku Shuppankai, 2006.

———. *Ranmai no chūsei: Shirabyōshi, ranbyōshi, sarugaku*. Tokyo: Yoshikawa Kōbunkan, 2016.

Ooms, Herman. *Imperial Politics and Symbolics in Ancient Japan: The Tenmu Dynasty, 650–800*. Honolulu: University of Hawai'i Press, 2008.

Ortolani, Benito. *The Japanese Theatre: From Shamanistic Ritual to Contemporary Pluralism.* Princeton, NJ: Princeton University Press, 1990.

Ōsone Shōsuke. "Fujiwara no Akihira." In *Kokushi daijiten.* Tokyo: Yoshikawa Kōbunkan. Online version. Accessed November 17, 2022. https://japanknowledge.com/psnl/display/?lid=30010zz416890.

O'Sullivan, Suzanne. *The Sleeping Beauties: And Other Stories of Mystery Illness.* New York: Pantheon Books, 2021.

Owen, Stephen. *Readings in Chinese Literary Thought.* Cambridge, MA: Harvard University Asia Center, 1992.

Pandey, Rajyashree. *Perfumed Sleeves and Tangled Hair: Body, Woman, and Desire in Medieval Japanese Narratives.* Honolulu: University of Hawaiʻi Press, 2016.

Partridge, Christopher. *The Lyre of Orpheus: Popular Music, the Sacred, and the Profane.* Oxford: Oxford University Press, 2013.

Pearson, Mike, and Michael Shanks. *Theatre/Archaeology.* London: Routledge, 2001.

Phelan, Peggy. *Unmarked: The Politics of Performance.* London: Routledge, 1996.

Piggott, Joan R. "Mō hitotsu no Heiankyō: Fujiwara no Akihira *Shinsarugakuki* no naka no toshi." In *Kōkyō suru kodai: Higashi Ajia no naka no Nihon*, edited by Ishikawa Hideshi, Hinata Kazumasa, and Yoshimura Takehito, 295–311. Tokyo: Tōkyōdō Shuppan, 2011.

Pinnington, Noel John. *A New History of Medieval Japanese Theatre: Noh and Kyōgen from 1300 to 1600.* London: Palgrave Macmillan, 2019.

Plutschow, Herbert E. *Chaos and Cosmos: Ritual in Early and Medieval Japanese Literature.* Leiden: Brill, 1990.

Pratt, Mary Louise. "Arts of the Contact Zone." *Profession* (1991): 33–40.

Rabinovitch, Judith N., and Timothy R. Bradstock, eds. and trans. *No Moonlight in My Cup: Sinitic Poetry (Kanshi) from the Japanese Court, Eighth to Twelfth Centuries.* Leiden: Brill, 2019.

"Rakuyō dengaku ki." By Ōe no Masafusa. Edited by Moriya Takeshi. In *Kodai chūsei geijutsu ron*, NST 23, 218–22. Tokyo: Iwanami Shoten, 1973.

Ranshōshō. In Gunsho Ruijū 26, 291–338. Tokyo: Zoku Gunsho Ruijū Kanseikai, 1939.

Raz, Jacob. *Audience and Actors: A Study of Their Interaction in the Japanese Traditional Theatre.* Leiden: Brill, 1983.

———. "Popular Entertainment and Politics: The Great Dengaku of 1096." *Monumenta Nipponica* 40, no. 3 (Autumn 1985): 283–98.

Record of Miraculous Events in Japan: The "Nihon ryōiki." By Kyōkai. Translated by Burton Watson. New York: Columbia University Press, 2013.

Ribu ōki. By Shigeakira Shinnō. Edited by Yoneda Yūsuke and Yoshioka Masayuki. Shiryō Sanshū 39. Tokyo: Zoku Gunsho Ruijū Kanseikai, 1974.

"Ryōjin hishō kudenshū, Volume 14." In *Ryōjin hishō*, edited by Sasaki Nobutsuna, 163–91. Tokyo: Iwanami Shoten, 1975.

Ryōjin hishō, Ryōjin hishō kudenshū. Compiled by Retired Emperor GoShirakawa. Edited by Shinma Shin'ichi and Tonomura Natsuko. In SNKBZ 42, 173–410. Tokyo: Shōgakukan, 2000.

Saitō Mareshi. *Kanbunmyaku: The Literary Sinitic Context and the Birth of Modern Japanese Language and Literature.* Edited by Ross King and Christina Laffin. Leiden: Brill, 2021.

Sakura Yoshiyasu. "Chūsei no retsujo: Sekai o hyōgen suru chi no shukusai." *Bungaku, gogaku* 222 (2018): 119–32.

Sakurai Yoshirō. "Geinō to bungaku: Girei kokka no hakai." *Kokubungaku kaishaku to kanshō* 681, no. 3 (1988): 104–9.

Sango, Asuka. *The Halo of Golden Light: Imperial Authority and Buddhist Ritual in Heian Japan.* Honolulu: University of Hawai'i Press, 2015.

Sankaiki. By Nakayama Tadachika. Vol. 3. ZST 28. Kyoto: Rinsen Shoten, 1965.

Sansom, George. *A History of Japan to 1334.* Rutland, VT: Charles E. Tuttle, 1963.

Sarashina nikki. Edited by Inukai Kiyoshi. In SNKBZ 26, 273–384. Tokyo: Shōgakukan, 1994.

Sasaki Nobutsuna. *Shintei Ryōjin hishō.* Tokyo: Iwanami Shoten, 1957.

Satō Michio. *Heian kōki Nihon kanbungaku no kenkyū.* Tokyo: Kasama Shoin, 2003.

Schafer, R. Murray. *The Soundscape: Our Sonic Environment and the Tuning of the World.* Rochester, VT: Destiny Books, 1994.

Schechner, Richard. *Performance Studies: An Introduction.* 2nd ed. New York: Routledge, 2006.

Schneider, Rebecca. *Performing Remains: Art and War in Times of Theatrical Reenactment.* London: Routledge, 2011.

———. *Theatre and History.* London: Red Glove, 2014.

Scott, James C. *Against the Grain: A Deep History of the Earliest States.* New Haven, CT: Yale University Press, 2017.

Scripture of the Lotus Blossom of the Fine Dharma (The Lotus Sūtra). Translated by Leon Hurvitz. New York: Columbia University Press, 1976.

"Seinō." In *Nihon kokugo daijiten*. Tokyo: Shōgakukan. Online version. Accessed February 5, 2023. https://japanknowledge.com/psnl/display/?lid=2002025aaf33lAsJ4YPK.

Sekiguchi Tsutomu. "Inari matsuri to shiten shōnin." In *Kōki sekkan jidai shi no kenkyū*, edited by Kodaigaku Kyōkai, 461–80. Tokyo: Yoshikawa Kōbunkan, 1990.

Shanks, Michael. *Experiencing the Past: On the Character of Archaeology*. London: Routledge, 1992.

Shibayama, Saeko. "Ōe no Masafusa and the Convergence of the 'Ways': The Twilight of Early Chinese Literary Studies and the Rise of Waka Studies in the Long Twelfth Century in Japan." PhD diss., Columbia University, 2012.

Shigeta Michi. "*Honchō monzui* shoshū 'Ben sangaku' no kisoteki kenkyū: Kaishaku oyobi sono geinōronteki kōsatsu." *Genesis: Kyoto Zōkei Geijutsu Daigaku kiyō* 21 (2017): 47–57.

Shigeta Shin'ichi. *Kakyū kizokutachi no ōchō jidai: "Shin sarugaku ki" ni miru samazama na ikikata*. Tokyo: Shintensha, 2018.

———. *Naguriau kizokutachi*. Tokyo: Kadokawa Gakugei Shuppan, 2008.

———. *Shomintachi no Heiankyō*. Tokyo: Kadokawa Gakugei Shuppan, 2008.

Shin sarugaku ki. By Fujiwara no Akihira. Edited by Kawaguchi Hisao. Tōyō Bunko 424. Tokyo: Heibonsha, 1996.

"Shin sarugaku ki." By Fujiwara no Akihira. Edited by Ōsone Shōsuke. In *Kodai seiji shakai shisō*, NST 8, 133–52, 301–307. Tokyo: Iwanami Shoten, 1979.

Shin sarugaku ki. By Fujiwara no Akihira. Sonkeikaku Zenpon Eiin Shūsei 42. Tokyo: Yagi Shoten, 2010.

Shin sarugaku ki, Unshū shōsoku. By Fujiwara no Akihira. Edited by Shigematsu Akihisa. Tokyo: Gendai Shinchōsha, 1982.

Shinzei kogaku zu. Edited by Yamada Yoshio. Fukkoku Nihon Koten Zenshū 2. Tokyo: Gendai Shichōsha, 1977.

Shohon shūsei Wamyō ruijū shō: Honbun-hen. Compiled by Minamoto no Shitagō. Edited by Kyoto Daigaku Bungakubu Kokugogaku Kokubungaku Kenkyūshitsu. Tokyo: Rinsen Shoten, 1999.

Shoku Nihongi. Vol. 2. Edited by Aoki Kazuo, Inaoka Kōji, Sasayama Haruo, and Shirafuji Noriyuki. SNKBT 13. Tokyo: Shōgakukan, 1990.

Shoku Nihongi. SZKT 2. Tokyo: Yoshikawa Kōbunkan, 2004.

Shoku Nihon kōki. SZKT 3. Tokyo: Yoshikawa Kōbunkan, 2004.

"Shōmonki." Edited by Takeuchi Rizō. In *Kodai seiji shakai shisō*, NST 8, 186–227, 315–26. Tokyo: Iwanami Shoten, 1979.

Shōyūki. By Fujiwara no Sanesuke. 3 vols. ZST, vols. 46–48. Kyoto: Rinsen Shoten, 1968.

Smits, I. B. "The Way of the Literati: Chinese Learning and Literary Practice in Mid-Heian Japan." In *Heian Japan, Centers and Peripheries*, edited by Mikael S. Adolphson, Edward Kamens, and Stacie Matsumoto, 105–28. Honolulu: University of Hawai'i Press, 2007.

Sorensen, Joseph T. "The Politics of Screen Poetry: Michinaga, Sanesuke, and the Court Entrance of Shōshi." *Journal of Japanese Studies* 38, no. 1 (2012): 85–107.

Sorgenfrei, Carol Fisher. "Reversibility as Historical Method: Japanese Theater and Its Doubles." In *Entangled Performance Histories: New Approaches to Theater Historiography*, edited by Erika Fischer-Lichte, Małgorzata Sugiera, Torsten Jost, Holger Hartung, and Omid Soltani, 167–89. London: Routledge, 2022.

Stallybrass, Peter, and Allon White. *The Politics and Poetics of Transgression*. Ithaca, NY: Cornell University Press, 1986.

"Statement Regarding Influenza." *Public Health Reports (1896–1970)* 43, no. 51 (December 1928): 3366–68.

Stavros, Matthew. *Kyoto: An Urban History of Japan's Premodern Capital*. Honolulu: University of Hawai'i Press, 2014.

Steininger, Brian. *Chinese Literary Forms in Heian Japan: Poetics and Practice*. Cambridge, MA: Harvard University Asia Center, 2017.

Strippoli, Roberta. *Dancer, Nun, Ghost, Goddess: The Legend of Giō and Hotoke in Japanese Literature, Theater, Visual Arts, and Cultural Heritage*. Leiden: Brill, 2018.

Suzuki Masataka, Tanaka Issei, Nomura Shin'ichi, and Matsuoka Shinpei. "Sairei to engeki: Kijin to okina no genryū e: Zadankai." In *Oni to geinō: Higashi Ajia no engeki keisei*, edited by Matsuoka Shinpei, 10–86. Tokyo: Shinwasha, 2000.

Taiheiki. 4 vols. Edited by Hasegawa Tadashi. SNKBZ 54–57. Tokyo: Shōgakukan, 1994–2002.

Takatori Masao. "Minzoku to geinō: Geinō mihatsu no bubun." In NG 1, 119–70. Tokyo: Hōsei Daigaku Shuppankyoku, 1996.

Takemoto Mikio. "Geinō ichiba to shite no jiin." *Chūsei bungaku* 20 (2020): 16–25.

The Tale of the Heike. Translated by Royall Tyler. New York: Viking, 2012.

Taylor, Diana. *The Archive and the Repertoire: Performing Cultural Memory in the Americas*. Durham, NC: Duke University Press, 2003.

Teeuwen, Mark. *Kyoto's Gion Festival: A Social History*. London: Bloomsbury Academic, 2024.

———. "Kyoto's Gion Festival in Late Classical and Medieval Times: Actors, Legends, and Meanings." *Religions* 13, no. 6 (2022): 545.

Thornbury, Barbara E. *The Folk Performing Arts: Traditional Culture in Contemporary Japan*. Albany: State University of New York Press, 1997.

Thornhill, Arthur T., III. *Six Circles, One Dewdrop: The Religio-Aesthetic World of Komparu Zenchiku*. Princeton, NJ: Princeton University Press, 1993.

Toda Yoshimi. "Shōen taisei kakuritsu ki no shūkyōteki minshū undō: Eichō Daidengaku ni tsuite." *Rekishigaku kenkyū* 378 (November 1971): 8–15.

Tōhokuin shokunin utaawase emaki. Edited by Kokuritsu Bunkazai Kikō. Accessed November 17, 2022. https://emuseum.nich.go.jp/detail?langId=ja&webView=null&content_base_id=100272&content_part_id=001&content_pict_id=010&x=5378&y=-18&s=1.

Tongdian. Compiled by Du You. Beijing: Zhonghua Shuju Chuban, 1984.

Toshiyori zuinō. By Minamoto no Toshiyori. Edited by Hashimoto Fumio. In SNKBZ 87, 13–246. Tokyo: Shōgakukan, 2002.

Tsuji Hirokazu. *Chūsei no yūjo: Nariwai to mibun*. Kyoto: Kyoto Daigaku Gakujutsu Shuppankai, 2017.

———. "GoShirakawa to 'toshimin.'" *Kodai bunka* 60, no. 3 (December 2008): 15–32.

Tsunoda Ichirō. *Ningyōgeki no seiritsu ni kansuru kenkyū*. Osaka: Asahiya Shoten, 1963.

———. "Sangaku no geinō." In NG 1, 289–314. Tokyo: Hōsei Daigaku Shuppankyoku, 1996.

———. "Sangaku sakumon kō." *Kokubungaku kenkyū* 2 (1950): 118–32.

Tsurezuregusa. By Kenkō. Edited by Nagazumi Yasuaki. In SNKBZ 44, 67–309. Tokyo: Shōgakukan, 1995.

Tu, Liwen. "Fujiwara no Akihira and *Shin Sarugakuki: Kanbun*, Heian Scholars, and Social Criticism." PhD diss., University of Oxford, 2020.

Turner, Victor. *The Ritual Process: Structure and Anti-Structure*. New York: Aldine De Gruyter, 1995.

Ueda Masaaki. "Kodai geinō no keisei." In NG 1, 171–228. Kyoto: Hōsei Daigaku Shuppankyoku, 1996.

Uejima Susumu. *Nihon chūsei shakai no keisei to ōken*. Nagoya: Nagoya Daigaku Shuppankai, 2010.

Ueki Yukinobu. *Chūsei geinō no keisei katei*. Ueki Yukinobu Geinō Bunkashi Ronshū 1. Tokyo: Iwata Shoin, 2009.

Uji shūi monogatari. Edited by Kobayashi Yasuharu and Masuko Kazuko. SNKBZ 50. Tokyo: Shōgakukan, 1996.

"Unshū shōsoku." By Fujiwara no Akihira. In *Nihon kyōiku bunko*, vol. 9, *Kyōkasho hen*, edited by Kurokawa Mamichi, 185–258. Tokyo: Dōbunkan, 1911.

Ury, Marian. *Tales of Times Now Past: Sixty-Two Stories from a Medieval Japanese Collection.* Ann Arbor, MI: Center for Japanese Studies, 1979.

Ushio Michio. *Ōtaue to taue uta.* Tokyo: Iwasaki Bijutsusha, 1968.

Von Verschuer, Charlotte. "Life of Commoners in the Provinces: The *Owari no gebumi* of 988." In *Heian Japan: Centers and Peripheries*, edited by Mikael Adolphson, Edward Kamens, and Stacie Matsumoto, 305–28. Honolulu: University of Hawai'i Press, 2007.

———. *Rice, Agriculture, and the Food Supply in Premodern Japan.* Translated by Wendy Cobcroft. London: Routledge, 2016.

Wakabayashi, Haruko. *The Seven Tengu Scrolls: Evil and the Rhetoric of Legitimacy in Medieval Japanese Buddhism.* Honolulu: University of Hawai'i Press, 2012.

Wakita Haruko. *Chūsei Kyoto to Gion matsuri: Ekijin to toshi no seikatsu.* Tokyo: Yoshikawa Kōbunkan, 2016.

———. *Josei geinō no genryū: Kugutsu, kusemai, shirabyōshi.* Tokyo: Kadokawa, 2014.

Waller, John. *The Dancing Plague: The Strange, True Story of an Extraordinary Illness.* Naperville, IL: Sourcebooks, 2009.

Watanabe, Takeshi. "Reexamining the *Yamai no Sōshi*: Who Gets Sick and Why?" In *Yamai no sōshi*, edited by Kasuya Makoto and Yamamoto Satomi, 225–58. Tokyo: Chūō Kōron Bijutsu Shuppan, 2017.

Watson, Burton. *Japanese Literature in Chinese*, vol. 1, *Poetry and Prose in Chinese by Japanese Writers of the Early Period.* New York: Columbia University Press, 1975.

Wen xuan, or Selections of Refined Literature. Compiled by Xiao Tong. Vol. 1. Translated by David Knechtges. Princeton, NJ: Princeton University Press, 1982.

Yamagami Izumo. "'Shidarajin' shinkō to sono wazauta no shiteki kōsatsu." *Fūzoku: Nihon Fūzokushi Gakkai kaishi* 4, no. 2 (December 1964): 21–35.

Yamaguchi, Masao. "The Dual Structure of Japanese Emperorship." *Current Anthropology* 28, no. 4 (August–October 1987): S5–11.

———. *Tennōsei no bunka jinruigaku.* Tokyo: Iwanami Shoten, 2000.

Yamaji Kōzō. *Chūsei geinō no teiryū.* Tokyo: Iwata Shoin, 2010.

———. "'Gakuko' no denryū: geinōmin sabetsu no genryū o kangaeru." *Geinōshi kenkyū* 172 (January 2006): 55–78.

———. "Nōfu, denpu no gaku." In NG 1, 270–289. Kyoto: Hōsei Daigaku Shuppankyoku, 1996.

———. *Uji sarugaku to rikyū sai: Uji no geinōshi.* Uji Bunko 8. Uji: Ujishi Rekishi Shiryōkan, 1997.

Yasar, Kerim. *Electrified Voices: How the Telephone, Phonograph, and Radio Shaped Modern Japan, 1868–1945.* New York: Columbia University Press, 2018.

Yasuda Tsuguo. *Jisha to geinō no chūsei.* Nihonshi Riburetto 80. Tokyo: Yamakawa Shuppansha, 2009.

Yiengpruksawan, Mimi Hall. "The Eyes of Michinaga in the Light of Pure Land Buddhism." In *The Presence of Light: Divine Radiance and Religious Experience*, edited by Matthew T. Kapstein, 227–61. Chicago: University of Chicago Press, 2004.

"Yūjo no ki." By Ōe no Masafusa. Edited by Ōsone Shōsuke. In *Kodai seiji shakai shisō*, NST 8, 154–56, 308. Tokyo: Iwanami Shoten, 1979.

Zeami, Zenchiku. Edited by Omote Akira and Katō Shūichi. NST 24. Tokyo: Iwanami Shoten, 1974.

Zeitlin, Judith T. "From the Natural to the Instrumental: Chinese Theories of the Sounding Voice before the Modern Era." In *The Voice as Something More: Essays Toward Materiality*, edited by Martha Feldman and Judith T. Zeitlin, 54–74. Chicago: University of Chicago Press, 2019.

Zokushi gushō. Compiled by Yanagiwara Motomitsu. SZKT 13. Tokyo: Yoshikawa Kōbunkan, 1999.

Zumthor, Paul. *Oral Poetry: An Introduction.* Translated by Kathryn Murphy-Judy. Minneapolis: University of Minnesota Press, 1990.

Index

Harvard East Asian Monographs
(most recent titles)

439. Eyck Freymann, *One Belt One Road: Chinese Power Meets the World*
440. Yung Chul Park, Joon Kyung Kim, and Hail Park, *Financial Liberalization and Economic Development in Korea, 1980–2020*
441. Steven B. Miles, *Opportunity in Crisis: Cantonese Migrants and the State in Late Qing China*
442. Grace C. Huang, *Chiang Kai-shek's Politics of Shame: Leadership, Legacy, and National Identity in China*
443. Adam J. Lyons, *Karma and Punishment: Prison Chaplaincy in Japan*
444. Craig A. Smith, *Chinese Asianism, 1894–1945*
445. Sachiko Kawai, *Uncertain Powers: Sen'yōmon-in and Landownership by Royal Women in Early Medieval Japan*
446. Juliane Noth, *Transmedial Landscapes and Modern Chinese Painting*
447. Susan Westhafer Furukawa, *The Afterlife of Toyotomi Hideyoshi: Historical Fiction and Popular Culture in Japan*
448. Nongji Zhang, *Legal Scholars and Scholarship in the People's Republic of China: The First Generation (1949–1992)*
449. Han Sang Kim, *Cine-Mobility: Twentieth-Century Transformations in Korea's Film and Transportation*
450. Brian Hurley, *Confluence and Conflict: Reading Transwar Japanese Literature and Thought*
451. Simon Avenell, *Asia and Postwar Japan: Deimperialization, Civic Activism, and National Identity*
452. Maura Dykstra, *Uncertainty in the Empire of Routine: The Administrative Revolution of the Eighteenth-Century Qing State*
453. Marnie S. Anderson, *In Close Association: Local Activist Networks in the Making of Japanese Modernity, 1868–1920*
454. John D. Wong, *Hong Kong Takes Flight: Commercial Aviation and the Making of a Global Hub, 1930s–1998*
455. Martin K. Whyte and Mary C. Brinton, compilers, *Remembering Ezra Vogel*
456. Lawrence Zhang, *Power for a Price: The Purchase of Appointments in Qing China*
457. J. Megan Greene, *Building a Nation at War: Transnational Knowledge Networks and the Development of China during and after World War II*

458. Miya Qiong Xie, *Territorializing Manchuria: The Transnational Frontier and Literatures of East Asia*
459. Dal Yong Jin, *Understanding Korean Webtoon Culture: Transmedia Storytelling, Digital Platforms, and Genres*
460. Takahiro Yamamoto, *Demarcating Japan: Imperialism, Islanders, and Mobility, 1855–1884*
461. Elad Alyagon, *Inked: Tattooed Soldiers and the Song Empire's Penal-Military Complex*
462. Börje Ljunggren and Dwight H. Perkins, eds., *Vietnam: Navigating a Rapidly Changing Economy, Society, and Political Order*
463. En Li, *Betting on the Civil Service Examinations: The Lottery in Late Qing China*
464. Matthieu Felt, *Meanings of Antiquity: Myth Interpretation in Premodern Japan*
465. William D. Fleming, *Strange Tales from Edo: Rewriting Chinese Fiction in Early Modern China*
466. Mark Baker, *Pivot of China: Spatial Politics and Inequality in Modern Zhengzhou*
467. Peter Banseok Kwon, *Cornerstone of the Nation: The Defense Industry and the Building of Modern Korea under Park Chung Hee*
468. Weipin Tsai, *The Making of China's Post Office: Sovereignty, Modernization, and the Connection of a Nation*
469. Michael A. Fuller, *An Introduction to Literary Chinese (Second Edition)*
470. Gustav Heldt, *Navigating Narratives: Tsurayuki's* Tosa Diary *as History and Fiction*
471. Xiaolu Ma, *Transpatial Modernity: Chinese Cultural Encounters with Russia via Japan (1880–1930)*
472. Yueduan Wang, *Experimentalist Constitutions: Subnational Policy Innovations in China, India, and the United States*
473. M. William Steele, *Rethinking Japan's Modernity: Stories and Translations*
474. Judith Vitale, *The Historical Writing of the Mongol Invasions in Japan*
475. Hang Tu, *Sentimental Republic: Chinese Intellectuals and the Maoist Past*
476. John D. Phan, *Lost Tongues of the Red River: Annamese Middle Chinese and the Origins of the Vietnamese Language*
477. Jungwon Kim, *Virtue That Matters: Chastity Culture and Social Power in Chosŏn Korea (1392–1910)*
478. Shiuon Chu, *Reinventing Examination and the State in Twentieth Century China and Taiwan*
479. Helen Hardacre, *Shinto Shrines in Prewar and Wartime Japan*
480. Wen-Chin Chang, *Echoes from the Sino-Burmese Borderlands: Untold Stories of Overland Chinese Migrants During the Cold War*
481. Talia Andrei, *Sacred Journeys and Institutional Rivalries: Pilgrimage Mandalas and the Art of Fundraising in Medieval Japan*
482. Ashton Lazarus, *Performing Transgression: Crowds and Bodies in Heian Japan*